Spirit-Filled Life®
New Testament
Commentary Series

EPHESIANS & COLOSSIANS

SPIRIT-FILLED LIFE®
NEW TESTAMENT
COMMENTARY SERIES

EPHESIANS & COLOSSIANS

Jack W. Hayford
David P. Seemuth

Jack W. Hayford and David P. Seemuth
General Editors

Spirit-Filled Life New Testament Commentary Series: Ephesians & Colossians
Copyright © 2005 by Jack W. Hayford and David P. Seemuth
Published in Nashville, Tennessee, by Thomas Nelson, Inc.

Unless otherwise indicated, Scripture quotations are from the New King James Version of the
Bible, © 1979, 1980, 1982, 1990, Thomas Nelson, Inc., Publishers

Book design and composition by *A&W Publishing Electronic Services, Inc.*, Chicago, Illinois

Spirit-Filled Life New Testament commentary series: Ephesians & Colossians/Jack W. Hayford
and David P. Seemuth

    Jack W. Hayford and David P. Seemuth, general editors
    ISBN 0-7852-4943-5
Printed in the United States of America
1 2 3 4 5 6 7—09 08 07 06 05

FOREWORD

Welcome to the Spirit-Filled Life® New Testament Commentaries. It has been my desire to combine solid biblical scholarship with a passionate embrace of kingdom living principles in a format accessible to pastors, students, and other readers of God's Word. If you have picked up this commentary you probably wish to become a more equipped servant of God through the thorough understanding of the Spirit's revealed Word to us.

God has led me at this stage of life to pour myself into the training of people fit for the task of kingdom ministry. Of course, this does not mean ministry in the "professional" sense. Ministry (service for the Master) occurs when people are moved by the Holy Spirit to advance as equipped warriors in a spiritual battle with evil forces to help deliver people from the realm of darkness and bring them into the kingdom of the Beloved Son of God. We know that this refers to outreach and evangelism. But such ministry extends far beyond that.

People must embrace the fullness of the kingdom of God for every aspect of life. Only by Spirit-filled living and moving will people be able to comprehend and connect with such a life. And only by Spirit-filled ministry will such work occur in the lives of others.

Key to the advancing of such kingdom ministry is the ministry of God's Word. To this end I have brought together individuals of significant biblical scholarship who also have an understanding of what it means to live the Spirit-filled life in order to form the Spirit-Filled Life® New Testament Commentary series. It should come as no surprise that biblical scholarship and an understanding of the Spirit-filled life are put together. Solid intellectual discovery of the Word of God leads to conclusions about the Spirit-filled life consistent with experience of God's empowering Spirit. The two are not to be in conflict. And they are not, in fact, in conflict. God's truth in the revealed Word (given by the Holy Spirit) is the same truth given in Spirit-empowered living. The Holy Spirit is the common denominator!

Some of the distinctives you will see in this series are:

- A commitment to renew our confidence in God's Word through solid scholarship in tune with current issues in New Testament studies
- A commitment to realized kingdom living through practical insights and application of God's Word.
- A commitment to reflect the inspiration of the text through seeing the Holy Spirit as Author even though God used human writers
- A commitment to reveal kingdom principles God has built into the Scriptures

Of course we know that the real purpose for knowing God's Word is to be transformed and equipped by it. We are not simply to accumulate intellectual facts about the Word. The end of study is not *knowledge* but *knowing God* by His Holy Spirit. This series will help you do just that.

So, it is with my joy to present these commentaries to you for your edification. May God use these to build you up for His service.

—*Jack W. Hayford*

PREFACE

It is such a joy to present this commentary on Ephesians and Colossians for the Spirit-filled Life® New Testament Commentaries. I have been under increasing conviction that these letters must be seen not only as wonderful truth about the church or of the nature of Christ. Along with that, we need to welcome a realization of Paul's prayer (Eph. 1:15-23), being open to see these Spirit-inspired epistles with a view that empowers the church of Jesus Christ to advance as Christ's body here on earth. That's the real first-century target of these letters: to challenge God's people to continue the ministry of God's Son, with confidence in Him and depending on the power He gives through the Holy Spirit.

The church consists of men and women who are positioned in Christ to be equipped to replicate His powerful ministry with nothing less than the full authority our exalted King has given with His commission. Believers thus will see themselves as *real* members in the dynamically destined, spiritually resourced *body of Christ*. A "Spirit-formed church" hereby becomes a current incarnation of Jesus' continuing ministry.

It is appropriate to link the epistles to the Ephesians and Colossians in this one volume. Certainly there is some overlap in themes between these letters of Paul. But the uniqueness of each provides wonderful insight into God's plan for the advancement and increase of His kingdom. Ephesians gives God's emphasis on the dynamic movement of the body of Christ; Colossians presents the glorious picture of the supremacy of Christ, the Lord of the church, over all creation to which His own are expectant heirs together with Him. Together these two epistles form a unit which links the pressing need of God's people to understand *how* they are to function as God's vehicle for kingdom advance with *Who* it is that authorizes their task, generating His adequacy to minister in His name.

I express my thanks to the brothers and sisters in Christ of The Church on the Way who have embraced much of this understanding of what it means to minister as Christ's body. They not only understand, but they act in accordance with God's kingdom authority. I also thank those within the International Foursquare Church, as well as the larger body of Christ with whom I partner on the front lines of the spiritual conflict, as we reach in love to the whole world.

I appreciate the work of Thomas Nelson Publishers for the partnership I have had with them in bringing the message of the Spirit-filled Life to many. Specifically I wish to thank copy-editor Daniel Partner and managing editor Lee Hollaway. Their work enabled this volume to be completed. However, most especially and profoundly, I express my gratitude to Dr. David Seemuth. David's dedication and help in bringing this whole commentary series into being is not only so pivotal to it's progress, but his brotherly help in bringing my own contributions into a form for publication is a gift of grace to me.

As you open this and other volumes, may you be enabled for the work Jesus has for you, gaining added power through His blessing and added insight through this commentary.

—*Jack W. Hayford*
February, 2005

THE EPISTLE TO THE

EPHESIANS

CONTENTS

INTRODUCTION

Some people have described Paul's Epistle to the Ephesians as the Grand Canyon of Scripture because of its splendor. It sets forth so grand a picture of our position, responsibilities, privilege, and calling in Christ that as we read and reread its pages we cannot help but be amazed at the magnificence of God's goodness in His plan for us.

God wishes us to understand and fully embrace the Holy Spirit's purposes described in the Epistle to the Ephesians. This embrace brings the church to full fruitfulness as she immerses herself in God's provision of power and effectiveness in the heavenly realms as described in this glorious book. Yet, the majority of commentaries about Ephesians have been theological, informational, or devotional. These are profitable, of course, and strengthen believers by helping them understand their salvation in Christ. However, they miss the ecclesiastical, incarnational, and dynamic dimensions of this letter. They fail to bring into focus the believer's ministry in Christ. This should accompany the understanding of salvation in Christ.

Set in its historic context this letter addresses the church in Ephesus, where a spiritual breakthrough not only penetrated intense pagan darkness but spread to impact a wide geographic region. This breakthrough is linked to a Spirit-filled, supernatural ministry. Paul's letter to the Ephesians is more than a warm, truth-filled exhortation. Here the founding pastor, under the Holy Spirit's inspiration, writes to the congregation with which he spent more time than any other except his home church in Antioch. In this epistle, Paul formulates something far beyond a collection of inspirational, ethical, or theological ideas. Rather, the Holy Spirit moved the apostle to frame a summary of the underlying grid of ideas on which the Ephesian congregation was founded.

THE CITY OF EPHESUS

This was a large and important city on the west coast of Asia Minor (modern-day Turkey). Here the apostle Paul founded a church (Acts 19). A number of factors contributed to the prominence of this city in the first century.

The first factor was economics. Situated at the mouth of the river Cayster, Ephesus was the most favorable seaport in the province of Asia and the most important trade center west of Tarsus. Today, because of silting from the river, the ruins of the city are in a swamp five to seven miles inland.

Another factor was size. Although Pergamum was the capital of the province of Asia in Roman times, Ephesus was the largest city in the province, having a population of perhaps 300,000 people.

A third factor was culture. Ephesus contained a theater that seated an estimated twenty-five thousand people. A main thoroughfare, some 105 feet wide, ran from the theater to the harbor, at each end of which stood an impressive gate. The thoroughfare was flanked on each side by rows of columns fifty feet deep. Behind these columns were baths, gymnasiums, and impressive buildings.

The fourth and perhaps most significant reason for the prominence of Ephesus was religion. The temple of Artemis (or Diana, her Roman name) at Ephesus ranked as one of the Seven Wonders of the Ancient World. As the twin sister of Apollo and the daughter of Zeus, Artemis was known variously as the moon goddess, the goddess of hunting, and the patroness of young girls. The temple at Ephesus housed the image of Artemis that was reputed to have come directly from Zeus (Acts 19:35).

One hundred and twenty-seven columns supported the temple of Artemis, each of them 197 feet high. The Ephesians took great pride in this grand edifice. During the Roman period, they promoted the worship of Artemis by minting coins with the inscription, "Diana of Ephesus."

The history of Christianity at Ephesus began about A.D. 50, perhaps because of the efforts of Priscilla and Aquila (Acts 18:18). Paul came to Ephesus in about A.D. 52, establishing a resident ministry for the better part of three years (Acts 20:31). During his Ephesian ministry, Paul wrote the Book of 1 Corinthians (1 Cor. 16:8).

The Book of Acts reports that "all who dwelt in Asia heard the word of the Lord Jesus" (Acts 19:10) while Paul taught in the lecture hall of Tyrannus (Acts 19:9). Influence from his ministry undoubtedly resulted in the founding of churches in the Lycus River valley at Laodicea, Hierapolis, and Colossae.

So influential, in fact, was Paul's ministry at Ephesus that the silversmiths' league, which fashioned souvenirs of the temple, feared that the preaching of the gospel would undermine the influence of the great temple of Artemis (Acts 19:27). As a result, one of the silversmiths, a man named Demetrius, stirred up a riot against Paul.

Something distinctive shines here. It is the concept of the church as Christ's body. This must be seen not only as a poetic truth, but also as a vital prophetic truth. The church is that agency that presently incarnates the ministry of Jesus Christ. She proclaims the merits and benefits of His saving and sanctifying work and delivers the power and love of His caring, healing, and deliverance. An incomplete definition of our mission prevails in the church. It is born of a limited view of our role as Christ's body and advanced by misapplied spiritual power.

Ephesians calls every church leader (4:11) to nurture those they serve, to the end that they perceive of themselves as members in the dynamically destined, spiritually resourced body of Christ. More than any other New Testament book, Ephesians holds the key to teaching and advancing the ministry and mission of the local church. Thereby, the truly Spirit-formed church incarnates Jesus' ministry.

Ephesians stands alone from the other books of Scripture. In none other is the purpose of the church condensed with such clarity and precision.

For most of his ministry, the apostle Paul was itinerant. He served only two churches for an extended period, and one of these was at Ephesus. The believers there existed as a small congregation before he came, but in the course of his three years, God shook the entire city and the gospel extended throughout the entire region that is now Turkey. This occurred because Ephesus was a trade center where hosts of people came in and out. The witness of believers there impacted this human tide. The Epistle to the Ephesians may have also circulated among other churches (see Col. 4:16).

During his stay in Ephesus, Paul encountered both great opportunities and great dangers. Paul indicates in 1 Corinthians 15:52, "I fought with beasts at Ephesus," something of the vicious nature of the demonic presence and human potential for "wild" evil he faced—doubtless in prayer's spiritual warfare as well as in threats related to human encounters. He baptized believers who apparently came

THE CAREER OF THE APOSTLE PAUL (1:5)

Origin:	Tarsus in Cilicia (Acts 22:3)
	Tribe of Benjamin (Phil. 3:5)
Training:	Learned tentmaking (Acts 18:3)
	Studied under Gamaliel (Acts 22:3)
Early Religion:	Hebrew and Pharisee (Phil. 3:5)
	Persecuted Christians (Acts 8:1–3; Phil. 3:6)
Salvation:	Met the risen Christ on the road to Damascus (Acts 9:1–8)
	Received the infilling of the Holy Spirit on the street called Straight (Acts 9:17)
Called to Missions:	Church at Antioch was instructed by the Holy Spirit to send out Paul to the work (Acts 13:1–3)
	Carried the gospel to the Gentiles (Gal. 2:7–10)
Roles:	Spoke up for the church at Antioch at the council of Jerusalem (Acts 15:1–35)
	Opposed Peter (Gal. 2:11–21)
	Disputed with Barnabas about John Mark (Acts 15:36–41)
Achievements:	Three extended missionary journeys (Acts 13—20)
	Founded numerous churches in Asia Minor, Greece, and possibly Spain (Rom. 15:24, 28)
	Wrote letters to numerous churches and various individuals that now make up one-fourth of our New Testament
End of life:	Following arrest in Jerusalem, was sent to Rome (Acts 21:27; 28:16–31) According to Christian tradition, released from prison allowing further missionary work; rearrested, imprisoned again in Rome, and beheaded outside of the city.

to know the gospel through disciples of John the Baptist (Acts 19:1–5), and he countered the strong influence of magic in Ephesus (Acts 19:11–20).

After Paul departed from Ephesus, Timothy remained to combat false teaching (1 Tim. 1:3; 2 Tim. 4:3; Acts 20:29). The challenges he faced in sustaining the development of this city-church in the face of pagan confusion are indicated by the fallacies he had to overcome with bold, pastoral teaching and faithful, servant-leadership. Many traditions testify that the apostle John lived in Ephesus toward the end of the first century. In the Book of Revelation, John describes the church of Ephesus as flourishing, probably more than two decades later than the time of Paul's ministry in and letter to them. By this time, carnality and corrupted teaching not only

infested parts of the body there, but their loss of "first love" reflected that worshipless climate and removal from simplicity and childlike humility that will weaken the church anywhere (Rev. 2:1–7).

Of interest, and though incidental to the text of scripture, evidence for the tradition of John's leadership in Ephesus is reinforced by the fact that in the sixth century A.D. the Roman Emperor Justinian (A.D. 527–565) raised a magnificent church to John's memory in this city. Ephesus clearly played a prominent role in the history of the church. A long line of bishops in the Eastern Church lived there. In A.D. 431, the Council of Ephesus officially condemned the Nestorian heresy, which taught that there were two separate persons, one divine and one human, in the person of Jesus Christ.[1]

---

[1] Ronald F. Youngblood, general editor; F. F. Bruce and R. K. Harrison, consulting editors, *Nelson's New Illustrated Bible Dictionary: An authoritative one-volume reference work on the Bible with full color illustrations* [computer file], electronic edition of the revised edition of *Nelson's Illustrated Bible Dictionary*, Logos Library System, (Nashville: Thomas Nelson) 1997, © 1995, p. 407.

Ephesians:
Christ Incarnate . . . Again

_____

We must understand that Paul's letter is given to us not simply to affirm the historic and didactic, but to actuate the apostolic and dynamic. The full embrace of the Holy Spirit's purposes through the Epistle to the Ephesians is the key to the church's immersion in that mindset that will bring her to fullest fruitfulness. The vast majority of commentary and preaching from Ephesians is either solely theological, informational or devotional (and as such is profitable and is strengthening to how believers understand their *salvation* in Christ). The result is that Ephesians is generally taught with a *limiting though life-giving* approach, but thereby misses the *ecclesiastical, incarnational and dynamic* dimensions of the letter (failing to bring into focus the believer's understanding of their *ministry* in Christ).

Paul's letter to the Ephesian church is more than a warm, truth-filled exhortation. Here is the founding pastor, under the Holy Spirit's inspiration, writing to the congregation he spent more time with than any other except his "home church" in Antioch. In his epistle to the Ephesians, Paul is formulating something far beyond a collection of inspirational, ethical, or theological ideas.

Rather, the Holy Spirit moved the apostle to frame a summary of that *undergirding grid* of ideas on which the Ephesian congregation was founded.

Something distinctive shines here. The central issue is Ephesians' exposition of the concept of *"the church as Christ's body;"* a term that must be seen as a *prophetic truth*, not only a *poetic term*. The church is that agency that presently incarnates the ministry of Jesus Christ. Her ministry *not only is to proclaim* the merits and benefits of His saving and sanctifying work, *but also to reach with continual ministry* in the power and love of His caring, healing, and delivering works. There is an incomplete definition that prevails in the church, concerning our mission (actually "unworthy," i.e., without full weight). It is born of a limited view of our role as "Christ's body," and advanced by a reticence born of misapplied "power" emphases concerning "Spirit-fullness."

The call of every servant leader (Ephesians 4:11) is to nurture those they serve in Christ's body to come to a perception of themselves as *real members* in the dynamically destined, spiritually resourced *body of Christ*. More than any other New Testament book, Ephesians holds the key to teaching and advancing *ministry mindset and mission* in the local church—thereby, the truly *Spirit-formed church*—incarnating Jesus' continuing ministry by the power of the Holy Spirit.

1. The Believer's Position of Security in Christ 1:1–14

Not merely for personal assurance, these verses establish the clear need for every believer *knowing* what God has done for us in Christ, and what our position in Him really is, but to use that secured confidence as the footings for an anticipated ministry in His name.

We must advance in a Spirit-empowered, Spirit-resourced ministry-mindset. This can rise as the believer *learns* "who I am" (through Christ's redemptive work in His Cross), and thereby *opens* to "what I can expect" (through Christ's ministry works by His Spirit in us today). In this light, "in Christ" moves beyond referencing our "acceptance" through His *saving work* for us, to "in Christ" *(Gk., en Christos—the Anointed One)*, referencing our "anointing" for His *Spirit's work* through us.

2. The Believer's Purpose and Destiny 1:15–23

This does not merely affirm God's divine design, personal intent, and warm desire toward believers in general, but also urges us to lay hold of His personal commitment to make each one of the redeemed (a) confident beyond doubts when weak, assailed, or discouraged, and (b) settled in the certainty of Christ's dominion flowing to and through them, as literal members of His body.

3. The Believer's Place of Authority 2:1–10

This does not merely describe the humbling position unto which we're lifted in Christ, notwithstanding our past deadness in sin, or the degree to which the power of evil manipulated or controlled our lives. God also declares the profound dimensions of partnership to which He has invited us "by grace" *(i.e., by the Spirit's flow to and through us)*, that within this grace *everything the Father created each of us to be* (v.10) can be fully expected—in character, vocation, and ministry.

4. The Believer's Call to Unity 2:11–22

God does not merely face a dated, cultural problem, nor to offer a call to "unity" as a generous thought to be embraced as "the Christian thing to do." He also confronts an essential priority that calls every believer to learn and live in that growing grace which transcends human habits of ethnic separatism. This is fundamental to the maximum release of the Spirit's power being released through Christ's body—making way for God's fullest habitation by His Spirit (vv. 20–22), and for His mightiest incursion against the darkness (chs. 3, 6).

5. The Believer's Revelation of the Mystery 3:1–21

Again, this is not merely a theological discourse enunciating (1) Paul's insight into God's global intent for the church (v. 1–13), and (2) the beauty of a resplendent glory to "ultimately" be revealed in the church (v. 14–21). God gives a two-edged focus on *strategy* and *capacity*—God's intended strategy to confound the Adversary by penetrating the darkness via His *kingdom mystery* working "in the church that functions by the Holy Spirit's power (love), and only becomes effective as each member welcomes its fullness and release in Him.

6. The Believer's Worthy Walk and Equipping for Ministry 4:1–16

The call is not merely a unity proposed as a possibility for consideration, as though it were but a noble ideal. This is a mandate to "earth-level" partnership if "heaven-level" dynamics ("according to the power working in you") would be realized, while making clear this unity requires the exercise of aggressive initiatives in order to be realized.

We also do not have merely an outline of officials assigned tasks for "church work," or merely a charge to leaders to train, resource, and prepare people for "Christian service." Rather this also is Christ's strategic plan for servicing every member of His body with servant-leadership that can/will (1) bring the body to wholeness and health, (2) strengthen the body with truth and confidence, and (3) mobilize the body through *both* earth-level and heaven-level resourcing. This cultivates a people with confidence in *how to minister* unto the building up of the local body of believers through (a) personal care and mutual ministry, and through (b) evangelism, as "ministering people." Such "ministering people" reach the lost with life, love, and hope and with effective prayer and healing ministry, as well as

THE CHURCH REALLY IS JESUS' BODY

In terms of believers conceiving of themselves as the embodiment of Jesus, in other words, as members of the body of Christ, we use "body of Christ" as a metaphor and not a conviction people think of. You pinch my finger and you have pinched me. "Members of my body" is not a metaphor—it's me. And "members of the body of Jesus" never was intended to be a poetic term to describe all these people who have been saved. But that's how people think about that term. It's a collective term to describe us all, rather than a literal term that describes Jesus in His people doing exactly what He did in His ministry—but doing it wherever they go, rather than wherever He went. People must be equipped to think of themselves that way and to function and live that way.

THE CHURCH REALLY IS AN ARMY

Generally speaking, believers are not trained to expect and pursue spiritual warfare. The invisible realm and the kind of warfare described in Ephesians 6, though believed in, is too seldom perceived or seen by leaders in Evangelicalism. To them, the invisible realm is an idea, not a reality. And the evidence of that is that if you talk about demons, for example, people look at you uneasily or suspiciously. If you talk about spiritual warfare, you'll get an argument that you're saying the Cross didn't obtain the victory and you're trying to add something. That's ridiculous to the proposition, and you can get in danger if you talk too much about that stuff. Spiritual warfare in the ministry of prayer and intercession is a pivot point in the church being the church. Ephesians shows that, and it shows it elsewhere.

solid, responsive verbal witness from "acquired platforms" for "a ready answer."

7. The Believer's Spirit-enabled Purity 4:17—5:14

God does not give us merely a set of requirements for a "worthy walk" in holiness of life, as though purity—though an appropriately godly objective—was an end in itself. Rather, He gives a summons to discern and confront, deny and find deliverance, from those things that diminish the capacity for Christ's life to flow through the believer in

THE CHURCH AS GOD'S ARMY

- RESOURCED by the Holy Spirit's gifting 1:3
- OVERFLOWED as Christ is incarnated in His "present body." 1:20–23
- ENFRANCHISED as "partnered" with Christ in His "present kingdom." 2:6 (unto the "good works" ministry, always intended for each one. 2:10)
- PREDESTINED to confound and overthrow the Adversary by the Spirit's power, *to the degree she (the church) invites and welcomes the release of that power; THEN,* walking and ministering in the path and pursuit of a liberated, discerning, and dedicated, practical daily *walk* in the Spirit, and a continual life of worship and obedience that sustains an enabling, ongoing *infilling* of the Spirit... *she*
- ENGAGES her warfare unto the spread of God's kingdom dominion everywhere.

The Follow-through Pattern for Pastors
The Ephesian Epistle Focuses on Developing

A. A body of people sensitized to spiritual realities, receptive of resources given by the Holy Spirit's gifts (1:3, *penumatika)*; a people who discern ministry in the spiritual realm (*epouranios*, 1:15–23; 2:6; 3:10; 6:10–18).

B. A body of people born of the Spirit (1:4–7), filled with the Spirit (1:8–14) as they become grounded in the certainty of their identity in Christ, and become enlightened to their mission and authority in Him (1:4—2:10).

C. A body of people who live out the unity intended by the Cross (2:11–18), that walls separating the body of Christ not be tolerated, but a unity of love give place to God's Spirit throughout the church (2:19–22).

D. A body aware of its role in the spiritual realm and its call to warfare in that invisible arena (3:1–13); becoming ever deepened and broadened (3:14–19) in the power-life of the Holy Spirit's enablement (3:20, 21).

E. A body united and mobilized by sensitive leaders who understand and serve their intended role to equip believers *unto ministry*—the life of Jesus showing *through* them as surely as His character grows *within* (4:1–16).

F. A body maturing in overcoming carnality and worldliness, committed to overcoming all carnal compromise that would cripple them for effective combat against the Adversary: "Don't give him place!" (4:17—5:14)

G. A body constantly pressed toward Spirit-fullness and worship (5:15–20). These two essentials are pivotal to experiencing the manifest *presence* of God *among* His people, and the manifest *power* of God *through* His people.

H. A body growing in the health of right and righteous domestic and social relationships, that the practical qualities of living faith be demonstrated in daily life, breeding credibility among onlookers (5:21—6:9).

I. A body effectively arriving at the prime focus of its ministry—engaging the power of darkness in the invisible (6:10–18), that the advance of the kingdom of God may occur in the world around them (6:19–24).

ministry; from those things that can concede ground to the Adversary and disable effective advance against him and his hordes.

8. The Believer's Understanding of the Will of God for Family and Lifestyle 5:15—6:9

This is not merely a set of guidelines,

instructions, and requirements regarding our pathway toward and pursuit of domestic order and ethical professional lifestyles. God gives an announcement that *these* traits of "divine order" for home and business life must be put in place if the church—the troops for battle—intend to succeed in the larger arena of overthrowing the "order" of the dark powers seeking to dominate our world.

9. The Believer's Warfare and Victory 6:10–24

God does not give merely a metaphorical description of a conflict of ideas we face as the church lives "in the world but not of it," and not merely a concluding set of observations. God, through Paul, presents this as the *point of it all: to see the church in the heavenlies.*

Opening Greeting

Ephesians 1:1, 2

Paul, an apostle of Jesus Christ by the will of God, to the saints who are in Ephesus, and faithful in Christ Jesus: Grace to you and peace from God our Father and the Lord Jesus Christ (1:1, 2).

Paul gives a typical greeting for first-century letters. Yet, for those in Christ, invoking the name of God the Father and the Lord Jesus Christ is never typical. Such a declaration situates the believer squarely under the realm of the reign of God on earth, which was ushered in with dramatic power upon the death and resurrection of Christ. Yet, the depth and dimension of meaning is expansively more grand for those in Christ. This declaration situates the believer squarely under and within the realm of the reign of God. *"In Christ" not only designates Jesus' person as Savior and Lord, but this and other recurrent use of His title as Messiah—the Christ, the Anointed One—point to the believer's enabling by that anointing. Just as surely as we may open to become recipients of the saving wealth of His redemption, so we may open to the dynamic of His overflowing us with the anointing of His Spirit and thereby His ministry and power. Jesus' death and resurrection have established joint blessings: (a) believers are declared "saints" (holy ones) by reason of the justifying power of the Cross's finished work, and (b) are bequeathed "grace" (the attendant favor of the Holy Spirit's presence and power available to them continually) and "peace" (the security of an unchallengable relationship with God and the unifying wholeness and health of soul it allows.* This perspective brings a new realization to the believer's life and helps the believer embrace the dynamic life in the Holy Spirit and engage in extending the kingdom of God.

Paul identifies himself as an apostle. *Apostle* means "sent one." Indeed, Paul was sent out by Jesus (Acts 9:15; 26: 7, 18). Paul recognized that Jesus gave him the ministry of an apostle for the sake of the people, and he wanted to do everything that he could to help them know their inheritance in Christ.

People tend to become what others think they are. Our Father God calls us saints, His holy ones. No person or institution can make you saintly; only the love of God in Jesus Christ can confer sainthood on us. Sainthood is not an accomplished perfection, but an established position that we have been given in Jesus Christ. Although the saints in Ephesus were still in the process of growing, Paul calls them faithful in Christ because they had put their full faith in Jesus.

Paul moves on to one of his favorite concepts: grace. This is God's favor that has been freely given to us.

WORD STUDY
APOSTLE

Apostle—*a special messenger of Jesus Christ; a person to whom Jesus delegated authority for certain tasks.* The word *apostle* is used of those twelve disciples whom Jesus sent out, two by two, during His ministry in Galilee. These men expanded Christ's ministry of preaching and healing. Evidently, when they were sent out they were first called apostles (Mark 3:14; 6:30).

The word *apostle* is sometimes used in the New Testament to mean *messenger* in a general sense. For instance, when delegates of Christian communities were charged with conveying contributions to a charitable fund, they were described as "messengers [apostles] of the churches" (2 Cor. 8:23).

The word *apostle* has a wider meaning than this in the letters of the apostle Paul. It includes people who, like himself, were not included in the original twelve disciples, but who saw the risen Christ and were specially commissioned by Him. Paul's claim to be an apostle was questioned by others. He based his apostleship, however, on the direct call of the exalted Lord who appeared to him on the Damascus Road and on the Lord's blessing of his ministry in winning converts and establishing churches (1 Cor. 15:10).

In 1 Corinthians 12:28 and Ephesians 4:11, apostles are listed along with prophets and other saints as part of the foundation of the household of God. In this strictly New Testament sense, apostles are confined to the first generation of Christians.

At an early stage in the church's history, it was agreed that apostles to the Jews and Gentiles should be divided into separate camps. Paul and Barnabas were to concentrate on the evangelization of Gentiles; Peter, John, and James (the Lord's brother) were to continue evangelizing Jews (Gal. 2:7–9).

As pioneers in the work of making converts and planting churches, apostles were exposed to special dangers. When persecution erupted, they were the primary targets for attack (1 Cor. 4:9–13). Paul, in particular, welcomed the suffering he endured as an apostle because it was his way of participating in the suffering of Christ (Rom. 8:17; 2 Cor. 1:5–7).[2]

---

[2] Ronald F. Youngblood, general editor; F. F. Bruce and R. K. Harrison, consulting editors, *Nelson's New Illustrated Bible Dictionary: An authoritative one-volume reference work on the Bible with full color illustrations* [computer file], electronic edition of the revised edition of *Nelson's Illustrated Bible Dictionary*, Logos Library System, (Nashville: Thomas Nelson) 1997, © 1995, pp. 91–92.

WORD STUDY
SAINTS

Saints—*people who have been separated from the world and consecrated to the worship and service of God.* Followers of the Lord are referred to as saints throughout the Bible, although the meaning of this word is developed more fully in the New Testament. Consecration (committed separation) and purity are the basic meanings of the term. Believers are called saints (Rom. 1:7) and saints in Christ Jesus (Phil. 1:1) because they belong to the One who provides their sanctification.

When Christ returns, the saints will be clothed in their righteous acts (Rev. 19:8) because they will have continued to live in faith through God's power (1 Sam. 2:9) and Christ's praying for them (Rom. 8:27). The saints are also those to whom the privilege of revelation (Col. 1:26; Jude 3) and the task of ministry (Eph. 4:12) are committed.[3]

We have done nothing to earn it. Grace is often defined as unmerited favor; it is a disposition of God towards us that we had nothing to do with. The Holy Spirit operates from the posture of grace (Acts 11:23). Paul pronounced an invocation of God's blessing by the power of the Spirit when he wrote, "Grace to you." This expresses one of the most important truths in the New Testament and reflects the early church's desire to see an ongoing work of the Holy Spirit in the lives of the saints.

Most people regard peace as the absence of conflict. This is not so with Paul. For him, peace marks the presence of God, for in His presence there is peace, harmony, and unity. The concept of peace describes the state where everything comes into full integration in the kingdom of God, whether it is a human personality, a home, or a society.

---

[3] Ronald F. Youngblood, general editor; F. F. Bruce and R. K. Harrison, consulting editors, *Nelson's New Illustrated Bible Dictionary*: An authoritative one-volume reference work on the Bible with full color illustrations [computer file], electronic edition of the revised edition of *Nelson's Illustrated Bible Dictionary*, Logos Library System, (Nashville: Thomas Nelson) 1997, © 1995, p. 1113.

WORD STUDY
THE WILL OF GOD

There are several facets of the will of God. First, there is the will of God that ordained all things. In the original creation, God's will was benevolent and it continues to be so. God willed that humankind would have a choice and be sovereign. He gave free will to humanity and thus put Himself at risk of being misjudged, for He has willed that everything that takes place on this planet shall pass through the grid of the human will. The worst consequence of the human will is mankind's partnership with Satan in rebellion against God. If a person's will sets itself against God, certain consequences are set in motion. God will not superimpose His will on self-will.

Chapter 1

Ephesians 1:3–14

THE BELIEVER'S POSITION OF SECURITY IN CHRIST

Paul begins his epistle with a list of all the benefits of redemption. Chapters 1–3 tell of the abundant blessings that are lavished upon the church. In chapters 4–6, Paul calls the church to act in accordance with the riches of the grace bestowed upon her. The first fourteen verses of chapter 1 constitute a declaration of full security in Christ. But Christ is more than simply a place to rest. The church's secure confidence in Christ is the basis of a Spirit-empowered ministry. This ministry results from the believer's understanding of Christ's redemptive work in His Cross. Our position in Christ is possible by our acceptance of His saving work. Its purpose is seen in the Spirit's anointing for His work through us.

Blessings of Full Redemption

Ephesians 1:3–8

———————

Blessed be the God and Father of our Lord Jesus Christ, who has blessed us with every spiritual blessing in the heavenly places in Christ, just as He chose us in Him before the foundation of the world, that we should be

WORD STUDY
ADOPTION

Adoption—This indicates the acceptance of believers as children of God. God brings us into a relationship not of servant to master or even guest to host but of son to father. The son becomes the heir of what the father possesses. Believers are in line to receive all the spiritual blessings of the heavenly Father because He has accepted us in the Beloved. The all-encompassing work of the Son of God accomplished redemption, thus bringing full acceptance by the Father. The verb *accepted* is a perfect, passive participle. This means that the phrase *accepted in the Beloved* is an accomplished fact in the past that extends into the continuous present. The Father sees us in the beloved Son and everything that is accomplished by His Son has been carried into our lives.

The phrase *He has made us accepted* is literally translated, "He has graced us with grace." We can claim no merit before the Father. Grace is found only in the beloved Son through faith. The fact that we are in Christ, in the Beloved, is a treasure. We stand only in the merits of Christ.

It was His will to bring us into His family. The good pleasure of His will indicates the spirit and mood of God's will towards us. His will is good and there is pleasure there. It is possible to know the will of God but not submit to it. No one will ever submit to God's will if it is less than good. When the Lord does what He wants He accomplishes wonderful things. This is His nature. God does not impose His will upon anyone, but is disposed toward revealing, unfolding, and working His will in every person who opens to it.

If the words *chosen, adopted,* and *accepted* possessed the believers' souls, it would transform the way we relate to one another. But our hearts have not been stretched by the grandeur of the love of God as expressed in Ephesians 1:4–6. To be possessed by the love of God is to be controlled by the revelation of Jesus' words to Nicodemus: "For God so loved the world that He gave His only begotten Son, that whoever believes in Him should not perish but have everlasting life" and Paul's words to the Romans: "But God demonstrates His own love toward us, in that while we were still sinners, Christ died for us" (John 3:16; Rom. 5:8). If God's love were to possess the church, the bonding, mutuality, and fellowship that God desires would be realized.

WORD STUDY
ELECTION

Election—Throughout the history of redemption, election has characterized God's saving activity. He chose and called Abraham from Ur to Canaan, making an everlasting covenant with him and his offspring (Gen. 11:31—12:7; Neh. 9:7; Is. 41:8). God also called Moses to lead His people out of bondage (Ex. 2:24—3:10; Deut. 6:21–23; Ps. 105). He chose Israel from among the nations of the world to be His special covenant people (Deut. 4:37; 7:6–7; Is. 44:1–2).

Election to salvation takes place in Christ (Eph. 1:4; 2:10) as a part of God's purpose for the human race. In His eternal plan, God allows us to use our freedom to rebel against Him. Thus, it is gracious of God to save those who find salvation through Jesus Christ. It is not unjust that God does not save everyone, since no one deserves to be saved (Matt. 20:14; Rom. 1:18; 9:15). Election is gracious; it is also unconditional and unmerited (Acts 13:48; Rom. 9:11; 1 Pet. 1:2). It is an expression of the eternal, sovereign will of God who cannot change (Rom. 8:29; 2 Thess. 2:13). Therefore, the salvation of the elect is certain (Rom. 8:28, 33).[4]

holy and without blame before Him in love (vv. 3, 4).

Believers invoke the word *blessing* in many ways. Most often blessings describe things people receive from God to benefit them. Here, however, Paul speaks of the blessedness of God Himself. We are to praise or *bless* God because He has spoken such beautiful things on our behalf. The Greek word *pnumatikos* is translated as *spiritual blessing* but is translated *spiritual gifts* in 1 Corinthians 14:1. This word is an umbrella term that encompasses the power, gifts, and the resources given to us in heavenly places.

The heavenly places are not found in another galaxy, or a distant location. This is the invisible realm. There is an immediate invisible realm around you. This is where your greatest enemies are (the demonic hosts) and where great hosts of angels are sent by God to come to your defense. It is also the realm where the promises of God's Word and the gifts of the Spirit are available. These are not only for you, but for others as well.

---

4   Ronald F. Youngblood, general editor; F. F. Bruce and R. K. Harrison, consulting editors, *Nelson's New Illustrated Bible Dictionary*: An authoritative one-volume reference work on the Bible with full color illustrations [computer file], electronic edition of the revised edition of *Nelson's Illustrated Bible Dictionary*, Logos Library System, (Nashville: Thomas Nelson) 1997, © 1995, pp. 389–90.

WORD STUDY
PREDESTINATION

Predestination—*the biblical teaching that declares the sovereignty of God over human beings in such a way that the freedom of the human will is also preserved.* God's predestination of human events does not eliminate human choice. A thorough understanding of how God can maintain His sovereignty and still allow human freedom seems to be reserved for His infinite mind alone. Great minds have struggled with this problem for centuries.[5]

In addition to blessing God for spiritual blessings, Paul points to God's choice to establish a people of His own. We must note two aspects of this choosing. First, it is a choice to create a group through whom He can work out His eternal plan. Second, since Paul focuses on the plural *us* in this text, he hints at the fact that individual election is not the issue here. God takes pleasure in enabling everyone to have the opportunity to enter into the elect community of God's people by faith. God chose to establish a people of His own before the world began. In other words, God was thinking about His redemptive plan of grace even before creation. It was a plan that was borne deep in His loving heart before the foundation of the world.

The point of being the chosen ones is to be holy and blameless. Some have called this *election*. God has chosen us because of His unconditional love toward those who believe. He knows that true peace and health can come only when we live out kingdom life here on earth. When we do that, we demonstrate and experience this love from the Father. While some refer to the elect or the chosen as if God chooses some individually to be saved and others to be damned, the Bible here is referring to God's gracious choice to have a group of people through whom the message and ministry of salvation may come. The individual is not in view. God calls the church the chosen ones.

Let us note what the text says and does not say. The church is elected, chosen, for a reason. That is, to embrace divine holiness. Similarly, the church is predestined for a reason: adoption as children of God. Each truth points to a reality that the church shall ultimately realize. The

---

5 Ronald F. Youngblood, general editor; F. F. Bruce and R. K. Harrison, consulting editors, *Nelson's New Illustrated Bible Dictionary*: An authoritative one-volume reference work on the Bible with full color illustrations [computer file], electronic edition of the revised edition of *Nelson's Illustrated Bible Dictionary*, Logos Library System, (Nashville: Thomas Nelson) 1997, © 1995, p. 1025.

Scriptures here do not suggest that some people are elected to receive salvation and others not. Nor is there a sense that some are predestined to salvation and others not. In 1:4–5, Paul focuses on the future reality of the church. This reality has been part of God's plan from before the beginning of time.

> Having predestined us to adoption as sons by Jesus Christ to Himself, according to the good pleasure of His will, to the praise of the glory of His grace, by which He made us accepted in the Beloved (vv. 5, 6).

Paul continues to list reasons for declaring the blessedness of God. Here he adds concepts that are rich in depth: predestination, adoption, grace, and acceptance. Each word deserves pause and reflection.

> In Him we have redemption through His blood, the forgiveness of sins, according to the riches of His grace which He made to abound toward us in all wisdom and prudence (vv. 7, 8).

With this verse, the blessings given to the people in Christ are heaped up. Redemption, forgiveness, grace, God's wisdom, and prudence come to those who believe. Again, each truth contains a wealth of encouragement for the followers of Christ. Christ's redemption purchased people from the domain of evil. The image here is of the slave who is purchased by a beloved master and then freed.

Our hands, which are without scars, can receive the gift of salvation because His hands were pierced upon the Cross. This gift of salvation is truly free and has infinite worth. Forgiveness through redemption is a tender theme that cannot

ACCENT ON APPLICATION
Predestination and Evangelism

God has chosen a people through whom He works out his eternal purpose. He has predestined these same people for adoption as sons. But this does not negate the need for evangelism. People have the choice of whether or not they will become part of this redemptive group. The church preaches the gospel and each individual chooses to believe or not. Every sinner can choose to be a follower of Jesus Christ through faith. God excludes no one from this opportunity. He is not willing that any should perish but that all come to repentance (2 Pet. 3:9). Thus, believers must take seriously their responsibility to be ambassadors of Christ, for God uses us in bringing people to Himself.

WORD STUDY
REDEMPTION

Redemption—*deliverance by payment of a price.* In the New Testament, redemption refers to salvation from sin, death, and the wrath of God by Christ's sacrifice. In the Old Testament, the word redemption refers to redemption by a kinsman (Lev. 25:24, 51–52; Ruth 4:6; Jer. 32:7–8), rescue or deliverance (Num. 3:49), and ransom (Ps. 111:9; 130:7). In the New Testament, it refers to loosing (Luke 2:38; Heb. 9:12) and loosing away (Luke 21:28; Rom. 3:24; Eph. 1:14).

Old Testament redemption was applied to property, animals, persons, and the nation of Israel as a whole. In nearly every instance, freedom from obligation, bondage, or danger was secured by the payment of a price, a ransom, bribe, satisfaction, or sum of money paid to obtain freedom, favor, or reconciliation. People may redeem property, animals, and individuals (slaves, prisoners, indentured relatives) who are legally obligated to God or in bondage for other reasons. God alone, however, is able to redeem from the slavery of sin (Ps. 130:7–8), enemy oppressors (Deut. 15:15), and the power of death (Job 19:25–26; Ps. 49:8–9).

The New Testament emphasizes the tremendous cost of redemption: "the precious blood of Christ" (1 Pet. 1:19; Eph. 1:7), which is also called an atoning sacrifice, "a propitiation by His blood" (Rom. 3:25). Believers are exhorted to remember the price of their redemption as a motivation to personal holiness (1 Cor. 6:19–20; 1 Pet. 1:13–19). The Bible also emphasizes the result of redemption: freedom from sin and freedom to serve God through Jesus Christ our Lord.

How can we fail to rejoice, having been freed from the oppressive bondage of slavery to sin (John 8:34; Rom. 6:18), the law (Gal. 4:3–5; 5:1), and the fear of death (Heb. 2:14–15)? "Therefore if the Son makes you free, you shall be free indeed" (John 8:36).[6]

be exaggerated. The power of God's redemption is as mighty as the blood of Christ that paid for our forgiveness and has broken the power of sin in us.

Forgiveness has at its root the canceling of a debt owed. God rightly could demand payment for sin. That payment is death according to Romans 6:23. But

---

[6] Ronald F. Youngblood, general editor; F. F. Bruce and R. K. Harrison, consulting editors, *Nelson's New Illustrated Bible Dictionary: An authoritative one-volume reference work on the Bible with full color illustrations* [computer file], electronic edition of the revised edition of *Nelson's Illustrated Bible Dictionary*, Logos Library System, (Nashville: Thomas Nelson) 1997, © 1995, pp. 1073–74.

WORD STUDY
FORGIVENESS

Forgiveness—*the act of excusing or pardoning others in spite of their slights, shortcomings, and errors.* Forgiveness in the New Testament is directly linked to Christ (Acts 5:31; Col. 1:14), His sacrificial death on the Cross (Rom. 4:24), and His resurrection (2 Cor. 5:15). He was the morally perfect sacrifice (Rom. 8:3) and the final and ultimate fulfillment of all Old Testament sacrifices (Heb. 9:11—10:18). Since He bore the law's death penalty against sinners (Gal. 3:10–13), those who trust in His sacrifice are freed from that penalty. By faith, sinners are forgiven—*justified* in Paul's terminology (Rom. 3:28; Gal. 3:8–9). Those who are forgiven sin's penalty are dead to its controlling power in their lives (Rom. 6:1–23).[7]

He instead frees the sinner from death through the payment of Christ's death. The riches of God's grace are poured forth in Christ. God holds nothing back from the church in general and the believer in particular. God delivers these blessings to us with wisdom and prudence.

Paul moves from *we* and *us*—a general presentation of salvation—to *you*. In this way, he brings the truth to bear on the readers. Salvation is not just a great spiritual truth; it enables believers to daily live in the Holy Spirit and strengthens them to engage in spiritual battle. This brings about the expansion of the kingdom of God.

Partnership In God's Purpose

Ephesians 1:9–14

Ephesians 1:3–14 constitutes one sentence in the Greek language in which it was written. In these verses, Paul moves the believer to the great realization of the church's partnership with God in bringing about His purpose.

Having made known to us the mystery of His will, according to His good pleasure which He purposed in Himself, that in the dispensation of the fullness of the times He might gather together in one all things in Christ, both which are in heaven and which are on earth—in Him (vv. 9, 10).

---

7   Ronald F. Youngblood, general editor; F. F. Bruce and R. K. Harrison, consulting editors, *Nelson's New Illustrated Bible Dictionary*: An authoritative one-volume reference work on the Bible with full color illustrations [computer file], electronic edition of the revised edition of *Nelson's Illustrated Bible Dictionary*, Logos Library System, (Nashville: Thomas Nelson) 1997, © 1995, pp. 461–62.

CROSS REFERENCE
1 Corinthians 1:20–25

"Where is the wise? Where is the scribe? Where is the disputer of this age? Has not God made foolish the wisdom of this world? For since, in the wisdom of God, the world through wisdom did not know God, it pleased God through the foolishness of the message preached to save those who believe. For Jews request a sign, and Greeks seek after wisdom; but we preach Christ crucified, to the Jews a stumbling block and to the Greeks foolishness, but to those who are called, both Jews and Greeks, Christ the power of God and the wisdom of God. Because the foolishness of God is wiser than men, and the weakness of God is stronger than men."

Paul declares in this section that God's wisdom and power is seen most in the message of the Cross and Resurrection. The supposed weakness of Christ when He died became true strength because His atoning death brings salvation to all who believe. Some people think that the message of the gospel is foolish. But it is actually the ultimate wisdom of God. In its simple message, God brings hope to all humanity.

The word *mystery* occurs six times in this book (1:9; 3:3, 4, 9; 5:32; 6:19). When Paul uses the word *mystery*, he does not mean secret, rather the opposite. God has fully disclosed His will to us. There is nothing mysterious about it. The disclosure does unfold step by step, but God never leaves us in the dark concerning His will. There are no secrets in God's will because He has made it known to us. He wants it to be understood so that we can participate in it.

God takes great delight in revealing the fullness of His love and the beauty of His plans to bring people back to Himself. It is His intention to fully reveal His love, not to keep it concealed. In this, we see the heart of God. He purposes in Himself to display the abundance of His kindness to the world. This emphasizes two realities. First, there is no outside power that forces the hand of God to save humanity. Second, only the magnificence of God's love for His creation moved Him to accomplish redemption.

The dispensation of the fullness of the times refers to how God works in the present age. The Greek word for dispensation (*oikonomian*) is the word from which we get the word *economy*. This is the administration of God's will. Similarly, an economy is the practical working of market and financial realities in the world. Paul does not have in mind a specific, measured period. He speaks of the purpose, or end, of the plan. That is, to

THE MEANING OF MYSTERY

In the last 150 years, the mystery novel evolved in American literature. This genre involves a crime, a detective, and a perpetrator of the crime. As the story proceeds, the detective uses various clues to try to solve the mystery of the crime. In the end of the story a full disclosure of the mystery is given. The term *mystery* was applied to this type of literature because when the reader reached the end of the story they knew who committed the crime. This pattern causes us to think about mystery from the point of view of *not* knowing the outcome of the story. But this is 180 degrees from what Paul intends. He revealed what used to be hidden. He made it clearly seen. So, we are not cast as detectives, straining to understand something that remains veiled. God has made known to us the mystery of His will.

bring together in one all things in Christ. The focus is upon putting people in Christ. This is the place of ultimate safety and fullness, not only for humanity, but also for all creation. Indeed, even creation benefits from redemption (Rom. 8:18–21).

In Him also we have obtained an inheritance, being predestined according to the purpose of Him who works all things according to the counsel of His will (v. 11).

We receive an eternal inheritance because a will has been signed in our interest. God signed this will when Jesus died for us on the Cross. The counsel of God's will means that anything that gets aligned with God's will is never going to be defeated because no one is more powerful or loving than God.

ACCENT ON APPLICATION
Love and the Plan of Salvation

Through an understanding of Ephesians 1:9 we see the fullness of God's love. In no way is God a mean old man who waits for people to slip up in order to bring punishment. Yet, this is how many perceive God. Others believe that God simply overlooks sin. In Ephesians, the plan for salvation is in full view. It highlights the amazing love of God. This tremendous love, which is a part of God's nature, provokes in Him the plan of salvation.

CROSS REFERENCE
Romans 8:28

"And we know that all things work together for good to those who love God, to those who are the called according to His purpose."

This verse has been an anchor for many people. It has also been seriously misunderstood throughout history. This is not a blatant announcement that everything that happens is God's desire. Evil still happens. But for those who have been reconciled to God, who love Him, true good will result from suffering. God is interceding by the Holy Spirit for those in weakness. No extreme experience is without consequent blessing from God because He brings gold out of the furnace of difficulty.

These sufferings work together for good. Isolated events may seem to be counterproductive to godly living; even contrary to God's ultimate plan. But put together by the loving hand of God, events work for God's design to bring blessing to believers. We may not know what is going on in our lives. But through this verse, God has given us His assurance that His ultimate plan for our lives will be worked out. Nothing escapes the eyes of God because His Spirit is within us. Therefore, He knows us intimately and knows what we need in the long run.

God works everything according to His will to what He made up His mind to do. He wants to unfold this purpose to us and then energize that purpose through us. He does not outwork His purpose independently from us; He works it through those who open up and allow Him to do the work. The will of God for every person is this: That something of God's life be ministered through us in this world. The great topic of the will of God concerns what pours out of our lives, not what we do as we pass through this life. The phrase *the counsel of His will*, is used to describe a plot, plan, or conspiracy. God is conspiring to get something done in our lives and in our world by placing us in Christ and working His will through us.

That we who first trusted in Christ should be to the praise of His glory (v. 12)

Paul usually uses the word Christ (Greek *christos*) without a definite article. In 1:12, however, he speaks of being part of that group who was the first to hope in *the* Christ. He uses the definite article with the

---

CROSS REFERENCE
Acts 19:1–6

"And it happened, while Apollos was at Corinth, that Paul, having passed through the upper regions, came to Ephesus. And finding some disciples he said to them, 'Did you receive the Holy Spirit when you believed?' So they said to him, 'We have not so much as heard whether there is a Holy Spirit.' And he said to them, 'Into what then were you baptized?' So they said, 'Into John's baptism.' Then Paul said, 'John indeed baptized with a baptism of repentance, saying to the people that they should believe on Him who would come after him, that is, on Christ Jesus.' When they heard this, they were baptized in the name of the Lord Jesus. And when Paul had laid hands on them, the Holy Spirit came upon them, and they spoke with tongues and prophesied."

This makes plain Paul's emphasis: A person's reception of the Holy Spirit is the sure benefit of salvation. Paul wrote to the Ephesians to clarify for them the fact that life is to be lived in the fullness of the Holy Spirit.

---

noun. Royalty fills this designation, for the essence of the idea of the Christ, i.e. Messiah, is found in the promises that a new king shall come and rule the kingdom. This king emerges from the seed of David and inherits David's throne forever. This kingdom never ends, nor does the reign of its king. With this in mind, it is no wonder that the essential posture of the believer, even one as great as Paul, is to be one of humble service. In this way, he highlights the present revelation of Jesus the Christ as the culmination of the heavenly plan of redemption. The first people who hoped in the Christ were also the first to embrace the plan for the ages. They are united in Him and are thus the first to be "in Christ people."

This is the goal of the universe according to God. This brings praise to God.

In Him you also trusted, after you heard the word of truth, the gospel of your salvation; in whom also, having believed, you were sealed with the Holy Spirit of promise, who is the guarantee of our inheritance until the redemption of the purchased possession, to the praise of His glory (vv. 13, 14).

Here Paul moves to the experience of the Ephesian believers. They also embraced the same message and the same Christ as Paul did. He recalls the sequence of events: They heard the gospel,

WORD STUDY
SEAL

Seal—*a device such as a signet ring or cylinder, engraved with the owner's name, a design, or both* (Ex. 28:11; Esth. 8:8). A medallion or ring used as a seal featured a raised or recessed signature or symbol so it could be impressed on wax, moist clay, or ink to leave its mark (Job 38:14).

The seal was strung on a cord and hung around the neck or worn on one's finger (Gen. 38:18, NRSV; signet ring, Jer. 22:24). A seal usually served to certify a signature or authenticate a letter or other document (Neh. 9:38; Esth. 8:8; John 3:33).[8]

they believed, they were sealed by the Holy Spirit, and were thus guaranteed the future inheritance planned by God for all who are in Christ. In telling of these things, Paul was referring to the events recorded in Acts 19 when he came and ministered to the Ephesians and they found fullness of joy in the circle of Spirit-filled living.

The Holy Spirit has been given as the guarantee or the down payment for our inheritance until we are fully possessed by God when Jesus returns. In a very real sense, we are now in escrow. The earnest payment has been made for our eternal dwelling place but we have not yet moved in.

WORD STUDY
GUARANTEE

Guarantee—*a promise or assurance; something given or held as security.* The apostle Paul declared that the Holy Spirit, who lives in our hearts, is the guarantee that we shall receive our full inheritance from God (2 Cor. 5:5).[9]

---

[8] Ronald F. Youngblood, general editor; F. F. Bruce and R. K. Harrison, consulting editors, *Nelson's New Illustrated Bible Dictionary*: An authoritative one-volume reference work on the Bible with full color illustrations [computer file], electronic edition of the revised edition of *Nelson's Illustrated Bible Dictionary*, Logos Library System, (Nashville: Thomas Nelson) 1997, © 1995, p. 1140.

[9] Ronald F. Youngblood, general editor; F. F. Bruce and R. K. Harrison, consulting editors, *Nelson's New Illustrated Bible Dictionary*: An authoritative one-volume reference work on the Bible with full color illustrations [computer file], electronic edition of the revised edition of *Nelson's Illustrated Bible Dictionary*, Logos Library System, (Nashville: Thomas Nelson) 1997, © 1995, p. 526.

QUESTIONS FOR PERSONAL REFLECTION AND GROUP DISCUSSION

Read Ephesians 1:3–14 and then answer the following questions.

1. How does the biblical idea of saint clash with a common understanding of the word?

2. To what is the believer predestined according to this section?

3. How would you explain redemption to someone who is not familiar with the Bible?

4. Explain how Paul uses the word mystery.

5. What does it mean to be in Christ according to Paul?

6. How does understanding verses 1–14 help us in our worship?

Chapter 2

Ephesians 1:15–23

THE BELIEVER'S PURPOSE AND DESTINY

God wants us to understand His commitment to make the redeemed confident beyond doubt when weak, assailed, or discouraged, and settled in the certainty of Christ's dominion flowing to and through them as members of Christ's body. We are to step forward in God's empowerment through the Holy Spirit. This does not minimize God's divine design, personal intent, and warm desire toward believers in general.

A Spirit of Wisdom and Revelation

Ephesians 1:15–18

Therefore I also, after I heard of your faith in the Lord Jesus and your love for all the saints, do not cease to give thanks for you, making mention of you in my prayers (vv. 15, 16).

Every time we read the word *therefore* in Paul's writing, something is being enunciated on the basis of what has gone before. All the wealth and riches that are ours in Christ—the magnitude of the truths in the previous verses—focus on this pivotal point: in the light of all this wealth we have in Christ, I am praying for you (v. 16).

The Ephesian believers were known for their love of the brethren.

ACCENT ON APPLICATION
Prayer for Other Believers

Here Paul is motivated by the truths of redemption to pray for the believers in Ephesus. He actively prays that they would have a spirit of wisdom and revelation. In this way, they know God.

He knows of their faith. This is the first step. But they are to move beyond simple faith to full kingdom living. This requires Paul to pray for the faithful, doing battle in the heavenly realms so that this might come to pass. Thus, we must give time to regular prayer for others so they will realize what has been given them in Christ through faith.

Just as the seal of the Spirit marks salvation, so also does love mark a life yielded to the Holy Spirit, for the Spirit brings such fruit (Gal. 5:22–23). Jesus promised to send the Spirit, and the fruit of the Spirit is the sure sign of a Spirit-filled believer.

> That the God of our Lord Jesus Christ, the Father of glory, may give to you the spirit of wisdom and revelation in the knowledge of Him (v. 17).

In this verse, Paul gives a glimpse of his practical requests on behalf of the Ephesian believers. Unpacking some of these concepts requires work because the truths are not immediately obvious. First, he asks that they receive the spirit of wisdom and revelation with the dual objective of their knowing Christ and understanding God's purpose and power in their lives. This wisdom increases as we reverence God; we reverence God as we learn who He is and know how He operates.

Revelation is an unveiling of our hearts that we may receive insight into the way God works in our lives. Revelation may be found in teaching or preaching that is especially anointed to tell of the glory of Christ and His purpose and power. But in making such a biblical use of the term as it appears here in Ephesians 1, it is wise to understand its alternate and grander use.

The Bible uses the word *revelation* in two ways. It is important to distinguish them to avoid confusion, humanistic ideas, and hopeless error. The Holy Scripture is the revealed Word of God. God's law (Deut. 29:29) and the words of the prophets (Amos 3:7) are the result of His revealing work. Essentially this means that the whole Old Testament is a revelation.

In the New Testament, this word is used of writings as well (Rom. 16:25; Eph. 3:3; Rev. 1:1)—writings that became part of the closed canon of the Holy Scriptures (Prov. 30:5, 6).

Wisdom and understanding, as well as sound, practical speech, recommend that today's believer know and clearly express what is meant if he or she speaks of certain revelations. The Holy Spirit does indeed give us revelation, as this text teaches. But such prophetic insight into the Word should never be considered as equal to the actual Holy Scripture itself. As helpful as insight into God's Word may be, the finality of the whole of the revelation of God's Holy Word is the only sure ground for building our lives (Matt. 7:24–29).[10]

The eyes of your understanding being enlightened; that you may know what is the hope of His calling, what are the riches of the glory of His inheritance in the saints (v. 18).

The Greek word here translated *understanding* can also be translated *heart*. Our deepest understandings are found in our hearts. The word *enlightened* (Greek, *photizo*) is easily recognizable as the root word for photography. If the apostle Paul were writing today he would have said something to this effect: "I would that God would cause your eyes to be opened to a massive flash of light so you could see His glory and purpose for you—that it would be burnt into the negative of your own life and create a positive

ACCENT ON APPLICATION
The Imprint of Christ

We may rephrase these ideas as follows: "That the lens of your heart would be wide open, that you would capture a vision, that into the darkness of your past and the darkness of your present struggle there would come the flooding light of the glory of the living God, that your heart would be exposed to the image of the Father's full-color purpose for your life."

This is a time exposure—you stay open to the light, and it keeps burning into your life, crowding out the dark places, and expanding His brightness. In this way, we understand that we must place ourselves continually under His light for on-going imprint of Christ in us.

10 Jack W. Hayford, general editor; consulting editors, Sam Middlebrook... [et.al.], *Spirit-filled Life Study Bible [computer file]*, electronic ed., *Logos Library System*, (Nashville: Thomas Nelson) 1997, © 1991, p. 1788.

WORD STUDY
CALL, CALLING

Call, Calling—*God's call of individuals to salvation, made possible by the sacrifice of Jesus Christ on the Cross* (Rom. 8:28–30; 1 Thess. 2:12). God's call to salvation also involves believers in the high calling of living their lives in service to others (1 Cor. 7:20).[11]

image of the purpose for which he created you."

He prayed that their hearts would be enlightened to capture in their understanding the great purpose of God. Paul desired that the knowledge they gained about God would become incarnate—that is, known in the intimate sense; that it would be the hope of their calling, the practical, penetrating application of God purpose in their daily lives.

The word *understanding* is not merely intellectual reasoning, but the ability to see how things work and integrate into the context of the human personality. It necessitates an understanding in the heart, a subjective grasp, a personal perspective that transcends mere analysis (*see* Prov. 23:7; Prov. 4:23; Matt. 9:4; Acts 8:22). Paul prays that every capacity we have will be trained, conveyed to the highest level, and brought under the dominion of the Holy Spirit who rules in our enlightened heart.

Paul highlights the importance of understanding the hope of God's calling. The call of God leads to the place of grace and the benefits of the kingdom of God. It is also linked to God's own inheritance. God delights in the church's glory and calls this His own inheritance. We must understand the glory and grandeur of the redeemed people called the church. If God is excited about the church, then we are to be just as thrilled. What an amazing thought that God would look to believers as His own special people through whom He will now work and whom He highly esteems. We are, of course, meant to live up to this view by the Spirit's working.

The Head Over All Things

Ephesians 1:19–21

And what is the exceeding greatness of His power toward us who believe,

---

[11] Ronald F. Youngblood, general editor; F. F. Bruce and R. K. Harrison, consulting editors, *Nelson's New Illustrated Bible Dictionary: An authoritative one-volume reference work on the Bible with full color illustrations* [computer file], electronic edition of the revised edition of *Nelson's Illustrated Bible Dictionary*, Logos Library System, (Nashville: Thomas Nelson) 1997, © 1995, p. 1030.

CROSS REFERENCE
Acts 2:36–38

The speeches of Acts show us the importance of the proclamation of the resurrection of Christ. In each of the major speeches of Acts, Luke, the author of Acts, highlights the Resurrection as the pivotal element that turned listeners toward repentance. In Acts 2 Peter preached Jesus as resurrected one whom God has made both Lord and Christ. In other words, he told the crowd to come to grips with the fact that they put to death the One who is exalted by God the Father. The people were cut to the heart and wondered what to do in response. Peter urged them to repent, be baptized, and gave them the assurance that they would receive the Holy Spirit.

Luke presents the common elements of the account of Jesus' holy, sacrificial life, His unjust death at the hands of the religious authorities, the resurrection of Christ as historical reality, the urgent plea to repent and believe in the Lord, and the response of the hearers. From this account of apostolic preaching we conclude that we must not shy away from calling to believe in the Lord based upon the revelation of His resurrection.

according to the working of His mighty power which He worked in Christ when He raised Him from the dead and seated Him at His right hand in the heavenly places (vv. 19, 20).

Paul continues pray that the Ephesian believers would have full knowledge and embrace the truths of the spiritual realm. In verse 19, Paul refers to "the greatness of His power" and "the working of His mighty power." What power is he talking about? The foremost event in human history is the resurrection of Jesus Christ from the dead. Just as the Cross is the pivot point of forgiveness and cleansing, the Resurrection is the pivot point of power. The Resurrection rolled back the power of death and neutralized its grip on humanity and on the universe. Paul prayed that that they would grasp with full perception that God has an intention for you and is committed to seeing it fulfilled, that everything you need is in the inheritance of His resources, and God will accomplish this by means of the same power that rolled back the death principle. Nothing of your own weakness, sin or carnality, or evil power can contain you any more than it could contain Jesus in the grave.

Far above all principality and power and might and dominion, and every name that is named, not only in this age but also in that which is to come (v. 21).

Jesus is not seated on a throne somewhere in the far corner of the universe. He is seated in this place of authority in the invisible realm. All principalities and powers with their evil works are beneath His feet. "The New Testament reveals an invisible hierarchy of evil powers who deceive and manipulate human behavior, thereby advancing satanic strategies. Christ and all who are in Christ are placed in authority above these powers. Only spiritual warfare can assert, demonstrate, and sustain this authority."[12]

The Church—Christ's Body

Ephesians 1:22, 23

And He put all things under His feet, and gave Him to be head over all things to the church, which is His body, the fullness of Him who fills all in all (vv. 22, 23).

The crowning achievement is expressed in these two verses. Yes, Christ is over all, and this is grand enough. But this is done for the sake of the church. The church is the authoritative extension of Christ with full power to act on His behalf in this age. The rule of Christ, guaranteed by the work of the Father, extends to the

WORD STUDY
PRINCIPALITY

Principality—*a powerful ruler, or the rule of someone in authority.* The word (often found in the plural) may refer to human rulers (Titus 3:1, KJV), demonic spirits (Rom. 8:38; Eph. 6:12; Col. 2:15), angels, and demons in general (Eph. 3:10; Col. 1:16), or (especially when used in the singular) any rule other than God's (Eph. 1:21; Col. 2:10). While Christians must often wrestle against evil principalities (Eph. 6:12), they can be victorious because Christ defeated all wicked spirits (Col. 2:15).[13]

---

[12] Jack W. Hayford, general editor; consulting editors, Sam Middlebrook...[et.al.], *Spirit-filled Life Study Bible [computer file]*, electronic ed., Logos Library System, (Nashville: Thomas Nelson) 1997, ©1991, p. 1788.

[13] Ronald F. Youngblood, general editor; F. F. Bruce and R. K. Harrison, consulting editors, *Nelson's New Illustrated Bible Dictionary: An authoritative one-volume reference work on the Bible with full color illustrations [computer file]*, electronic edition of the revised edition of *Nelson's Illustrated Bible Dictionary*, Logos Library System, (Nashville: Thomas Nelson) 1997, © 1995, p. 1030.

church. The church is the place where Christ freely moves without any opposition. The demonic powers resist and seek to deceive believers, but Christ's reign is extended through the believing community. Our only revelation of Jesus today, outside of what is disclosed in His Word, is through His church in which He is fully invested.

QUESTIONS FOR PERSONAL REFLECTION AND GROUP DISCUSSION

Read Ephesians 1:15–23 and then answer the following questions.

1. How does Paul's prayer set an example for a believer?

2. What does it mean to have the spirit of wisdom and revelation?

3. Explain the concept of principalities and powers.

4. How should an understanding of the position of the resurrected Christ affect a believer's everyday life?

5. What is the role of the church according to verses 15–23?

Chapter 3

Ephesians 2:1–10

THE BELIEVER'S PLACE OF AUTHORITY

Dead in Trespasses and Sins

Ephesians 2:1–3

In Ephesians 2:1–10 Paul describes the profound partnership into which God has invited us by grace. This occurs by the gracious movement of God's Spirit to and through us, notwithstanding our past deadness in sin or the degree to which the power of evil manipulated or controlled our lives. Within this grace, everything that the Father created us to be can be fully realized in character, vocation, and ministry.

And you He made alive, who were dead in trespasses and sins, in which you once walked according to the course of this world, according to the prince of the power of the air, the spirit who now works in the sons of disobedience (vv. 1, 2).

Paul emphasizes the Ephesians' sorry state before God invaded their lives through grace. While the word order in the text above puts the focus on being made alive, the word order in the original Greek puts a spotlight on the trespasses and sins that bound the Ephesians before coming to Christ.

The pervading influence of evil overshadows any freedom of choice that an unbeliever may claim. The power of evil enslaves humanity to sin through diabolical means. Yet, God

CROSS REFERENCE
Ezekiel 28:1-19; Isaiah 14:12-21

"Your heart was lifted up because of your beauty; you corrupted your wisdom for the sake of your splendor; I cast you to the ground, I laid you before kings, that they might gaze at you. You defiled your sanctuaries by the multitude of your iniquities, by the iniquity of your trading; therefore, I brought fire from your midst; it devoured you, and I turned you to ashes upon the earth in the sight of all who saw you. All who knew you among the peoples are astonished at you; you have become a horror, and shall be no more forever" (Ezek. 28:17-19).

"How you are fallen from heaven, O Lucifer, son of the morning! How you are cut down to the ground, you who weakened the nations! For you have said in your heart: 'I will ascend into heaven, I will exalt my throne above the stars of God; I will also sit on the mount of the congregation on the farthest sides of the north; I will ascend above the heights of the clouds, I will be like the Most High.' Yet you shall be brought down to Sheol, to the lowest depths of the Pit" (Is. 14:12-15).

When we speak of Satan, we are not referring to some abstract force of evil. This is a very real being. Ezekiel 28:1-19 and Isaiah 14:12-21 record the birth of evil in Satan's heart. He is the author of all sin and confusion for it was birthed in him. Therefore, he is the personification of evil. Satan is not omnipresent; he is not always there (Matt. 4:11), though the Lord is (Ps. 139:7-10). Nor is Satan omniscient. He does not know everything (1 Cor. 2:8).

Satan is not omnipotent; not all-powerful, though he is more powerful than any other being in the universe except for the Almighty God. Miraculously, the omnipotence of Almighty God has come to dwell in us. The dominion of the Lord can overcome anything (1 John 4:4).

makes such people, with such evil influences and tendencies, alive.

Several words in this text require attention. The words *trespasses* and *sins* cover the spectrum of misdeeds. *Trespasses* (Greek *paraptoma*) highlights general transgression of explicit commands of God and the violation of the conscience. The word *sins* (Greek *harmartia*) denotes missing the mark, that is, falling short of what God expects. The breadth of sinfulness is part and parcel of the experience of the Ephesian believers before coming to know Christ.

Paul uses the word *walked* to describe the unbelievers' manner of life. In other words, sins and trespasses were not one time, or even rare actions; rather, sins and trespasses were a manner of continued behavior. Of course, Paul often uses the idea of walking to describe the Christian's experience. Both the sinner's walk and the Christian's walk spring from deep-rooted behavior patterns that bear distinctive fruit.

The phrase *the course of this world* indicates the patterns and way of the world. *The prince of the power of the air* is Satan. Here the *air* is not referring to the earth's atmosphere, but the general climate of the culture. These people lived like dead people because they were dead in sin. They had no recourse. An unregenerate person is under the domination of the adversary. This does not mean that every unbeliever is possessed by demons, nor do they worship Satan, but their whole thought system and pattern of life is motivated, animated, and manipulated by God's adversary. People are not free. A master puppeteer, the adversary of the soul, manages them. The puppet strings, however, are invisible so people assume that they are in control of their lives. When they try to get truly free, the strings in the puppeteer's hands restrain them.

Paul uses the word *spirit* here to refer to Satan. This is a rare use of this word. But Paul contrasts the almighty, authoritative Christ who is seated at the right hand of God and under whom are all powers and authorities and the puny dominion of Satan. However, they are both spirit. Certainly, Satan has some power to inflict evil. But Christ's dominion is infinitely more powerful. This is shown by the Holy Spirit's power in and through Christ and the church.

Among whom also we all once conducted ourselves in the lusts of our flesh, fulfilling the desires of the flesh and of the mind, and were by

ACCENT ON APPLICATION
The Children of Wrath

There was a time when we all lived in the world's system. Outside of Christ, all of us were managed and manipulated by the lusts of our flesh. As fallen people, we were born into this way of life. This is why we must be reborn. People outside of Christ are not necessarily demon-possessed, but the spirit of this world manipulates them. The living church, which is the salt of the earth, preserves the world from being overwhelmed by that dominion.

CROSS REFERENCE
Romans 1:18—3:20

"For the wrath of God is revealed from heaven against all ungodliness and unrighteousness of men, who suppress the truth in unrighteousness, because what may be known of God is manifest in them, for God has shown it to them... You are inexcusable, O man, whoever you are who judge, for in whatever you judge another you condemn yourself; for you who judge practice the same things. But we know that the judgment of God is according to truth against those who practice such things" (Rom. 1:18, 19; 2:1, 2).

Paul in this section describes the evil state and demeanor of the Gentiles as well as the Jews. Ethnicity does not shield a Jew from God's judgment. Nor is a Gentile saved from righteous judgment because he or she lacks the knowledge of the Law of Moses. A Gentile will be judged through the law of the heart written on the conscience. A Jew will be judged according to the Mosaic Law. Each will be found guilty based on sinful behavior as measured by the law they have. None will be declared righteous before God by behavioral standards because they can never meet God's standard of behavior. Thus, everyone is justly destined for the wrath of God.

---

nature children of wrath, just as the others (v. 3).

Paul carefully avoids any we-versus-they comparisons. Paul counts himself along with all his fellow Jewish believers to be among those who were bound in trespasses and sins. Paul's conduct was exactly like the Gentile unbeliever's walk (most of the Ephesian church consisted of Gentiles). He and they were in the same category before Christ liberated them from the bondage to sin.

We should note here that *lust* is not used here only in a sexual sense. It describes any desire that is contrary to the will of God. This certainly can be sexual, but it is not limited to the sexual area. In fact, Paul broadens the focus to speak of the *flesh*, that part of us which simply desires to do what is evil. Paul does not condemn himself and others because of disobedience and lust. He carefully points out that he fulfilled such sinful desires. Because Paul lived in this way before Christ, he describes himself and others as children of wrath. While that may seem harsh, it is a fact. Paul and the believers in Ephesus would be awaiting wrath from God if something dramatic had not happened to him and to the world.

WHAT IS GRACE?

Grace can be defined as favor or kindness shown without regard to the worth or merit of the one who receives it. It is one of the key attributes of God. The Lord God is "merciful and gracious, long-suffering, and abounding in goodness and truth" (Ex. 34:6). Therefore, grace is usually associated with mercy, love, compassion, and patience.

In the Old Testament, the supreme example of grace is the redemption of the Hebrew people from Egypt and their establishment in the Promised Land. This did not happen because of any merit on Israel's part. It was in spite of their unrighteousness (Deut. 7:7–8; 9:5–6). Although the grace of God is always free and undeserved, it must not be taken for granted. Grace is only enjoyed within the covenant—God gives the gift, and it is received through repentance and faith (Amos 5:15). Grace is to be humbly sought through the prayer of faith (Mal. 1:9).

The grace of God was revealed and given in the person and work of Jesus Christ. Jesus was not only the beneficiary of God's grace (Luke 2:40), but was also its very embodiment (John 1:14), bringing it to humankind for salvation (Titus 2:11). By His death and resurrection, Jesus restored the broken fellowship between God and His people, both Jew and Gentile. The only way of salvation for anyone is through the grace of the Lord Jesus Christ (Acts 15:11).

The Holy Spirit, who is called the Spirit of grace (Heb. 10:29), applies the grace of God to human beings for their salvation. The Spirit is the One who binds Christ to His people so that they receive forgiveness, adoption to sonship, and newness of life, as well as every spiritual gift or grace (Eph. 4:7).

The theme of grace is especially prominent in the letters of Paul. He sets grace radically against the law and the works of the law (Rom. 3:24, 28). Paul makes it abundantly clear that salvation is not something that can be earned; it can be received only as a gift of grace (Rom. 4:4). Grace, however, must be accompanied by faith; a person must trust in the favor of God, even though it is undeserved (Rom. 4:16; Gal. 2:16).

The Law of Moses revealed the righteous will of God in the midst of pagan darkness; it was God's gracious gift to Israel (Deut. 4:8). But His will was made complete when Jesus brought the gospel of grace into the world (John 1:17).[14]

---

[14] Ronald F. Youngblood, general editor; F. F. Bruce and R. K. Harrison, consulting editors, *Nelson's New Illustrated Bible Dictionary*: An authoritative one-volume reference work on the Bible with full color illustrations [computer file], electronic edition of the revised edition of *Nelson's Illustrated Bible Dictionary*, Logos Library System, (Nashville: Thomas Nelson) 1997, © 1995, p. 522.

Made Alive Together in Christ

Ephesians 2:4–10

But God, who is rich in mercy, because of His great love with which He loved us, even when we were dead in trespasses, made us alive together with Christ (by grace you have been saved) (vv. 4, 5).

After reading verses 1–3 the first two words of verse 4, *But God*, are beautiful to encounter. God has not left sinners to wallow in the shame, slavery, and desperation of a child of wrath. No, God enters in to rescue the perishing, motivated by His own love and grace. His mercy embraces the pitiful. His love works for the unlovely. His grace extends to the most needy of all.

Paul highlights God's abundant mercy and the double measure of God's love. Nothing can stop the power of God's gracious plan. The dead are made alive together with Christ. The same enlivening power that raised Jesus from the dead makes

CROSS REFERENCE
Romans 1:17–20

"Indeed you are called a Jew, and rest on the law, and make your boast in God, and know His will, and approve the things that are excellent, being instructed out of the law, and are confident that you yourself are a guide to the blind, a light to those who are in darkness, an instructor of the foolish, a teacher of babes, having the form of knowledge and truth in the law."

The Jewish questioner of the Epistle to the Romans tries to argue his special relationship with God, even to the point of boasting in that relationship. The Jew obviously places his trust in something more than blood heritage. He is in the embrace of the law as the embodiment of the knowledge of God. He boasts in God's special posture towards Israel, a well-known fact of history and clearly testified in the Old Testament. From the Jew's knowledge of the law comes knowledge of God's will. Through possessing the law he has quite a superior posture: He knows God's will; He approves the things that are excellent; He confidently guides the blind, gives light to those in darkness and instructs the foolish; and He teaches "babes."

Yet, this superior posture does not exempt this Jew from the same expectations he brings upon others. And the Jewish questioner is found "guilty" of sin just as the Gentile "sinner" was.

a dead sinner alive as well. Only God has the power to raise the dead to life. The sinner, dead through sin, becomes alive again to reign with Christ in the heavenly realms. The saving power of God is the resurrection power of Christ, and God intends that this power produce in us a resurrection lifestyle. We shall this see later in the letter. All of this is by grace.

And raised us up together, and made us sit together in the heavenly places in Christ Jesus, that in the ages to come He might show the exceeding riches of His grace in His kindness toward us in Christ Jesus (vv 6, 7).

Paul uses three verbs that have *with* as part of their prefixes. By this, he emphasizes our union with Christ. God makes us alive together with Christ, raises us up together with Christ, and seats us together with Christ at the right hand of God the Father. Thus, believers are graced with amazing benefits purely because of the overwhelming love of the Father. In the face of persistent disobedience and errant ways, God in his sovereignty intervenes with an outpouring of mercy. God's Word describes how His grace brings us from death to life, and how He has elevated us to be seated with Christ. This is not something that will come at the day of our rapture—the time when we will go to be in God's presence eternally—this is our present experience. Those who have accepted Christ as Savior are now in Christ and function from that position.

The heavenly places are the invisible realm. This is not some place in a distant corner of the universe. We have been raised up to reign with Him in the invisible realm. Because we have been seated in this heavenly place, we have been given the ultimate high ground against the adversary. We can look down at all those things that come against us because the Lord has lifted us above them by His great grace and power. We are seated with Him and all things are under His feet (1:22).

For by grace you have been saved through faith, and that not of yourselves; it is the gift of God, not of works, lest anyone should boast (vv. 8, 9).

This is perhaps one of the best-known verses in the New Testament. Yet, we must not let its familiarity cause us to pass it over. First, note that the Ephesian believers have been saved. The verb tense of the original language signifies that this is an accomplished event with continuing results. It is also something that God did and the believers received. This happened through faith.

Note the negatives here. Paul is careful to exclude human effort. The work is totally of God. All the believer does is respond by exercising faith in Christ. There is no ground for

WORD STUDY
WORKMANSHIP

Workmanship (Greek *poiema*)— *that which is manufactured, a product, a design produced by an artisan.* From it comes the word *poem.* Workmanship emphasizes God as the master designer of the universe as His creation (Rom. 1:20), and of the redeemed believer as His new creation (Eph. 2:10). Before conversion, our lives had no rhyme or reason. Conversion brought us balance, symmetry, and order. We are God's poem, His work of art.[15]

boasting. It matters not whether one is a Jew or Gentile, all one can do is receive. The sinner cannot do anything to cause God to grant salvation. Boasting of one's relationship with God is especially excluded.

For we are His workmanship, created in Christ Jesus for good works, which God prepared beforehand that we should walk in them (v. 10).

Believers, both Jew and Gentile, are totally the work of God. No claim of extraordinary effort to be godly can be claimed by the believer. The Holy Spirit declares us God's workmanship His special projects, as it were. He is on the job accomplishing His divine task. His is a creative task to bring the dead to life again. Those who were dead in sin God makes alive. In this way, He returns to the role of Creator, forming people in Christ to do good works. Good works do not bring salvation. However, through salvation a believer brings good works to the world.

Paul provides a contra-bookend to his comments in 2:1–2. There, he spoke of the sinner's walk in sins and trespasses. Here he speaks of the believer's walk in good works. These foreordained paths of righteousness bring truly good things to the world. Having received grace from God, the forgiveness of sins, and the gift of salvation, we can enter into the purpose of God for our lives and destiny in Christ. We set about certain tasks, or works, that God has prepared specifically for us to do. It is critical for believers to understand the principle of this truth, because many have misunderstood it. Grace and works have unfortunately become divorced in the minds of some believers.

---

[15] Jack W. Hayford, general editor; consulting editors, Sam Middlebrook... [et.al.], *Spirit-filled Life Study Bible [computer file]*, electronic ed., *Logos Library System,* (Nashville: Thomas Nelson) 1997, © 1991, p. 1789.

QUESTIONS FOR PERSONAL REFLECTION AND GROUP DISCUSSION

Read Ephesians 2:1–10 and then answer the following questions.

1. How does the Evil One influence people to sin?

2. Why might people be called children of wrath?

3. What caused God to bring forth salvation through Christ?

4. According 2:1–10, how do faith and obedience relate to a believer's life?

5. What is the role of good works according to verse 10?

Chapter 4

Ephesians 2:11–22

The Believer's Call to Unity

Paul next calls every believer to live in that grace which transcends ethnic separatism. This leads to the release of the Spirit's power through Christ's body, the church, and makes way for God's full indwelling (2:20–22). This section does not merely address a dated, cultural problem. Nor does it call for unity as a generous thought to be embraced as the Christian thing to do. Instead, by smashing all things that separate people, God assaults the powers of darkness.

Alienated and Hopeless

Ephesians 2:11, 12

Therefore remember that you, once Gentiles in the flesh—who are called Uncircumcision by what is called the Circumcision made in the flesh by hands—that at that time you were without Christ, being aliens from the commonwealth of Israel and strangers from the covenants of promise, having no hope and without God in the world (vv. 11, 12).

Paul reminds the Gentile Ephesian believers that they were formerly alienated from the Jews. Here he hints that the Circumcision, those people who are of Jewish descent who still emphasize adherence to the Mosaic

---

WORD STUDY
FLESH

Flesh (Greek *sarx*)—*the substance of the body, whether of animals or persons* (1 Cor. 15:39; 2 Cor. 12:7). In its idiomatic use, the word indicates the human race or personhood (Matt. 24:22; 1 Pet. 1:24). In an ethical and spiritual sense, *sarx* is the lower nature of a person, the seat and vehicle of sinful desires (Rom. 7:25; 8:4-9; Gal. 5:16-17).[16]

Law, focus on the flesh just as much as the Gentiles. The Gentiles are in the flesh and the Jews promote the circumcision made in the flesh by hands. The Jew's empty ritual that does not acknowledge the reality of Christ's sacrifice and the Gentiles life of sinful behavior are both far off from God.

Paul describes the particularly desperate state of the Gentiles, however. They are described first as being without Christ. Jews expected the Messiah to come in the future. Gentiles expected no such deliverer. Israel at least had the Old Covenant through which God worked and by which they could relate to God. Gentiles had no such covenant with God. Thus, Gentiles were *aliens* and *strangers*. Paul promotes a picture of one being outside of the realm of God's gracious hand of protection and promise. This results in a life totally without hope and without God. The Jews experienced hope and God, though this was to point to the embrace of Jesus as Messiah.

At Peace in Christ

Ephesians 2:13–18

But now in Christ Jesus you who once were far off have been brought near by the blood of Christ (v. 13).

The Gentiles embraced Christ so they were no longer far off from God or from the believing Jews. The phrase *but now* signifies not only a movement in the writer's thought, but also more importantly, a dramatic breakthrough in the history of the ages and the expectations for the future. Paul used these words in Romans 3:21 to mark out the change of epoch inaugurated by Christ's work of redemption. Here they emphasize that the Gentiles are no longer alienated from the things of God because of the blood of Christ. In other words, the atonement required to make peace with God applies to

---

[16] Jack W. Hayford, *Hayford's Bible Handbook [computer file]*, electronic ed., *Logos Library System*, (Nashville: Thomas Nelson) 1997, © 1995, p. 612.

CROSS REFERENCE
2 Corinthians 5:16-17

"Therefore, from now on, we regard no one according to the flesh. Even though we have known Christ according to the flesh, yet now we know Him thus no longer. Therefore, if anyone is in Christ, he is a new creation; old things have passed away; behold, all things have become new."

Paul recognized that he too had a view of Christ that was according to the flesh. Indeed, the apostle regarded everyone according to the flesh prior to knowing Christ. He distinguished between Jews and Gentiles, circumcised or uncircumcised. Even Christ's death was viewed from a fleshly point of view. Paul viewed Jesus in His death as a criminal, cursed by God. But through his dramatic encounter with Christ on the road to Damascus, Paul's paradigm shifted. Being placed in Christ changes everything. All things become new in Him.

God has established a new order in the kingdom of God. Those who have embraced the Lord Jesus by faith enjoy the benefits of a new society—the society of the people of God. In this society there are new standards to live by. Perhaps one of the most important is that "from now on, we regard no one according to the flesh." This means that we embrace the truth that earthly distinctions mean little in the kingdom of God. There is now "neither Jew nor Greek . . . slave nor free . . . male nor female; for you are all one in Christ Jesus." Racial distinctions are removed. Class distinctions are nullified. And the limitations or advantages based upon gender are also eliminated. This provided the church with a radical opportunity to have impact in all sectors of the Roman Empire as people realized they were brought to an equal level through the work of God. We are admonished to make sure that the world's distinctions don't enter our own perspective of other people.

People evaluated Jesus by a purely human perspective while He was on earth. Even those who should have known better, the Jewish religious leaders, focused upon how Jesus did not live up to their own expectations of a leader who was to liberate them from bondage to Rome or on how Jesus did not fulfill their own understanding of the Mosaic law. Jesus was also crucified, which, to the Jewish leaders, brought Jesus under a curse (Gal. 3:13; Deut. 21:23). But Jesus is transformed through His resurrection to be the obviously victorious king, fully vindicated from any notion of being "cursed." Just as Jesus is seen in a new way as the resurrected Messiah, freed from simply earthly evaluation, so also believers are to regard no one from an earthly perspective.

The Significance of Circumcision

The act of circumcision was required as a sign of the covenant established with Abraham (Gen. 17:10). This was not a new covenant but an external sign that Abraham and his descendants were to execute to show that they were God's covenant-people. The fact that this was performed upon the male reproductive organ had twofold significance. The cutting away of the foreskin spoke of the cutting away of fleshly dependence. Also, hope for the future posterity and prosperity was not to rest upon human strength. Circumcision was a statement that one's confidence was placed in the promise of God and His faithfulness rather than in personal strength and ability, that is, the flesh.[17]

Gentiles as well as Jews. This profound truth is often lost on the Gentile community of the twenty-first century. In the first century, only Jews expected to be part of God's covenant community. Gentiles were excluded unless they became part of the covenant community through conversion and circumcision. God changed all this with the New Covenant.

No Blood, No Atonement

"For the life of a creature is in the blood, and I have given it to you to make atonement for yourselves on the altar; it is the blood that makes atonement for one's life" (Lev. 17:11). This verse gives the clearest statement of the necessity of blood as it relates to sacrificial offerings. The life of a creature is in the blood, so an animal's life and blood were given upon the altar for the specific purpose of attaining reconciliation with God. Apart from the shedding of blood there was no atonement. This ordinance is reaffirmed in the New Covenant in Hebrews 9:22. The New Covenant in Christ's blood fulfilled the requirements of the Old Covenant for redemption. The blood of Christ surpasses the blood sacrifices of the Old Covenant and eternally satisfies the requirements of a holy God (Heb. 9:12).[18]

---

[17] Jack W. Hayford, *Hayford's Bible Handbook [computer file]*, electronic ed., *Logos Library System*, (Nashville: Thomas Nelson) 1997, © 1995, p. 561.

[18] Jack W. Hayford, *Hayford's Bible Handbook [computer file]*, electronic ed., *Logos Library System*, (Nashville: Thomas Nelson) 1997, © 1995, p. 562.

For He Himself is our peace, who has made both one, and has broken down the middle wall of separation (v. 14).

Gentiles were not allowed within the Jewish temple. A literal wall of separation existed there. The Romans would destroy this wall in A.D. 70. The literal destruction of this wall of separation only provided visual proof of its earlier obliteration by Christ's atoning work.

The Greek text is very emphatic here: "He Himself is our peace." We must note also that Paul does not speak of *your peace*, referring to the Gentiles. No, he recognizes that the peace so desperately needed by Gentiles is the same peace needed by Jews. In the process of breaking down the wall of separation, God brings the two groups together into one. Together they are at peace with one another and with God. The radical nature of this transformation is lost to many in our day. Separation of Jew and Gentile existed in the first century ethnically, culturally, religiously, and physically as many Jews lived in enclaves to protect their cultural distinctiveness.

Having abolished in His flesh the enmity, that is, the law of commandments contained in ordinances, so as to create in Himself one new man from the two, thus making peace (v. 15).

The enmity is the hostility that resulted from transgressing of the law of the commandments. Christ abolished this through His own flesh, that is, the atoning death on the Cross. As the perfect man who adhered to every demand of the law of God, He could make atonement for those who sinned. Christ also abolished the legal demand that one must conform to all the scriptural ordinances. Only through Christ does one find the fulfillment of the law. His holy life

CROSS REFERENCE
Galatians 3:28

"There is neither Jew nor Greek, there is neither slave nor free, there is neither male nor female; for you are all one in Christ Jesus."

The Holy Spirit through Paul declares the great message of equality in Christ. No distinctions that people normally make to separate humanity exist in Christ. The church is the place where the oneness in Christ is celebrated and lived out in everyday life.

becomes the believer's life when that person believes in Him. His atoning death becomes the believer's as well. So there are no distinctions between Jew and Gentile based on law-orientation. These are obliterated in Christ. Thus, those in Christ are brought together no matter the ethnic, gender, or class distinctions that exist in the world.

And that He might reconcile them both to God in one body through the Cross, thereby putting to death the enmity (v. 16).

God delights in bringing estranged parties together in peace. He does this by making peace with mankind through the Cross. Secondly, God provides reconciliation for those who would not normally be united. Jews and Gentiles are brought together in Christ. Their enmity was destroyed at the Cross. Christ's death was

thought to have been an ignominious one marked by God's curse. But it has become the triumphant entry of the kingdom of God with great power.

And He came and preached peace to you who were afar off and to those who were near. For through Him we both have access by one Spirit to the Father (vv. 17, 18).

God designed the message of Christ through the Spirit of God to apply to those who were near to Him (the Jews) and those who were afar off (Gentiles). Jesus' earthly ministry, His sacrificial death, and His resurrection each proclaim the peaceful work of God to break down barriers. Access to God is through one Spirit. This accentuates the connection between Jewish and Gentile believers. It is one and the same Spirit who accomplishes the ministry of Christ in

HE IS OUR PEACE

The word *peace* has several different meanings in the Old and New Testaments. The Old Testament meaning of peace was completeness, soundness, and well-being of the total person. This peace was considered God-given, obtained by following the Law (Ps. 119:165). Peace sometimes had a physical meaning, suggesting security (Ps. 4:8), contentment (Is. 26:3), prosperity (Ps. 122:6–7), and the absence of war (1 Sam. 7:14). The traditional Jewish greeting, *shalom*, is a wish for peace.

In the New Testament, peace often refers to the inner tranquility and poise of the Christian whose trust is in God through Christ. This understanding was originally expressed in Old Testament writings about the coming Messiah (Is. 9:6–7). The peace that Jesus Christ spoke of was a combination of hope, trust, and quiet in the mind and soul brought about by reconciliation with God. The host of angels proclaimed such peace at Christ's birth (Luke 2:14), followed by Christ Himself in His Sermon on the Mount (Matt. 5:9) and during His ministry. He also taught about this kind of peace at the Lord's Supper, shortly before His death (John 14:27). Such peace and spiritual blessedness is a direct result of faith in Christ (Rom. 5:1).[19]

both peoples. This in and of itself provides unity and peace. No group can claim superiority in standing before the God of gracious peace.

The Church—God's Building

Ephesians 2:19-22

———

Now, therefore, you are no longer strangers and foreigners, but fellow citizens with the saints and members of the household of God (v. 19).

The word *you* in this verse denotes the Gentile Ephesian believers. Based upon Paul's previous argument, these believers must in no manner consider themselves second-class citizens in the household of God. Nor ought the Jewish believers think of themselves as superior to the believing Gentiles. No, those who were once considered strangers and foreigners are part of God's household. A citizen has rights and responsibilities in the community of God. A member of the household has a place of belonging and a familial relationship with God and others.

19 Jack W. Hayford, *Hayford's Bible Handbook [computer file], electronic ed., Logos Library System*, (Nashville: Thomas Nelson) 1997, © 1995, p. 716.

ACCENT ON APPLICATION
Oneness in the Household of God

We have been made members of God's household (v. 14). Although there are many walls in this world, there is an entrance door into the household of God. Within there is one family with no division. Instead, there is understanding and mutuality because through Christ we all have access by one Spirit to the Father (Eph 1:18). In the household of God, people do not build walls. Do not let anything come between you and your brothers and sisters in Christ or in your family relationships.

Having been built on the foundation of the apostles and prophets, Jesus Christ Himself being the chief cornerstone (v. 20).

Paul moves from the concept of a household to the image of a building. The familial relationship has been established. Now the stability and nature of the church as God's temple find the spotlight. While the apostles and prophets are important, the most important element of the structure is the cornerstone. This joins it together and gives it ultimate stability. Jesus Christ joins together Jewish and Gentile believers in a way that gives

WORD STUDY
FOREIGNERS

Foreigners (Greek *paroikoi*)—This word, which stems from "to dwell" or "dwelling," denotes an alien who dwells in a land without the rights of citizenship. It describes Abraham and Moses, sojourners in a land that was not theirs (Acts 7:6, 29), and the Christian who is traveling through this world as an alien whose citizenship and ultimate residence are in heaven (1 Pet. 2:11).[20] In Ephesians 2:19, the point is that from God's point of view we believing Gentiles are no longer aliens among the people of God. Contrariwise, we are members of God's household.

---

[20] Jack W. Hayford, general editor; consulting editors, Sam Middlebrook. . . [et.al.], *Spirit-filled Life Study Bible [computer file]*, electronic ed., *Logos Library System*, (Nashville: Thomas Nelson) 1997, © 1991, pp. 612–13.

WORD STUDY
CORNERSTONE

Cornerstone—*a stone placed at the corner, or the intersecting angle, where two walls of a building come together.* In biblical times, buildings were often made of cut, squared stone. By uniting two intersecting walls, a cornerstone helped align the whole building and tie it together.

In his address before the Jewish Sanhedrin, the apostle Peter quoted Psalm 118:22 and boldly proclaimed that Jesus Christ of Nazareth, crucified and raised from the dead, was the stone rejected by the builders who has now become the chief cornerstone (Acts 4:11; capstone, NIV; Eph. 2:20). This chief cornerstone, Jesus Christ, is the foundation of the church, because "there is no other name under heaven given among men by which we must be saved" (Acts 4:12). In Him, "the whole building, being joined together, grows into a holy temple in the Lord" (Eph. 2:21). All who believe in Jesus find a solid Rock on which to build their lives.[21]

security and soundness to the structure called the church.

In whom the whole building, being fitted together, grows into a holy temple in the Lord, in whom you also are being built together for a dwelling place of God in the Spirit (vv. 21, 22).

Two strong ideas emerge from the picture of the church as the building of God. First, once joined together, the church becomes a growing entity. The building continually increases in stature through the stability of the Chief Cornerstone, Jesus Christ, and through the work of the apostles, prophets, and others. In addition, this construct is to be the dwelling place of God in the Spirit. God dwells on earth through His Spirit because the church is on earth. The church is the building in which God dwells. Paul is not thinking of physical church buildings. There were no such things in his day. The church everywhere and in all ages constitutes the one building of God where He dwells by His Spirit.

We are fitted together as believers when we acknowledge our peaceful, built-up relationship to one another.

---

21 Ronald F. Youngblood, general editor; F. F. Bruce and R. K. Harrison, consulting editors, *Nelson's New Illustrated Bible Dictionary: An authoritative one-volume reference work on the Bible with full color illustrations* [computer file], electronic edition of the revised edition of *Nelson's Illustrated Bible Dictionary*, Logos Library System, (Nashville: Thomas Nelson) 1997, © 1995, p. 304.

THE LIVING STONES IN GOD'S HOUSE

Peter used the term *spiritual house* to describe Christians as a corporate entity (1 Pet. 2:4–10). Christ is the chief cornerstone of this house (v. 6). He is "a stone of stumbling and a rock of offense" (v. 8), a "living stone, rejected . . . by men, but chosen by God and precious" (v. 4). Like Christ, Christians are living stones that are being built into this spiritual house (v. 5). Peter combines the metaphor of the spiritual house with that of a holy priesthood that offers spiritual sacrifices (v. 5). This royal priesthood of believers is a holy nation, God's new people who proclaim His praises (vv. 9–10; Ex. 19:6).[22]

Congregations of believers enable people to realize and live out their need for one another. Life in the Holy Spirit requires a point of relationship with others. The church provides this connecting point.

---

[22] Ronald F. Youngblood, general editor; F. F. Bruce and R. K. Harrison, consulting editors, *Nelson's New Illustrated Bible Dictionary: An authoritative one-volume reference work on the Bible with full color illustrations* [computer file], electronic edition of the revised edition of *Nelson's Illustrated Bible Dictionary*, Logos Library System, (Nashville: Thomas Nelson) 1997, © 1995.

QUESTIONS FOR PERSONAL REFLECTION
AND GROUP DISCUSSION

Read Ephesians 2:11–22 and then answer the following questions.

1. What characterized a Gentile according to Paul?

2. How does breaking down the middle wall of separation illustrate what God has done between Jews and Gentiles in Christ?

3. How is the concept of *far off* helpful in communicating an unbeliever's position before God?

4. How do the images Paul uses in verses 19–22 help round out our understanding of the church?

5. Why is the idea of the church being a dwelling place for God so important for Paul in the context of Ephesians?

6. How should Paul's view of the church revolutionize relationships among Christians?

Chapter 5

Ephesians 3:1–21

The Believer's Revelation
of the Mystery

In Ephesians 3 Paul reveals God's strategy to confound the Evil One by His kingdom mystery that works in the church. Here we find deep theological truths concerning God's global intent for the church and the resplendent glory that will be revealed in the church. The overall movement of Paul's argument creates the expectation that the church will assault the realms of darkness. In this brief section (3:1-7), the emphasis is on the message of the gospel set in the context of God's cosmic plans.

Paul's Stewardship

Ephesians 3:1–7

For this reason I, Paul, the prisoner of Christ Jesus for you Gentiles . . . (v. 1).

Paul was imprisoned in Rome but uses this terminology because his life was governed by God's providence. He also knew that Jesus would work through his life while he was imprisoned. The phrase *prisoner of Christ Jesus* may also be translated *prisoner for Christ Jesus*. In fact, Paul may have

CROSS REFERENCE
Galatians 1:11–12

"But I make known to you, brethren, that the gospel which was preached by me is not according to man. For I neither received it from man, nor was I taught it, but it came through the revelation of Jesus Christ."

In the midst of apostasy among the Galatian believers, Paul vigorously opposed any dilution of the radical message of the gospel of Christ. He boldly stated his reason for his aggressive message: he received his message from Christ Himself through revelation. Due of this, Paul viewed his message as epoch-making. His message tells of the kingdom inaugurated through the powerful work of God in Christ. No other message triumphs over this gospel.

been intentionally ambiguous here. Paul had appealed to Caesar to protect himself from premature judgment (Acts 25:11–12) and sentencing. But all the while Paul knew his fate was in the hand of God. No matter if he is in chains or free, he lives for Him.

Paul's imprisonment was a result of his ministry to the Gentiles. The Jews in Acts 21:17—23:35 incited a riot with the intention of killing Paul. The primary issue was Paul's involvement in Gentile ministry. Even though Paul was careful to follow Jewish law and custom, he infuriated the religious leaders with his description of Christ and his own ministry. As a result, he was seized and eventually extricated from Jerusalem and taken to Caesarea and eventually to Rome. Paul gladly ministered for the sake of Christ; he was imprisoned at least partially because of his work for Gentile believers like those in Ephesus.

If indeed you have heard of the dispensation of the grace of God which was given to me for you, how that by revelation He made known to me the mystery (as I have briefly written already, by which, when you read, you may understand my knowledge in the mystery of Christ) (vv. 2–4).

In the first eight verses of this chapter, Paul mentions God's mystery three times. His intention is to convey the mystery to the Ephesians. God's economy depends on our willingness to receive this mystery so that the resurrected Christ will function through us. The revelation of this mystery begins in Acts 9. We are not told how many other times God revealed His message of salvation. Certainly, nuances of understanding came continually through Paul's worship of Christ and his study of the Scriptures.

Which in other ages was not made known to the sons of men, as it has now been revealed by the Spirit to His holy apostles and prophets (v. 5).

In Christ's death and resurrection God inaugurated the new age of the kingdom of God where the Spirit reigns. This contrasts with previous ages where the plan was hidden. The word translated *ages* (Greek *geneais*) is more appropriately understood as *generations*. Paul does not claim any superiority in being born at the right time. He simply points out that previous generations did not have the knowledge that he and others received through Christ. The phrase *has now been revealed by the Spirit* describes the

fact that Paul and others are simply receivers. They watch the mystery being made known.

Here the apostles and prophets are described as *holy*. Unfortunately, just as the word *mystery* has a different meaning in current language than in the original Greek, so also the word *holy* carries different meanings. *Holy* (Greek *hagiois*) describes a people set apart for God. This leads to a change of lifestyle so that the apostle and prophet become more and more like God in actions and motives. But the contemporary view of *holy* implies a level of purity that is nearly otherworldly and, therefore, unattainable.

That the Gentiles should be fellow heirs, of the same body, and partakers of His promise in Christ through the gospel, of which I became a minister according to the gift of the grace of God given to me by the

Accent on Application
Less than the Least of All Saints

Before he became a Christian, Paul had violently opposed the gospel of God and the Christians who preached it. On the road to Damascus, he learned that he was actually persecuting Jesus (Acts 9:3–5). This is probably why Paul considered himself less than the least of all saints. He had once been an oppressor of the church who conspired to murder (7:58—8:1). But his life was a testimony to the believers that even such a person as he could have a part in the ministry of Christ. Paul's life is proof that people can never fall so deeply that God cannot use them in His eternal plan.

WORD STUDY
MYSTERY

The Greek meaning of the word *mystery* is this: A secret has been revealed and there is no longer anything mysterious about it. God did not intend that His plan be hidden from anyone and Paul wanted to be sure that people saw it. The word *fellowship* means "stewardship" and indicates that a person has the right disposition to a gift. Jesus is identified as the Creator here and is placed with God the Father before time began. Thus, the plan of the ages was formed by the Father and Son and empowered by the Holy Spirit.

effective working of His power (vv. 6–7).

It is very difficult to translate into in English the dramatic words Paul uses to describe the changes inaugurated by the gospel. But the words *fellow heirs, of the same body,* and *partakers* each use a prefix meaning *with.* So, the Gentiles are heirs with Jews. Gentiles are of the same body with Jews. Gentiles become partakers with Jews of the great things God planned for His people. But these Gentiles did not simply become Jews. God created a new man out of the two races (2:15). In this plan, one does not have superiority over the other.

Paul called himself a minister—a transmitter of Christ as if he was a waiter serving, or ministering, food. Here is the will of the Lord for humankind: He is "not willing that any should perish but that all should come to repentance" (2 Pet. 3:9). God wants people to be reached with the gospel. God empowered Paul for this purpose.

The Fellowship of the Mystery

Ephesians 3:8–13

The mystery of the gospel now moves from apostles and the prophets to the church as a whole. The assault on the principalities and powers begins with the apostles but finds ultimate effectiveness when each believer operates within the Holy Spirit's empowerment. Power and effectiveness God assures through the accomplished work found in Christ Jesus.

To me, who am less than the least of all the saints, this grace was given, that I should preach among the Gentiles the unsearchable riches of Christ, and to make all see what is the fellowship of the mystery, which from the beginning of the ages has been hidden in God who created all things through Jesus Christ (vv. 8, 9).

ACCENT ON APPLICATION
The Kingdom Vision

The key to having a kingdom vision is this: No matter how dark the force or tough the circumstance, you recognize by faith the ultimate triumph of Jesus Christ. This enables His work in your life to emanate from you. By the grace and the power of God, this has an effect on the world's darkness.

When he was Saul of Tarsus, Paul had been a horrible Jewish sectarian. Throughout history, the Jews were the only repository of life and light in God's truth. But God brought through the Jewish people the world's Redeemer. Thus life exploded throughout the whole world. It burst over every ethnic, sectarian, and racial boundary. When that happened, Paul had to overcome his own smallness, which is indicative of our own need to tear down the walls that would divide us from other people. Paul never portrays himself as an impressive man. His Roman surname *Paulus* means "small". His opponents were singularly unimpressed with Paul. But his apostolic mantle and power were unmistakable.

To the intent that now the manifold wisdom of God might be made known by the church to the principalities and powers in the heavenly places, according to the eternal purpose which He accomplished in Christ Jesus our Lord (vv. 10, 11).

The concept of the manifold wisdom of God can be likened to a diamond ring whose radiance is so marvelous that no matter which way you turn it radiance shines forth. God's wisdom is available in any situation. It shines into any circumstance and drives back the works of darkness. The church is comprised of all the people that know the living God and have come to life in Jesus Christ. Such people have been given God's wisdom.

The phrase *principalities and powers* describes the works of hell in the invisible realm where spiritual activity occurs. The Lord desires that these demons would see the glory of His power in the church. In fact, this wisdom is made known through the church.

God's plan from the beginning of time was to assault the powers of darkness through the church. The believer's blessings described in the first three chapters of Ephesians lead to a posture of warfare against the invisible realm where evil forces reside. This plan of attack is part of God's eternal

WORD STUDY
MANIFOLD

Manifold—(Greek *Polupoikilos*) *"many-colored"*—This word pictures God's wisdom as varied, with many shades, tints, hues, and colorful expressions. God embodies variety. He enters the human arena displaying many-sided, multicolored, and variegated wisdom both to His people and through His people.[23]

purpose that is fulfilled in Christ's perfect life, sacrificial and atoning death, and empowered resurrection life.

In whom we have boldness and access with confidence through faith in Him. Therefore I ask that you do not lose heart at my tribulations for you, which is your glory (vv. 12, 13).

God accomplished His redemptive and epoch-changing work in Christ. Paul, therefore, moves with tremendous vigor; his whole manner changes from his previous manner of life to focus completely upon the Redeemer. Formerly, Paul thought Jesus Christ was cursed before he received the revelation on the road to Damascus. Faith and trust in Christ changed everything for him.

Boldness comes from Christ; access to the Father comes from Christ; confidence comes through this access.

Paul did not lose boldness or confidence in God while imprisoned. He knew that his life was in God's hand from first day until last breath. So, if Paul did not lose heart, nor should the Ephesian believers. In fact, the Ephesians should glory in the fact that Paul is fulfilling his divine task, even if it involves tribulations for them. Suffering and service often go hand in hand.

Paul's Prayer for the Believers

Ephesians 3:14–19

In order to be effective in the assault upon the powers of darkness believers need supernatural empowerment through the Holy Spirit. In addition, because of the fullness of the love of God in Christ, God fully inhabits believers and the church is triumphant in the battle over evil. But first things are first. The church must embrace these important aspects of God.

---

[23] Jack W. Hayford, general editor; consulting editors, Sam Middlebrook. . . [et.al.], *Spirit-filled Life Study Bible [computer file]*, electronic ed., Logos Library System, (Nashville: Thomas Nelson) 1997, © 1991, p. 1791.

ACCENT ON APPLICATION
Spiritual Leaders Pray as Well as Teach

Spiritual leaders must pray for people as well as teach them. Paul prayed that his fellow believers might know the strength of the Spirit in the inner person, just as a storm-tossed ship on which he once sailed was strengthened by braces and cables (Acts 27:17). The strength of Christianity is not outward laws but inward character. So Paul prayed that Christ might enter through the open door of faith, dwell in their hearts, and imprint His nature upon their minds, wills, and emotions. When Christ enters a life, He brings His life—the very soil in which we take root and blossom, the ground in which our lives are founded. Prayer begets prayer. A believer into whom Christ's love brings the fullness of God will ask and expect great things from God! [24]

For this reason I bow my knees to the Father of our Lord Jesus Christ, from whom the whole family in heaven and earth is named (vv. 14, 15).

The focus of this chapter is Paul's prayer that begins in this verse. He begins the chapter with the same phrase, "For this reason," only to digress for thirteen verses out of the overflow of the Holy Spirit in his heart. This is another glimpse into Paul's prayer life, however. He is never far from petitioning the Father. Paul fully recognizes that prayer is an integral part of assaulting the principalities and powers. He accomplishes his purpose through prayer and writing to the Ephesians.

In identifying God as Father, Paul highlights that we are members of God's family, born into it through faith in Jesus Christ. So, we are to live solidly, established in the certainty of the Lord's life in us.

That He would grant you, according to the riches of His glory, to be strengthened with might through His Spirit in the inner man (v. 16).

God's strengthening only happens through the person and work of the Holy Spirit. God's reserves for blessing are inexhaustible. The riches of His glory show that believers may draw upon God's power at any time, place, or in any circumstance. Power failure is

[24] Jack W. Hayford, general editor; consulting editors, Sam Middlebrook. . . [et.al.], *Spirit-filled Life Study Bible [computer file]*, electronic ed., *Logos Library System*, (Nashville: Thomas Nelson) 1997, © 1991, p. 1791.

impossible with God. The place of His ministry is deep within the believers. The inner man is similar to the heart in verse 17. It is the very seat and center of every human being whom God empowers and changes by His Holy Spirit. In fact, no lasting change can come without a change in the inner man.

That Christ may dwell in your hearts through faith; that you, being rooted and grounded in love, may be able to comprehend with all the saints what is the width and length and depth and height—to know the love of Christ which passes knowledge; that you may be filled with all the fullness of God (vv. 17–19).

The dwelling place of Christ is in the heart, the very center of one's being. In using the word *dwell* (Greek *katoikeo*) here, Paul emphasizes a permanent residence. Paul could have used a related word (Greek *paroikeo*), which refers to a temporary dwelling place. But God abides within the believer as the Holy Spirit. This is a permanent dwelling place through faith. Because God dwells in people by faith, they grow in His love.

Thus, Paul prayed that the believers in Ephesus be filled with all the fullness of God, and so experience stability rather than a transient experience of Christ. Nothing firms this up more clearly than the term *rooted and grounded*. Being rooted and grounded in the Lord makes possible the growth of Jesus' life in us. God's love is a believer's roots and ground that lead to growth and fruit-bearing.

Paul prays that the believers will have a comprehension of God's love that transcends knowledge. He describes the width, length, depth, and height of God's love to show that God's love is inexhaustible. No one is far from His love; no one is in too deep a hole to experience Him; no one will ever reach the end of the demonstration of God's love. Such knowledge of God's love surpasses knowledge.

Paul prays for the knowledge of love that surpasses knowledge. This is a play on words. He hopes that the Ephesian believers will have such a comprehension of the love of God in the inner man that simple explanation is inadequate. The goal is that all the fullness of God may dwell in the believer. This is the Christian's goal. God accomplishes this in love by the power and work of the Holy Spirit.

Glory in the Church

Ephesians 3:20–21

Now to Him who is able to do exceedingly abundantly above all that we ask or think, according to the power that works in us, to Him be glory in the church by Christ Jesus to all generations, forever and ever. Amen (vv. 20, 21).

While verse 20 usually is quoted in the context of an individual's petition to God, the focus here is the church. The power mentioned here is the power of Christ working through the church through His Holy Spirit. Victories in the spiritual realm go far beyond what people think or imagine. So, Paul gives us a glimpse of the effectiveness of spiritual assault on the realms of darkness. This brings glory to God, just as victory in battles brought glory to earthly kings. This glory in the church will return to Him because of His work in the church. The concept of glory is the concept of excellence because it excels over every other power. This glorious power extends to the end of time through the church.

QUESTIONS FOR PERSONAL REFLECTION AND GROUP DISCUSSION

Read Ephesians 3:1–21 and then answer the following questions.

1. How are Gentile believers described in verses 1–7?

2. What does the term *dispensation of grace* (v. 2) mean?

3. Why might Paul regard himself as less than the least of all the saints (v. 8)?

4. Why isn't Paul concerned about the tribulations (v. 13) he is experiencing as he writes to the Ephesians?

5. How is Paul's prayer in verses 14–21 an example for believers? How can you incorporate this pattern in your own life?

Chapter 6

Ephesians 4:1–16

THE BELIEVER'S WORTHY WALK AND EQUIPPING FOR MINISTRY

If heavenly dynamics join with the earthly ministry of unity in the body of Christ, aggressive initiatives against the powers are set in motion. A life that is worthy of Christ's presence is the first step toward this dynamic partnership. This is not merely a noble ideal or a vague possibility. The church is called out of the world to live in union with the Holy Spirit. All believers are one in Him.

The Diligent Pursuit of Unity

Ephesians 4:1–6

I, therefore, the prisoner of the Lord, beseech you to walk worthy of the calling with which you were called, with all lowliness and gentleness, with longsuffering, bearing with one another in love (vv. 1, 2).

In Ephesians 1—3, Paul has built a wonderful case for the provisions God has made to bring people to Himself to form a new entity called the church. God has done this purely on the basis of His good pleasure. This constitutes great news for sure. But Paul's real desire is to bring the Ephesian believers to the realization that God has empowered them to establish the kingdom of God.

Thus, the word *therefore* points back to Paul's detailed argument concerning God's enthronement of Christ in the spiritual realm above all things and the believers' place in Christ at the right hand of the Father. These things are already accomplished and people can embrace their reality by faith in Christ. In this way people appropriate on earth what is already true in heaven.

Paul calls himself a prisoner of the Lord. This is slightly different from the wording in 3:1. Paul was writing in Greek, which literally says *in the Lord* rather than *of the Lord*. While the change of meaning may be slight, its nuance indicates the security that is in Christ. The issue of being a prisoner of Rome is secondary; it merely hinders earthly movement. The letter to the Ephesians is about strategic realities in the heavenly realms, so physical location matters little to the apostle.

The English text of this verse places the words *beseech you* later in the sentence, but Paul placed this phrase first. This highlighted the importance of the request. In fact, it is not simply a request, but a strong urging, a begging of the believers to take stock of the truths of Ephesians 1—3 and live in a manner that embraces all that God has done. *Beseech* is the same word that Paul uses in Romans 12:1—"I beseech you therefore, brethren, by the mercies of God, that you present your bodies a living sacrifice, holy, acceptable to God, which is your reasonable service."

CROSS REFERENCE
Romans 12:1

"I beseech you therefore, brethren, by the mercies of God, that you present your bodies a living sacrifice, holy, acceptable to God, which is your reasonable service."

Here in Romans 12 Paul beseeches the Christians. The Greek word for beseech is *parakalo*. It bears the sense of a strong urging or pleading with the reader to act upon what has been said. Paul connects this exhortation with the word *therefore* as the key link to what goes before. All of Romans 1:18—11:36 is in view here. For it is by the mercies of God that one is challenged to excel in living for Christ in daily life. In fact the whole letter to the Romans tells of mercy coming after justice. Justice left humanity dead, condemned, and expecting wrath. But the just One, Jesus Christ, provides the way of being justified before God purely by grace through faith. His holy life is ours; His atoning, sacrificial death is ours; His resurrection life is ours. We have all we need to live for Christ in the present day.

WORD STUDY
MEEKNESS

Meekness—an attitude of humility toward God and gentleness toward people, springing from recognition that God is the sovereign Creator. Although weakness and meekness may rhyme and look similar, they are not the same. Weakness springs from negatives such as lack of strength or lack of courage. But meekness is a person's conscious choice. It is strength and courage under control, coupled with kindness.

The apostle Paul once pointed out that the spiritual leaders of the church have great power, even leverage, in confronting a sinner. But he cautioned them to restrain themselves in meekness (Gal. 6:1; 5:22–23). Even toward evil men, the people of God should be meek, knowing that God is in control. Meekness is a virtue practiced and commended by our Lord Jesus (Matt. 5:5; 11:29). As such, it is part of the equipment of the believer (2 Cor. 10:1; Gal. 5:23; 6:1; Eph. 4:1–2).[25]

In Romans, Paul carefully argued the case that God is fully justified and just in His dealings with humanity. He justly judges sinners. He justly redeems them as well. There is no way that people can bring a charge of arbitrariness or fickleness against God. His gracious way of saving people totally by faith and His provision for daily, righteous living should yield in a believer the willingness to follow Paul's admonitions. So, the apostle says, "I beseech you" in Romans 12:1. Paul continues with this pattern—moving from God's benefits to our responsibilities as receivers of these benefits—here in Ephesians as well.

The calling we have received from God is this: we are called saints, God's holy ones (1:1). This verse (4:1) serves as a pivot to the entire book. In the first three chapters, Paul writes about the believers' calling and in the last three he writes about their walk. God calls believers to walk in a worthy fashion. The church should live in a manner that is consistent with the provisions made in Christ and consistent with the truths of the heavenly realms where Christ reigns supreme and the church is given power over evil. He further defines what it is to live in a worthy fashion in the following verses. Paul returns to a familiar word here translated *walk*. He urges

25 Jack W. Hayford, *Hayford's Bible Handbook [computer file]*, electronic ed., *Logos Library System*, (Nashville: Thomas Nelson) 1997, © 1995, p. 698.

believers to walk in a fashion that is totally opposite to the walk they were used to (see 2:2).

According to Paul, God calls with a calling. While this may seem to be odd wording, it is natural from Paul's perspective. He was called to be an apostle with a calling directly from the Lord Jesus Christ. The Ephesian believers experienced God's call to a particular role, a calling. This calling is to live in a worthy manner and fulfill their calling as people of the new order, the kingdom of God.

Paul did not exhort the believers to act with great brashness and a posture of authority and arrogance because of their newfound knowledge of what is true in the heavenly realms. This is not the way God works. Paul's words were not at all like those used by the authoritative leaders of the day. In fact, Paul intentionally communicated attributes that were despised by the people of power and influence in Greek society. Yet, these originate from the Holy Spirit and reflect the way of the Triune God.

In verse 2, the words are less than impressive in this world of bravado and flash. Each word carries with it the very essence of what God is like. We can look at the Gospels to see how Christ exhibits such qualities. The world may call these qualities weak, yet they are part of the strength of God. The first two are related in manner. Lowliness and gentleness signify the posture of the heart and mind. *Lowliness* (Greek *tapeinophrosunes*) literally means "lowliness of mind." There is no attitude of superiority when people are lowly of mind. Jesus did not walk the earth with arrogance and pride. He was pleased to empty Himself and take the form of a man, becoming a servant. What humility! The truth is that He is the divine King. Yet He serves.

The second word, *gentleness* (Greek *prautetos*), points to a strong person's control. There is no weakness associated with this word. People of truly great power are in such control of their power that they can

SIX SAINTLY CHARACTERISTICS

Ephesians 4:1–3 is a procession of saintly characteristics. We walk worthy of God's calling with all *lowliness* of mind, with all *meekness*, with *longsuffering*, bearing with one another *in love*, striving to keep the *unity* of the Spirit in the bond of *peace*.

The first five characteristics are attitudes that reside deep within us and bear fruit in our relationships with others. The final two are evidence of Christ within us functioning dynamically within the church.

ACCENT ON APPLICATION
Guidelines for Growing in Godliness

Godliness is living the way God wants us to live. Few books speak as clearly and succinctly to this subject as does Ephesians. Here godliness is described in terms of behavior, motivating dynamic, and example. Godly behavior is modeled after God Himself, especially as He has revealed Himself in His fullness in Jesus Christ.

In 4:1, you are to understand that your conduct is the most effective sermon you will ever preach. Therefore, live a life that gives consistent, undeniable evidence of the truth of the gospel.

In 5:1, 2, you model your life after Jesus, imitating Him rather than others and understand that He is the perfect example of the love God requires.

In 5:18–20, you are to be continually filled with the Holy Spirit and overflow with a continual song of praise and thanksgiving in order to maintain a Spirit-filled flow in your life.

In 6:18–20, you give yourself to constant, faithful prayer and let God change your prayer life to a life of prayer.[26]

serve without relying on such power. This Greek word is sometimes translated *meekness*.

The third phrase, *with longsuffering*, is another interpersonal trait. Some have translated this as *long-term patience*. We are to exercise the same patience God has toward the ungodly, which is designed to lead people to repentance (Rom. 2:4). This trait demonstrates itself when repeated infractions are graciously handled and received. Paul is not here advocating being a doormat. He wants our behavior to reflect Christ, who did not give evil for evil.

Closely related to this is the phrase *bearing with one another in love*. The attitude of the believer toward other believers is one of love, unconditional love. If love is truly unconditional, then one can continually bear with a difficult person. The church is a new society with a new way of handling relationships.

Endeavoring to keep the unity of the Spirit in the bond of peace (v. 3).

We are to work hard, do our best, to keep the unity of the Spirit in the

---

[26] Jack W. Hayford, *Hayford's Bible Handbook [computer file]*, electronic ed., Logos Library System, (Nashville: Thomas Nelson) 1997, © 1995, p. 385.

THE GIFTS OF THE GODHEAD

Each member of the Godhead plays a distinct role in giving gifts to mankind. Foundationally, the Father gives us our existence—human life (Gen. 2:7; Heb. 12:9). He also gave His only begotten Son as the redeemer for mankind (John 3:16). Redemptively, Jesus is the giver of eternal life (John 5:38–40; 10:27–28). He gave His life and shed His blood to gain the privilege of giving eternal life (John 10:17–18; Eph. 5:25–27). Further, the Father and Son have jointly sent the Holy Spirit (Acts 2:17, 33) to advance the work of redemption through the church's ministry of worship, growth, and evangelism.

Romans 12:3–8 describes the gifts given by God as Father. They exemplify inherent tendencies that characterize each individual because of the Creator's unique workmanship in their birth. While only seven categories are listed, few people are fully described by only one. More commonly, a mix is found. Different traits of each gift are present to some degree, while one is the dominant trait of a particular person. These gifts are related to our place in God's created order and are foundational.

In 1 Corinthians 12:7–11 the nine gifts of the Holy Spirit are listed. Their purpose is specific—to profit the body of the church. The word *profit* (Greek *sumphero*) means "to bring together, to benefit, to be advantageous." This is experienced as the body is strengthened in its life together and expanded through its ministry of evangelism. These nine gifts are available to every believer as the Holy Spirit distributes them (1 Cor. 12:11). They are not to be merely acknowledged in a passive way, but rather are to be actively welcomed and expected (1 Cor. 13:1; 14:1).

The gifts that the Son of God gives are pivotal in assuring that the first two categories of gifts are applied in the church. Ephesians 4:7–16 indicates the so-called office-gifts Christ has placed in the church, along with their purpose. The ministry of these leaders equips the body by assisting each person to perceive the place the Creator has made him to fill by His creative workmanship in him, and the possibilities of what he was made to be; and to receive the power of the Holy Spirit, and begin to respond to His gifts, which are given to expand each believer's capabilities beyond the created order and toward the redemptive dimension of ministry, for edifying the church and evangelizing the world.

So, there are clearly designated categories of gifts: the Father's (Rom. 12:6–8), the Son's (Eph. 4:11), and the Holy Spirit's (1 Cor. 12:8–10). The understanding of this helps in two ways. First, we see the distinct interest and work of each member of the Trinity in providing for our unique purpose and fulfillment. Second, it prevents us from confusing our foundational motivation in life and service for God with our purposeful quest for and openness to His Holy Spirit's full resources and power for service and ministry.[27]

bond of peace. The church is to strive to make sure that the heavenly truth of the unity of the Spirit between all believers is a reality in the earthly realm. The phrase *unity of the Spirit* points to the unity that the Holy Spirit brings. He is the author and provider of unity between believers. The *bond* spoken of here (Greek *sundesmo*) may be a play on words. In 3:1 and 4:1, Paul describes himself as a prisoner (Greek *desmios*). Here the believers are bound together as if they are prisoners for Jesus, for the sake of the church and the world. But, rather than being in prison at the hands of Roman guards, believers are bound together in the peace of Christ.

There is one body and one Spirit, just as you were called in one hope of your calling; one Lord, one faith, one baptism; one God and Father of all, who is above all, and through all, and in you all (vv. 4–6).

These verses state the basis for earthly unity among believers everywhere. All Christians affirm the reality of these truths. Here Paul appeals to the Ephesians experience of life in the church and in the Holy Spirit, their participation in the earthly reality that reflects heavenly truth.

The believers look forward to their ultimate salvation and rescue from the present evil age. This constitutes the hope of their calling. They look only to the one Lord Jesus Christ for hope. Their unique faith is in this same Jesus. Because of their faith, they all were baptized in water. And, of course, only one God is the origin of all things in heaven and on earth; the ruler above all things; who is not limited by anything in heaven or on earth; who inhabits each of the believers as the Spirit.

The final three words, *in you all*, have true impact. The same God who, in the heavenly realm, creates, provides, protects, perpetuates, and empowers unity in the church is the One

27 Jack W. Hayford, *Hayford's Bible Handbook [computer file]*, electronic ed., *Logos Library System*, (Nashville: Thomas Nelson) 1997, © 1995, p. 644.

who inhabits the believers, enabling them to walk worthy of their calling.

The Building of the Body of Christ

Ephesians 4:7–16

The Holy Spirit through Paul presents Christ's strategic plan for equipping every member of His body with the gifts of service and leadership so that the body of Christ can be whole and healthy, strengthened with truth and confidence, and mobilized through both earthly and heavenly resources. Such people are confident in their ministry for the building up of the local church through personal care and mutual ministry. They reach out to the lost with life, love, hope, effective prayer, healing ministry, and a solid, responsive verbal witness. Thus, Paul is not simply

describing the officials who are assigned to the task of church work or presenting a charge to leaders to train, resource, and prepare people for service.

———————

But to each one of us grace was given according to the measure of Christ's gift (v. 7).

The translation here properly follows the word order of the original Greek text. Each believer has received grace. No believer has been omitted. Because of this, every believer is responsible to take the position accorded to him or her. The measure of the grace is in proportion to Christ's gift. The Greek text says "the gift of Christ." This may refer to the gift that comes from Christ or the gift that is Christ Himself. Paul may have

THE DESCENT INTO HADES

Christ's journey to the place of the dead following His crucifixion is called the descent into Hades. Some interpreters see this descent in Paul's reference to the "lower parts of the earth" (Eph. 4:9). Both Peter (Acts 2:27) and Paul (Acts 13:35) quote Psalm 16:10, declaring that Jesus experienced death but was kept from the corruption of the grave (Acts 2:27). From the heights of heaven's throne Jesus descended to earth and even to death itself to provide for our redemption.

The Bible does not teach of this descent as a part of the completion of salvation's plan. Christ announced at Calvary, "It is finished." This reveals that Jesus' death was a full victory over sin, death, and hell (Heb. 2:14–15).[28]

———————

[28] Jack W. Hayford, *Hayford's Bible Handbook [computer file], electronic ed., Logos Library System,* (Nashville: Thomas Nelson) 1997, © 1995, p. 585.

WORD STUDY
GIFTS

Paul speaks of spiritual gifts elsewhere in his writings. While the focus here in Ephesians is on the gifts of the Son of God, Paul also refers to gifts of the Holy Spirit particularly in 1 Corinthians 12—14. There the Greek word for the word "gift" is *charisma* from which we have the plural *charismata*, "gifts." The word "charismatic" in English often signifies a person of significant influence who has an ability to persuade through personal power or oratory. We sometimes hear of the "charismatic" gifts often referring to the so-called "sign" gifts of tongues, prophecy, healing, etc. Some people even evaluate themselves to find out what gifts they have. But we should understand the word *charisma* before we try to bring application of certain "gift" texts to our lives. The word *charisma* is constructed from the root *charis*, which means "grace," and the particle, or suffix, *ma*. This suffix brings a sense of movement to the noun that it is attached to. Thus, it would be appropriate to understand the word "gift" as a "movement of grace." Think about how this would revolutionize our understanding of the "spiritual gifts" if we would think of these as "movements of God's grace" in our lives. No longer would we think in terms of what "gifts" we have. We would be moved to consider being open to any movement of the grace of God in ways that build up the body of Christ. The debates of what "gifts" are "best" (which the Corinthians were concerned about in 1 Corinthians 12—14) fade into the background as we make ourselves available in any way for God's gracious actions taking place in us for the benefit of others. We become channels of the grace of God, not the possessors of certain gifts.

intended both meanings. He links the individual believer's grace with the gift that comes from Christ, that is salvation, and the gift that is Christ Himself. In other words, there is no shortage of grace when you consider the author of grace—Christ.

———

Therefore He says:
 "When He ascended on high,

He led captivity captive,
And gave gifts to men" (v. 8).

Paul quotes from Psalm 68:18 in support of his proposition that there is abundant grace inherent in Christ's gift. The glorification of Christ to the right hand of God the Father, with full authority and splendor, proves the measure of Christ's authority. He is the victorious king who not only

The Gifts of the Son to Equip the Body of Christ

Apostle

- In apostolic days, this term was applied to a select group chosen to carry out the ministry of Christ; a few of these completed the sacred canon of the Holy Scriptures.
- This title implies the exercise of a distinct representative role of broad leadership.
- Such a person functions as a messenger or spokesman of God.
- In contemporary times apostles are those who display the spirit of apostleship in their ability to extend the work of the church, open fields to the gospel, and oversee large sections of the body of Christ.

Prophet

- This is a spiritually mature spokesperson for God with a special, divinely focused message to the church or the world.
- Such a person is sometimes gifted with insight into future events.

Evangelist

- This person has a special gift of preaching or witnessing in a way that brings unbelievers into the experience of salvation.
- Functionally, the gift of evangelist operates for the establishment of new churches, while pastors and teachers follow up to organize and sustain.
- An evangelist operates to establish converts and to gather them spiritually and literally into the body of Christ.

Pastor-teacher

- The word pastor comes from a root-word meaning "to protect." From this we get the word shepherd.
- This person nurtures, teaches, and cares for the spiritual needs of the body.

Missionary

- Some people see the apostles and evangelists as missionaries.
- A missionary participates in the practical unfolding of God's plan for spreading the gospel to the world (Rom. 1:16).
- Such people have an attitude of humility. This is necessary for them to serve in remote areas and unknown situations (Is. 6:1–13).
- The missionary has an inner compulsion to bring the whole world to know Jesus Christ (2 Cor. 5:14–20).[29]

---

[29] Jack W. Hayford, *Hayford's Bible Handbook [computer file]*, electronic ed., *Logos Library System*, (Nashville: Thomas Nelson) 1997, © 1995, pp. 646–47.

WORD STUDY
EQUIP

The Greek word for *equip* implies recovered wholeness, as when a broken limb is set and mends. It also indicates a discovered function, as when a physical member is properly operating. The work of ministry is the enterprise of each member of the body of Christ and not the exclusive charge of select leaders. Taken together, verses 11 and 12 reveal that the task of the gifted leader is to cultivate the individual and corporate ministries of those he or she leads.[30]

brings captives back from the battle, but also captivity itself. Psalm 68 speaks of the victory of God over those who would keep the Israelites captive. The psalm references God's victory over Egypt and the exodus of all the enslaved people with all the spoils of their captors. Thus, the treasures of the Egyptians were given to God's people through the victory of God. Likewise, because of the victory of Christ, the spoils garnered through His triumph over the principalities and powers are given to God. Then God gives them back to people. The measure of the believers' gifts is directly compared to the triumph of Christ over all the powers. Since the triumph is great, so is the gift.

(Now this, "He ascended"—what does it mean but that He also first descended into the lower parts of the earth? He who descended is also the One who ascended far above all the heavens, that He might fill all things) (vv. 9, 10).

Paul explains that for Christ to ascend, he had to first descend. And he asks the question that may arise in his readers' mind: what does "He descended into the lower parts of the earth" mean?" Some have thought that this refers to a descent into hell, or Hades. However, this text probably is reminiscent of Philippians 2:5–11, which chronicles the movement of the Son of God from the place of enthronement with God the Father down to the place of death. Philippians says God rewarded Jesus and exalted Him to the highest place with the Father on the throne of God.

After His descent into the lower parts of the earth, Christ resurrected and ascended to His rightful place of authority over all things. He did this in

30 Jack W. Hayford, general editor; consulting editors, Sam Middlebrook... [et.al.], *Spirit-filled Life Study Bible [computer file]*, electronic ed., *Logos Library System*, (Nashville: Thomas Nelson) 1997, © 1991, p. 1793.

order to fulfill His purpose to fill all things. This purpose is finalized through His body, the church: Christ gave gifts to the church so that that Christ might be all and in all.

And He Himself gave some to be apostles, some prophets, some evangelists, and some pastors and teachers (v. 11).

Christ Himself is the giver of these gifts to the church. They are listed in a similar order to that in 1 Corinthians 12:28, although that list adds other gifts as well.

In the early church, apostolic ministry was both based in a local church and addressed beyond the local church. Apostles have a voice beyond a local church. Prophets bring a message from heaven to earth. Everything that a prophet says makes the Word of God come alive in a way that is contemporary and powerful. An element of this ministry is present in those who are pastor-teachers, but a different level of authority is present with prophetic ministry. An evangelist is a missionary that penetrates another culture. Such a person is able to mobilize others for evangelism, and is a miracle worker because supernatural signs follow the good news.

These gifted people are examples for others to follow. All five of these offices are presently functioning in the church of Jesus Christ today, although only three are regularly mentioned.

For the equipping of the saints for the work of ministry, for the edifying of the body of Christ (v. 12).

Paul explains the purpose of the gifts of apostles, prophets, evangelists, and pastors and teachers. In typical fashion, Paul piles phrase upon phrase to accomplish this. Since it is easy to get lost among all these phrases, we look at the structure of verses 11–13 here.

God gives the church five main gifts: apostles, prophets, evangelists, and pastors and teachers. Their function is to equip the saints. These believers can then do two things: the work of ministry and the edifying of the body of Christ. The goal of this ministry and edification is twofold: to bring the church to the unity of the faith and to the knowledge of the Son of God. This is further described in two ways: A perfect man and the measure of the stature of the fullness of Christ.

Thus, we can see that the work of ministry, or *service* as it could be translated, results in the edifying the body of Christ. Conversely, edifying the body of Christ is part of the work of ministry.

Till we all come to the unity of the faith and of the knowledge of the Son of God, to a perfect man, to the measure of the stature of the fullness of Christ (v.13).

Each of the four concepts in this verse points to the time when our knowledge of Christ and of each other will be complete. We strive to make this a reality now through the gifts of the Son of God. The unity of the faith is not a unity of a systematic doctrine. It is simply Jesus Christ the Son of God. Jesus is the measure for our growth in relationship to God. We should not measure our spirituality by those who are our spiritual heroes. Instead, measure it by Jesus.

The knowledge of the Son of God is not simply intellectual knowledge. In fact, here Paul uses a more intensive form of the noun that is normally translated knowledge. The Greek word *epignoseos* describes a more experiential knowledge of the fullness of Christ. Through a complete knowledge of Christ and a unity of the faith the church becomes complete, a perfect man. Then, we as the body of Christ will find the fullness of the experience of all that Christ is.

That we should no longer be children, tossed to and fro and carried about with every wind of doctrine, by the trickery of men, in the cunning craftiness of deceitful plotting (v. 14).

The perfect man, whom the church is destined to become is contrasted with

ACCENT ON APPLICATION
What Is a Minister?

Ministry is not a professional office. Someone who ministers is administrating the life of Jesus throughout society. Ministry has to do with taking what you have and giving it in the interests of other people. In this world in desperate need, ministry has very little to do with church as we usually think of it. It does have to do with the church reaching out and serving Christ to the world.

The gifts described in Ephesians are given to people who can lead others into the knowledge of Christ for the work of ministry. These gifts are not given to everyone, but are distributed in God's economy. Such leading ministers are not superior to others, rather they are the servants of all. They are the instruments that Jesus uses to equip the saints for the building up of His church.

WORD STUDY
FULLNESS

Fullness (Greek *pleroma*)—*full number, full complement, full measure, copiousness, and plenitude; that which has been completed.* The word describes a ship with a full cargo and crew, and a town with no empty houses. *Pleroma* strongly emphasizes fullness and completion.[31]

the children that the believers once were. The work of the gifts of the Son, the apostles, prophets, etc., anchor the believers so they will not be swayed by false teachers who are constantly looking to deceive. This anchoring is accomplished as each person is built up and ministering in the church. Deceitful plotting originates in the realm of darkness and is perpetrated by those who are under the sway of the Evil One. Effective ministry provides security for the church, which is constantly under attack.

But, speaking the truth in love, may grow up in all things into Him who is the head—Christ (v. 15).

Speaking the truth in love is a great challenge. Some people use the truth like a sword and hack at people with it. But in love it is used as surgeon uses a scalpel to perform life-saving surgery. We must learn how to minister truth in love. Sometimes this means that we wait, speak carefully, all the while not hiding behind half-truth, lies, or deceit.

The goal is maturity, to become the complete man that the church is destined to be. We must be careful not to interpret this passage too individualistically. The person who grows up is the church! This growth requires that all believers do their part in the Lord's ministry. It won't happen on its own. The ministry of darkness wishes to derail any attempt to bring about a mature church.

The church is people growing in the love of God because only love will enable us to accept one another. Love is the only thing that evidences true growth. We must never buy into a religious program that focuses upon human perfection at the expense of divine affection, for it miscalculates what the gospel is about.

From whom the whole body, joined and knit together by what every joint supplies, according to the effective

---

[31] Jack W. Hayford, *Hayford's Bible Handbook [computer file], electronic ed., Logos Library System,* (Nashville: Thomas Nelson) 1997, © 1995, p. 614.

working by which every part does its share, causes growth of the body for the edifying of itself in love (v. 16).

The church, Christ's body, depends upon Christ, who is the head. Christ Himself causes the growth of the body. But He does this through the individual parts. The gifts bring forth ministry. This brings forth growth into perfection.

So, the various members of the body depend upon what others supply. The motivation we see here is the love of Christ. The church will be anchored in maturity through a deep experience of His love and the gifts He has given to the church in love. The church will be anchored in maturity as each person does his or her part in the Lord's ministry to His body.

QUESTIONS FOR PERSONAL REFLECTION AND GROUP DISCUSSION

Read Ephesians 4:1–16 and then answer the following questions.

1. How might one follow Paul's admonition to *walk worthy* in verses 1–3? What makes this difficult to incorporate within the church?

2. What is the point of the repeated use of the word *one* in verses 4–6?

3. List the gifts given to the church by the Father, by the Son, and by the Spirit.

4. Does verse 9 say that Jesus went to hell? Why or why not?

5. What is the idea behind the word *equip*?

6. How does the structure of verses 12–16 help us to understand the church's ministry and growth?

7. Describe the tasks of each gifted person listed in verse 11.

Chapter 7

Ephesians 4:17—5:14

THE BELIEVER'S SPIRIT-ENABLED PURITY

In this section, Paul summons the believers to discern, confront, deny, and find deliverance from those things that diminish the capacity for Christ to flow through them in ministry, he calls them to flee from those things that give ground to the Adversary, and he sets forth the requirements for a worthy walk in holiness. This way of life exclusively holds God as its objective. Holiness must not be an end in itself.

Put On the New Man

Ephesians 4:17–32

This I say, therefore, and testify in the Lord, that you should no longer walk as the rest of the Gentiles walk, in the futility of their mind, having their understanding darkened, being alienated from the life of God, because of the ignorance that is in them, because of the blindness of their heart; who, being past feeling, have given themselves over to lewdness, to work all uncleanness with greediness (vv. 17-19).

Here is the reason to forsake the old life: it is futile. The emptiness of the unbeliever's life shouts from these verses, which describe the nature of life before salvation. They are linked to Romans 1:18–32, which expands on them. Paul uses his favorite verb to describe how life is lived: *to walk* (Greek *peripatein*). This word connotes a continuous pattern of life. Gentile believers are to distinguish themselves from the rest of society, not with a holier than thou attitude, but in genuine purity and holiness.

Here are the characteristics of the way of darkness: *Futility of mind*: emptiness of purpose and a hollow manner of thinking; *darkened understanding*: people intentionally move outside of the revealed intentions of God; *alienated from the life of God*: a choice to follow a path that is against God's desire and displays a willful disregard of God—the rejection of a life

CROSS REFERENCE
Romans 1:28–32

"And even as they did not like to retain God in their knowledge, God gave them over to a debased mind, to do those things which are not fitting; being filled with all unrighteousness, sexual immorality, wickedness, covetousness, maliciousness; full of envy, murder, strife, deceit, evil-mindedness; they are whisperers, backbiters, haters of God, violent, proud, boasters, inventors of evil things, disobedient to parents, undiscerning, untrustworthy, unloving, unforgiving, unmerciful; who, knowing the righteous judgment of God, that those who practice such things are deserving of death, not only do the same but also approve of those who practice them."

We must be clear that these verses do not describe a progression of depravity, but the continuing manifestation of the fruit of rejecting the knowledge of God. In this section, the more run-of-the-mill sins come to light. These vices are clearly against God's law and deserve punishment.

God gave people over to a debased mind because they did not want to reckon with God. They found that the knowledge of God did not fit their own minds. Therefore, God allowed their minds to yield what debased minds yield: actions that are not befitting godliness. It is important here to maintain the divine perspective: Wrong behavior results from wrong thinking; wrong thinking results from hearts hardened toward God; hard-heartedness towards God results from the rejection of the revelation of God that leads to the worship of God. Too often people simply ask others to stop their ungodliness. But Paul does not ask people to stop behaving in a certain way. He points out the verdict on such behavior: guilt requiring God's wrath.

CROSS REFERENCE
Galatians 5:19—21

"Now the works of the flesh are evident, which are: adultery, fornication, uncleanness, lewdness, idolatry, sorcery, hatred, contentions, jealousies, outbursts of wrath, selfish ambitions, dissensions, heresies, envy, murders, drunkenness, revelries, and the like; of which I tell you beforehand, just as I also told you in time past, that those who practice such things will not inherit the kingdom of God."

God gives us an organized list of vices in Galatians 5:19–21. While we might add more to the list, this section of Scripture includes sexual sins (adultery, fornication, uncleanness, lewdness), religious sins (idolatry and sorcery), relational sins (contentions, jealousies, outburst of wrath, selfish ambitions, dissensions, heresies, envy, murders), and indulgences of the body (drunkenness and revelries). Paul concludes by saying, "and the like," to include other sins not listed. We may add greed or covetousness to the list (Col. 3:5) and have a complete list. Often people have specific areas of weakness in one or more of these areas. Encouragement, prayer, and other means of support should be made by and on behalf of people succumbing to such influences.

The specific vices listed are arranged in four groups. The first two groupings are qualified with the words "full of" indicating the depth of the problems in these areas. The third group aggressively states what people do to propagate wickedness and the final group denotes what people don't do. This last group has the negating "un-" before the attribute.

that leads to the fullness of divine life; *ignorant of God*: not only a life that is outside God's revelation, but a choice to ignore the inner testimony of God.

Blindness of heart: Paul here says *blindness* rather than *hardness* of heart. These terms are probably interchangeable in his mind. To reject the light of truth that is available to one's heart is the same as rejecting the influence God could have on a soft heart. The unbelieving lifestyle comes from a heart problem *and* a mind problem. The center of the human being is the heart, which is lived out through the mind. If both are set against God, this leads to the following characteristics.

Being past feeling: sensitivity to the deeds of darkness is gone, the conscience no longer sends strong warnings about the posture, attitude, and demeanor toward the life that God gives. *Given to lewdness*: indecent behavior marked with shamelessness.

To work all uncleanness with greediness: the insatiable desire that overwhelms a person when they feel they cannot get enough because they have moved past feeling. This is the essence of covetousness.

Paul warned the people who were walking in Christ to not retreat to the greediness and covetousness that gratify the lusts of the flesh and the desires of the mind.

As in Romans 1:18–32, Paul does not imply that Gentiles are evil simply because they do evil deeds. The issue is far deeper than that. Paul looks at the root issues. These deal with the matters of mind, heart, soul, and openness to God. An unbeliever's posture against God includes a mind, heart, and soul that reject God's revelation. This is the essence of the Gentiles' problem. It inevitably leads to ungodly behavior.

Renewed Behavior

Behavior comes from the center of one's being and is played out through the thoughts patterns of the minds. If there are fundamental problems with the heart and mind, then ungodly behavior is guaranteed. Such was the case with the Ephesian believers before knowing Christ. But now they have broken from the past. They are in Christ and exhibit behavior that emanates from the renewal of their mind by the Holy Spirit.

> **But you have not so learned Christ, if indeed you have heard Him and have been taught by Him, as the truth is in Jesus (vv. 20, 21).**

Four verbs control the thought of these two verses: *learn, hear, is,* and *teach.* With these words, Paul provides the antidote to the Gentile way of life and its destructive response to the revelation of God.

The Ephesian believers have embraced Christ in these ways: They have become learners; they have *learned Christ.* We must not miss the sentence construction here. Paul does not say that they learned about Christ. No, they learned Christ Himself.

The word *learned* (Greek *emathete*) is related to the term *disciple.* They have become true followers of Jesus, imitating His life and thought. They are schooled in Him. We must be careful to not think of school in a twenty-first century sense. Paul is not thinking of classroom study—of lectures and textbooks. This kind of learning comes from walking with Jesus, learning at the feet of Jesus.

The Ephesian believers were not among the Twelve. Those original disciples certainly had an advantage in the "school of Christ." But the Ephesian believers had the advantage of Paul's presence for over two years. He could tutor them in the school of Christ. Paul taught them the revelation he had received of

Christ. The Ephesians' greatest advantage over the original twelve disciples was the presence of the Holy Spirit who would lead them into all truth. Indeed, the original disciples received the Holy Spirit, but while Jesus walked the earth, they did not have the power and revelation of the indwelling Holy Spirit.

The Ephesians also *heard Him.* Again, the issue is not focused on hearing about Christ. They responded to Christ's call themselves. The calling went out to these Gentiles in Ephesus and they heard and responded in faith. So, it is for all believers. They hear Christ's call and respond.

They were also *taught by Him.* One's own efforts cannot bring about true change. Only God can do that. It is true that Paul, along with prophets, evangelists, pastors and teachers, have a role in teaching. But if the resurrected Christ teaches a person, change results. That is God's promise.

We could easily miss the fourth verb: *is.* The truth of the universe and the truth of the unseen world are embodied in Jesus. Of all the things people study, Christ is the first truth. The Ephesians apprehended this. They knew they were grounded in Christ. They were schooled well.

That you put off, concerning your former conduct, the old man which grows corrupt according to the deceitful lusts, and be renewed in the spirit of your mind, and that you put on the new man which was created according to God, in true righteousness and holiness (vv. 22–24).

Here are three controlling verbs: *put off, be renewed,* and *put on.* Well-schooled disciples of Christ exhibit certain behaviors. They put off the bad conduct, they are renewed in their minds, and they put on the new way of life. The overall context of the letter urges believers to bring the truths of the spiritual realm into reality on earth. Christ is ruler over everything and believers are seated in the heavenly realm with Him. So, we display the rule of Christ in our practical lives.

First, believers jettison the old man along with all the conduct that was part of their former life. This old man is like the body of death that Paul refers to in Romans 7:24. The old man is corrupt according to deceitful lusts. The deceiving thing about lust is that it never satisfies. When we pursue lust, we never find satisfaction. We generally think of lust in only a sexual connotation, but lust is at the heart of our desire to have more—the quest for control. Any mode of selfishness is in one way or another an expression of lust.

Believers may be tempted to think that the old man is still in control. This is a lie. The new man is in charge. Paul describes the Gentile's conduct as a natural outgrowth of deceitful lusts. No wonder Gentile behavior is bad. It emanates from the nature that focuses on evil desires. Paul does not exclude Jews from this. He deals with them in Romans 2:1—3:20. But the issue of Jewish sinfulness is irrelevant in this epistle to a church made up of Gentiles.

Believers then will find that they can be *renewed in the Spirit*. The translation in the NKJV does not capitalize the "s" in *spirit*. However, Paul pressed the point that the renewal of the mind comes by the Holy Spirit. True, the adjective *holy* does not precede the word *spirit*. But Paul many times uses the construction *in the Spirit* (Greek

Cross Reference
Romans 6:10—13

"Likewise you also, reckon yourselves to be dead indeed to sin, but alive to God in Christ Jesus our Lord. Therefore, do not let sin reign in your mortal body, that you should obey it in its lusts. And do not present your members as instruments of unrighteousness to sin, but present yourselves to God as being alive from the dead, and your members *as* instruments of righteousness to God."

God intends that our reality be like Jesus' resurrected reality. In this verse, the Holy Spirit gives us one of the few commands in this section of Romans. He uses a term that is reminiscent of the earlier flow of thought. We are to reckon (*logizomai*) ourselves dead to sin.

Since the reign of Christ is secure in our lives by faith, we can use our will, by the Holy Spirit, to say "No" to sin's desire to rule us. We have a long history of sin's deadly reign. Our bodies are still mortal due to the pervasive effects of the fall of humanity. But that does not mean we are doomed to live in continual misery. Sin still wishes to rule in us, however, even though its chains are broken. We feel this in the pull sin still has in our lives. Nonetheless, the power rests in us, not in sin. So, we have moved from the reckoning of the mind to the decision of the will to not let sin reign.

We may easily see the progression of thought in this way:
1. *Reckon* is a movement in the mind of the believer (v. 11).
2. *Don't let sin reign* is an action of the will of the believer (v. 12).
3. *Stop presenting* and *present* are done with the body of the believer (v. 13).

Thus, mind, will, and body are the focus of Paul's concern to bring righteousness into life every day by the Holy Spirit.

CROSS REFERENCE
Zechariah 8:16—17

"'These are the things you shall do: Speak each man truth to his neighbor; give judgment in your gates for truth, justice, and peace; let none of you think evil in your heart against your neighbor; and do not love a false oath. For all these are things that I hate,' says the LORD."

In the days of Zechariah, God wanted to establish a new relationship with the people of Israel. This relationship was not marked by the pre-exilic ways. That manner led to being carried away into exile. No, a new manner of life ensued. God longs to relate to Israel based on this new way.

to pneumati) to refer to the movement of the Holy Spirit. Any change in the mind comes by the Holy Spirit. Of course, renewal of the mind also involves renewal through the understanding of the truth. We can avoid many problems in our minds by the input of the truth. But the Lord will never allow us to merely accumulate information. If we pursue this course, we will discover that truth slides through our fingers.

In reality, every believer is a new man. The old man is cast off in order that the new reality of what we are in Christ may be embraced in all its fullness. This will inevitably lead to a life of true righteousness and holiness. The new man is perfect in every way, just as Adam was in the first creation. Now believers must bring this truth into everyday life.

Therefore, putting away lying, "Let

each one of you speak truth with his neighbor," for we are members of one another (v. 25).

We see both the negative and the positive here. In putting off the old man we put off lying. In urging truthfulness, Paul quotes from Zechariah 8:16. This recalls the days when exiled Israel was called back to Jerusalem. They were to live with a new ethic, pleasing to God and nurturing to the people. Likewise, we are to speak the truth and to not give place to lying. Nothing is more at the core of the kingdom of darkness than the lie.

The fact that we are members of one another reflects another truth of the spiritual realm that must be lived out in the physical realm. The church is the one new man. No longer are there Jews and Gentiles. Relationships must be marked by honesty because we are members of one body.

Accent on Application
Keys to Godly Relationships

Ephesians has much to say about building godly relationships. This is one of the major themes of the New Testament. Our relationships are to be loving, truthful, selfless, and submissive. Simply put, Ephesians exhorts that we relate to others as Jesus relates to the Father and to us.

- 4:25–27—Diligently practice honesty and truthfulness in all your relationships. Deal with anger quickly, not allowing it to influence your treatment of others.
- 5:21—6:4—Maintain a selflessly submissive attitude in all your family relationships. Understand that this will provide evidence that Christ rules your home.
- 6:5–8—Do not be a people-pleaser at work! Serve the Lord in all you do. Recognize that He assigned you to that job.[32]

"Be angry, and do not sin": do not let the sun go down on your wrath, nor give place to the devil (vv. 26, 27).

These are among the most instructive and therapeutic words in the entire Bible. They constitute a passive command that allows anger, but not sin. Our human nature is incapable of not becoming angry or frustrated. Anger or wrath is an expressed trait of God's own nature. God becomes angry and yet He never sins.

Verse 26 refers to Psalm 4:4. There is a place for anger. Jesus Himself was angry. God was angry and brought forth wrath. But here the command is to deal with anger in a way that leads to righteousness and not to sinfulness. Paul also urges the Ephesian believers to refuse to carry anger in their hearts for any extended length of time. Grudges are excluded from the life of the people of God. It is no accident that verse 26 is followed by verse 27.

This shows that place can be given to the devil by carrying grudges. Satan loves to disintegrate demonstrations of unity and goodwill. His task as deceiver and destroyer is to cripple the one new man, the church. He will do anything in his power to bring this to pass. When people do not deal with their disagreements, Satan will enter and implement his destructive strategy. The writer was addressing those who had been sainted in Christ and

---

32 Jack W. Hayford, *Hayford's Bible Handbook [computer file], electronic ed., Logos Library System,* (Nashville: Thomas Nelson) 1997, © 1995, p. 385.

ACCENT ON APPLICATION
How to Control Wrath and Anger

The Bible doesn't give us license to put people on emotional trial—we are all sinners saved by grace. Therefore, we do not carry our anger toward others through the night and into the next day. God has forgiven us in Jesus Christ, and He doesn't wait till tomorrow to say, "It's okay." Today is the day of salvation, and today is the day when we should release others from wrath, lest it bind them and us in a circumstance that is contrary to God's will.

this admonition would not be made if it were not possible for place to be given to the devil. The Greek word for "place" (*topos*) is the root of the word topography, referring to a literal terrain. If a place has been given to him, the devil will not go out without being evicted. Believers, however, are not able to become demon-possessed because the Holy Spirit possesses them.

_____

Let him who stole steal no longer, but rather let him labor, working

CROSS REFERENCE
Psalm 4:3—8

"But know that the LORD has set apart for Himself him who is godly; The LORD will hear when I call to Him. Be angry, and do not sin. Meditate within your heart on your bed, and be still. Offer the sacrifices of righteousness, and put your trust in the LORD. There are many who say, 'Who will show us any good?' LORD, lift up the light of Your countenance upon us. You have put gladness in my heart, more than in the season that their grain and wine increased. I will both lie down in peace, and sleep; for You alone, O LORD, make me dwell in safety."

This quote speaks of the satisfaction of the righteous person in knowing that the Lord is his defender. Many slanderers falsely accuse godly people. But God will bring peace and righteousness. The picture painted here dramatically shows how it is possible to rest in God and release the need for revenge. The antidote to the desire for revenge is resting in God and meditating upon who He is. Any action coming out of that meditation will be mixed with righteousness, not wickedness.

ACCENT ON APPLICATION
Work vs. Vocation

The believer's work is not simply to earn a living, but it is a vocation. We are called to exercise the particular gift He has given to each of us. When serving the Lord with our talents He allows us to realize a financial return on the investment of our time. In a real sense, the earning is simply the fruit of His work in us. Trees that bear fruit do not earn the fruit, and in a similar way, we bear money as part of our wage-earning capacity. Part of that we use for ourselves, but the objective is how much beyond our need can we use to minister to others. We need to learn to regard our work as a vocation—in that we have been called and gifted by God to do something that turns us into a ministering agent, not only in the work that we do, but also with the resources that are derived from it.

with his hands what is good, that he may have something to give him who has need (v. 28).

In contrast to the greediness and covetousness of the unregenerate Gentile, the conduct of the new man in Christ shows industriousness and generosity. Honest labor, doing what is good in every endeavor, leads to the righteous life of God's desire. Generosity fights against covetousness and greed. When one gives to another, the old man is put off and the new man is put on. Integrity is compromised when we are indifferent toward irresponsible behavior, lack accountability, and are not faithful to principles of honesty and morality.

___

Let no corrupt word proceed out of your mouth, but what is good for

necessary edification, that it may impart grace to the hearers. And do not grieve the Holy Spirit of God, by whom you were sealed for the day of redemption (vv. 29–30).

The word *corrupt* used here means "rotten" and refers to something that is fouled and gone bad. It is used elsewhere in the New Testament for dead bodies that have decayed (John 11:39). Garbage talk is not only that which is corrupt, but also that which has a corrupting influence. Words themselves may not be foul, but a foul atmosphere can be created by words because of the attitude that attends them. We are to speak words that will build people up. To impart grace to the hearer means that one imparts something to others that has no relationship to what they have earned or deserved. That's what God does to us.

The Bible does not say we are to respond in kind, otherwise we would receive nothing but judgment from God. Yet, how often do we return judgment to one another?

God, by the Holy Spirit, put His seal of ownership and protection upon the believers. Thus, behaviors that provoke decay grieve the Holy Spirit who resides in us. Paul will talk further about the fullness of the Holy Spirit that works against decay. But here Paul simply asks the believers to live in a way that brings joy to the Holy Spirit who resides in them.

Let all bitterness, wrath, anger, clamor, and evil speaking be put away from you, with all malice. And be kind to one another, tenderhearted, forgiving one another, even as God in Christ forgave you (vv. 31, 32).

Tossing off the old and clothing oneself with the new are the themes in these two verses. Kindness and tenderheartedness both work against the old way of life. Kindness overwhelms wrath and anger. Tenderheartedness does not allow us to engage in clamor or slander. Forgiveness defuses malice. Here the word *forgive* (Greek *charis*) means "to extend grace" to another person and when grace is extended, peace rules. The whole point is to live as Christ lived, to exhibit His qualities, the qualities of the new man.

There are ten imperatives or commands given in this passage (vv. 25–32). Two of them are passive, which means that you are to allow a certain thing to happen to you. These are seen in verse 26—be angry, and verse 31—be put away. The other eight commands are in the present imperative, and when the Bible gives

ACCENT ON APPLICATION
How to Tame the Tongue

Proper speech is crucial to effective Christian living. Proverbs points out that life and death are in the power of the tongue. How important it is for us to realize that our speech can be spiritually motivated.

- 4:29—Be careful how you speak and what you say. Reject evil attitudes; and develop compassionate, forgiving attitudes toward others.
- 5:3–7—Avoid and reject any impure or immoral speech or behavior because it contradicts your profession of faith in Christ.[33]

---

[33] Jack W. Hayford, *Hayford's Bible Handbook [computer file]*, electronic ed., *Logos Library System*, (Nashville: Thomas Nelson) 1997, © 1995, p. 385.

THE SEVEN STEPS TO SUCCESS

1. Be graciously truthful and never lie (v. 25).
2. Tame your temper and refuse to hold a grudge (v. 26).
3. Don't give the devil a place (v. 27).
4. Do not steal and make your work a ministry (v. 28).
5. Stop garbage talk and make your words life-giving (v. 29).
6. Honor God's private dealings with your soul (v. 30).
7. Replace negative traits with positive ones (v. 31–32).

such a command, it is understood as being continuously incumbent upon us, conveying the idea of ongoing accountability.

Be Imitators of God

Ephesians 5:1–7

Paul continues to bring to the fore the things that will bring health to the body of Christ. The believers must be trained in basic, healthy living. In this section, Paul furthers his training of his Ephesian brothers and sisters.

Therefore be imitators of God as dear children (v. 1).

It is unfortunate that the chapter division occurs here because *therefore* points back to 4:32. God is in His very nature kind, tenderhearted, and forgiving. Jesus Christ, God incarnate, demonstrated this not only with His life, but also in His death. Everything about God points to the beauty of the

new way of life that believers are to embrace. The words *be imitators* derive from the Greek *mimetai*, the word from which we derive *mimic.* We are to mimic God's behavior and character. The motivation for such imitation is that we are the objects of His love. So, we who are loved by the Father wish to become like the Father.

And walk in love, as Christ also has loved us and given Himself for us, an offering and a sacrifice to God for a sweet-smelling aroma (v. 2).

The Christian walks in love as Christ also walked. The disciple follows the Master. The Master on this earth followed the way of love perfectly. His love was totally self-sacrificing. Just as Christ lived as a sacrificial offering to God, so Christians are to do the same. No person lives unto himself or herself. Each is to be an offering to God.

No one who has a reasonable understanding of Christ's sacrifice should shy away from living in self-giving love for others. Just as the Gentiles gave themselves to lewdness, so Christ gave Himself as a sacrifice. The contrast could not be greater. The Gentiles should acknowledge their Creator through submission to His will. Instead, they reject His control. The Savior, who ought to be worshiped, is scorned by humanity. Yet, He sacrifices Himself for those who disregard Him. Believers are to imitate Christ in this fashion.

But fornication and all uncleanness or covetousness, let it not even be named among you, as is fitting for saints; neither filthiness, nor foolish talking, nor coarse jesting, which are not fitting, but rather giving of thanks (vv. 3, 4).

Fornication means sexual impropriety or any sexual intercourse outside of marriage. All uncleanness has to do with death-dealing impurity. The Greek word used for *impurity* was used to describe diseases that people would contract by digging up graves. If we involve ourselves with things of death, we become polluted, impure. Those who have been called to be holy should not be associated with these actions.

The list of forbidden activities is daunting. But a believer walks by the Holy Spirit, so these are not even issues. In the Old Testament, God showed His displeasure with such activities in giving the Law. But the believer does not need the Law, since the Spirit now rules from within.

For this you know, that no fornicator, unclean person, nor covetous man, who is an idolater, has any inheritance in the kingdom of Christ and God. Let no one deceive you with empty words, for because of

CROSS REFERENCE
Galatians 5:18, 22, 23

"But if you are led by the Spirit, you are not under the law... But the fruit of the Spirit is love, joy, peace, longsuffering, kindness, goodness, faithfulness, gentleness, self-control. Against such there is no law."

Law is unnecessary for those led by the Holy Spirit because the Holy Spirit only leads in the direction of righteousness. Each of the items listed in Galatians 5:22–23 cuts against the grain of sin. The religious person enacts regulations to produce ethical behavior; the person of the Spirit lives by the Holy Spirit and righteousness is assured. Thus, law is irrelevant.

these things the wrath of God comes upon the sons of disobedience. Therefore do not be partakers with them (vv. 5–7).

Paul presents a list of vices that shows the contrast between what believers once were and what they are now. The old way of life was part of the old man who was put to death. Believers put off the manners of the old man in the process of living for Christ. The Ephesian believers ought to be rejoicing at this point because they are not named among those upon whom the wrath of God comes. Because of their transformation from death to life, they must separate themselves from such behavior. Paul urges them not to partake with such people.

The children of God never participate in evil behavior, though association with evil people is sometimes necessary. God did not take us out of the world. He left us in it. But we are not to be of the world. The Holy Spirit will give grace when we must associate with godless people. He will also give grace to us when we must flee people who are practicing evil.

Walk as Children of Light

Ephesians 5:8–14

After contrasting the way of those who practice evil with the way of the Lord, Paul shows how believers may shine in the midst of darkness. The world is a very dark place. Believers are called to live in the kingdom of light and life. This is a very different lifestyle compared to that of those outside the kingdom. It is a winsome witness.

For you were once darkness, but now you are light in the Lord. Walk as children of light (for the fruit of the Spirit is in all goodness, righteousness, and truth), finding out what is acceptable to the Lord (vv. 8, 9).

Paul brings the Ephesian believers back to reality. They are light in the Lord. What is true in the heavenly realms must be lived out in the physical domain. Just as Christ has glory at the right hand of God the Father, so also the believers who are seated in the heavenlies with Christ shine like the sun. We emanate light on earth just as it is in heaven. The only claim one has to such light is through faith in the Lord. Apart from that reality, people are darkness and live out the deeds of darkness.

Paul's greatest challenge was to enable believers to become what God had prepared them to be. The same is true today. The command *walk as children of light* brings focus to this issue. Life in the Holy Spirit is totally consistent with the life of light. Goodness, righteousness, and truth emanate from Spirit-filled believers. It can neither be stopped nor denied. It

ACCENT ON APPLICATION
How to Walk in the Light

1. Demonstrate the fruits of the Spirit (v. 9), rather than anger in the name of so-called righteousness.
2. Discern what is acceptable to the Lord (v. 10).
3. Let the light in you make clear the meaninglessness of the darkness (v. 11).
4. The exposure of the darkness is not the recitation of a litany of sins (vv. 12, 13)—where there is a bright light shining, people will find their way home.
5. Let divine life enlighten a dead world and do not become trapped in the world's ways (v. 14).
6. Learn to discern what is going on around you (v. 15).
7. Watch for redemptive opportunities and stand against the pressures to conform to this world (v. 16).

simply happens. This is always the will of God. It is acceptable to Him. The believer, therefore, lives a life of transparency to those around him. Light will not be a threat, for the light will test and approve the believer's actions.

And have no fellowship with the unfruitful works of darkness, but rather expose them. For it is shameful even to speak of those things which are done by them in secret (vv. 11, 12).

Christian fellowship does not include fellowship with the deeds of darkness. In fact, a life lived in the Holy Spirit will bring Christ's light upon all darkness. Paul admonishes the believers to live in such a way that the brightness of the life they live will expose and shame those living in darkness. This is not to be judgmental and does not lead to a life of legalism. In fact, Paul may be cautioning the Christians not to present a litany of misdeeds to unbelievers in order to expose their evil. Their glorious, pleasant life will be enough to expose the deeds of darkness.

But all things that are exposed are made manifest by the light, for whatever makes manifest is light. Therefore He says:
"Awake, you who sleep,
    Arise from the dead,
And Christ will give you light"
(vv. 13, 14).

The Holy Spirit through Paul proclaims two great truths here. First, God will, by the light of His presence, expose evil deeds for all to see. The second great truth is this: The revealing work of the light of God through the church by the Holy Spirit brings light into darkness. The church's light illuminates for many the path of redemption.

It is not clear where the quotation in verse 14 comes from. It may very well be an early hymn or a baptismal saying. The point of the text is to support the contention that when the light of Christ shines upon a person, change occurs. The dead are brought to life as if awakening from a deep sleep. God dispels the darkness of sin by the light of His presence found in the body of Christ.

QUESTIONS FOR PERSONAL REFLECTION AND GROUP DISCUSSION

Read Ephesians 4:17—5:14 and then answer the following questions.

1. Why do unbelievers engage in such sinful behavior as is listed in verses 17–19? What other portions of Scripture help us understand this behavior?

2. How is a person renewed in the spirit of their mind (v. 23)?

3. How can the improper handling of anger give room for the devil to work according to verses 26–27?

4. What are the characteristics of one who is an imitator of God (vv.1–7)?

5. How is it possible to grieve the Holy Spirit?

6. What does it mean to expose the works of darkness?

7. Why did Paul include verse 14 in this section?

Chapter 8

Ephesians 5:15—6:9

THE BELIEVER'S UNDERSTANDING OF THE WILL OF GOD FOR FAMILY AND LIFESTYLE

Redeeming the Time

Ephesians 5:15–17

———

See then that you walk circumspectly, not as fools but as wise, redeeming the time, because the days are evil. Therefore do not be unwise, but understand what the will of the Lord is (vv 15–17).

This short section sets up the commands that are to follow. The believers have a choice. They can live foolishly, in the world's fashion, without any care or discernment, or they can live in a wise fashion. Paul urges the believers to watch how they live their life. They must watch the path with extra care, as if walking an unknown path at night. This may be common sense, but not in this present age, for the present age is marked with evil and deception. The Evil One is a master at deceiving people into thinking that all is well when it isn't.

Believers are to redeem the time. The word *redeeming* here (Greek *exagorazomenoi*) means to buy back. There is an ever-present tendency to let time slip away without giving attention to God's purpose. Thus, we

CROSS REFERENCE
Acts 2:2–8, 12–17

"And suddenly there came a sound from heaven, as of a rushing mighty wind, and it filled the whole house where they were sitting. Then there appeared to them divided tongues, as of fire, and one sat upon each of them, and they were all filled with the Holy Spirit and began to speak with other tongues, as the Spirit gave them utterance. And there were dwelling in Jerusalem Jews, devout men, from every nation under heaven. And when this sound occurred, the multitude came together, and were confused, because everyone heard them speak in his own language. Then they were all amazed and marveled, saying to one another, 'Look, are not all these who speak Galileans? And how is it that we hear, each in our own language in which we were born?' ... So they were all amazed and perplexed, saying to one another, 'Whatever could this mean?' Others mocking said, 'They are full of new wine.' But Peter, standing up with the eleven, raised his voice and said to them, 'Men of Judea and all who dwell in Jerusalem, let this be known to you, and heed my words. For these are not drunk, as you suppose, since it is only the third hour of the day. But this is what was spoken by the prophet Joel:

And it shall come to pass in the last day, says God.
That I will pour out My Spirit on all flesh;
Your sons and your daughters shall prophesy,
Your young men shall see visions,
Your old men shall dream dreams.'"

Ephesians 5:18 probably refers to this section in Acts 2 when the Spirit came upon the scene signaling that a new era had begun. The Jews should have expected this new era, for the prophet Joel, among other prophets, predicted this event. The signs manifested by the Holy Spirit were misinterpreted. The record in Acts shows that some people mocked the coming of the Spirit, claiming that new wine had simply had its effect. But it was not so. A new power had taken control. The inauguration of the new era of the Holy Spirit brought new power and effectiveness to believers. It also brought in the era of speaking in tongues.

are to be sensitive to what is going on around us and keep on target with God's plan for the ages.

The word *evil* does not describe something sinister or suspect. Evil has sufficient force so that we feel the pressure of it. It can be likened to siege laid against an ancient city. We must buy up opportunities to minister because our world is pressed full with so many cares.

We redeem the time so that these cares will not crowd us out of God's plan. In keeping watch, we will understand what the will of the Lord is and will be full of the wisdom that comes from living in the light of God's presence.

Be Filled with the Spirit

Ephesians 5:18–21

This extremely important section issues the mandate for a life full of the Father's blessings. Many errors within churches and in believers' lives emanate from a misunderstanding and misapplication of this text. Here is the manifesto for effective life: be filled with the Spirit.

And do not be drunk with wine, in which is dissipation; but be filled with the Spirit (v. 18).

Paul contrasts reckless drunken living with fulfilled spiritual living. It is not hard to see why Paul uses intoxication from wine as a contrast to the filling of the Spirit. The intoxicated person has given control of his life over to a foreign power. This results in a destructive manner of life. Paul here focuses on wine, but the controlling power could be anything. Any outside force apart from the Spirit of God can take control of one's life. There can be only one end to this: dissipation.

We are presented with twin commands here. One is a prohibition and the other is an authorization. The present-tense verb in the prohibition implies that the Ephesians are not to be known for their drunkenness or for being controlled by anything other than God Himself. The present tense also indicates that they should be filled and keep on being filled by the Holy Spirit. It

Accent on Application
Five Reasons to Be Filled with the Holy Spirit

1. Jesus promised the Helper-Comforter to be beside you to complete God's purpose by His power in you.
2. Jesus commanded His disciples to receive the promised Spirit so that He might replicate His life in them.
3. The fullness of the Holy Spirit overflows into the emptiness of our spiritual capacities and expels the world's spirit.
4. The power of the Holy Spirit gives birth to an evangelistic passion to reach the unsaved and a compassion that can love people to life.
5. Spiritual language begets praise and prayer that exalts Christ, breaks evil bonds, and builds up believers.

ACCENT ON APPLICATION
Encouraging One Another in Praise

Paul tells the Ephesians to speak to one another using psalms and hymns and spiritual songs. If we come to a gathering of believers with a small offering of praise, it is magnified as we join with others. Their voices encourage us, and we inspire them. Separation from the local assembly deprives a person of this relationship and its strength. Let us assemble often and praise much—encouraging one another in praise.[34]

is up to the believers to always receive the fullness of the Holy Spirit.

We are not to get our exhilaration or our fulfillment in the way the world does; we are to be filled with the Holy Spirit. Being filled with the Spirit does not mean that you are filled always. Therefore we must keep on being filled with the Spirit.

... speaking to one another in psalms and hymns and spiritual songs, singing and making melody in your heart to the Lord (v. 19).

Paul shows the manner in which the Holy Spirit's fullness is made manifest to the church. First, it is found in a new way of relating to one another. The believers are known for their style of speech. This is focused around worship. The Book of Psalms was the hymnbook of the Old Testament. No wonder Paul underlines the importance of such

scriptural songs. But Paul does not limit these songs to the Old Testament Book of Psalms. *Psalms* indicates a broad category of songs that are often accompanied by various forms of instruments. Paul also does not give us a strict definition of what a hymn is. Clearly, it is sung in the context of public worship. The believers are united in praise to God. The third element mentioned in this verse is spiritual songs. These are songs motivated by the Holy Spirit. The word that modifies *song* is *pneumatikois*, which is better translated "in the Spirit."

Having been filled with the Spirit (v. 18), we are to worship in the Spirit. Psalms are scriptural songs, hymns are songs that have a lyric with a doctrinal content, and spiritual songs come from the Holy Spirit and are able to penetrate the spiritual realm. Such worship and fellowship guarantees a new manner of interpersonal relationships that are rooted in the worship of God.

---

[34] Jack W. Hayford, general editor; consulting editors, Sam Middlebrook...[et.al.], *Spirit-filled Life Study Bible [computer file]*, electronic ed., Logos Library System, (Nashville: Thomas Nelson) 1997, © 1991, pp. 1794–95.

Of course, there is also a private element to worship. Worship must be connected to a person's heart. Thus, making melody in one's heart enables the Christian to carry worship into everyday life. It is not limited to the public setting. Private heart-adoration is portable.

Giving thanks always for all things to God the Father in the name of our Lord Jesus Christ (v. 20).

This does not mean that we are to be thankful for everything that happens to us, both positive and negative. Rather, we give thanks to God that He is greater than all things. The Bible reveals in Psalm 22:3 that God is enthroned in the believers' praise. Here, worship and thanksgiving, provoked by the movement of the Holy Spirit, point to the glory of the Father and the Son. In this section, then, we have powerful reference to the working of the triune God.

The Holy Spirit moves us to praise. We offer praise and thanksgiving in the name of our Lord Jesus Christ, who provides us access to the Father. The divine economy works for the benefit of the worshiper.

Submitting to one another in the fear of God (v. 21).

In this atmosphere of being filled with the Spirit (v. 18) and in worship (v. 19) and thanksgiving (v. 20), we are to submit to one another. The fear of God has to do with reverencing God's order. This is a fundamental requirement of maturity and dynamic in a believer's life. It is a team principle that makes each of us mutually dependent on one another for far more than just the loving acceptance and mutual affirmation we all need. These are essential points of beginning: we must be completely accepting of the

THE SPECIFICS OF SUBMISSION

1. Submission to God the Father—Hebrews 12:5–9, James 4:6, 7.
2. Submission to the Truth—Romans 10:3 (The receiving of God's provision of righteousness through Christ alone, without works).
3. Submission to the Body of Christ. This refers to submission to Jesus as the Head—Ephesians 1:20–23; Colossians 2:18, 19; local eldership—Hebrews 13:17; 1 Corinthians 16:16; individuals in the church—Ephesians 5:21; 1 Peter 5:5.
4. Submission to others such as: Parents—Luke 2:51; Ephesians 6:1–3; Colossians 3:20; civil authority—1 Peter 2:13–23; Romans 13:1–8; employers—Colossians 3:22; Ephesians 6:5–7; husband or wife—Ephesians 5:22–33; Colossians 3:18, 19.

ACCENT ON APPLICATION
The Marriage Commitment

Responsibility to our marriage precedes responsibility for our ministry, since our ministerial and leadership qualifications are founded upon the model and quality of our marriages.

The church does not understand its relationship to Jesus until it understands the marriage commitment. It involves living through pain, committing to stay, learning to yield and to serve, and seeing beyond the imperfect. It involves answering the call to grow up and stop supposing that abundant life means personal convenience, the avoidance or escape from problems, the absence of trial or struggle, or the instant fulfillment of every wish. True abundance is in grace that learns graciousness, love that learns to die, faith that learns to wait, and trust that God can do all things.

---

weakness, the imperfection, and the learning process that is found in relationships.

The verb *submitting* means that submission is a person's voluntary choice to be under the influence of another. Spirit-filled people never demand others to submit to them. True submission protects, insures, and secures. It never demands, though it is demanding of our fallen nature. It never dominates, though it teaches the pathway to dominion.

marked by legalistic boundaries or rigid demands. On the contrary, God desires individuals in the fellowship of believers to express His manner of life. In so doing, His troops are prepared for spiritual battles. Thus, the following guidelines, instructions, and requirements regarding domestic order and ethical lifestyle are not ends in themselves, but preparatory to being effective in confronting the powers of evil.

The Great Mystery—Christ and the Church

Ephesians 5:21—6:9

There is orderliness to a life that is lived in the Holy Spirit and is ready to do spiritual battle. This order is not

Wives, submit to your own husbands, as to the Lord. For the husband is head of the wife, as also Christ is head of the church; and He is the Savior of the body. Therefore, just as the church is subject to Christ, so let the wives be to their own husbands in everything (vv. 22–24).

These verses have provoked many to decry the apostle Paul for holding un-liberated, chauvinistic views of women. Nothing could be further from the truth. Verse 22 does not contain the word *submit* in the original text. It is implied from verse 21 and appropriately carried through in this verse. But Paul specifically provides practical instructions for both wife and husband on what mutual submission looks like.

Such mutual submission was necessary because, in Paul's day, the subjugation of women was a fact of everyday life. Domination by the husband was simply assumed. Paul told married couples to submit to one another. This inaugurated a radical cultural shift in which wife and husband are on the same level in Christ. She can function in the body of Christ according to her gift and faith. She can pray and prophesy in the public fellowship (1 Cor. 11:2–16), as long as she does it in a culturally sensitive way, not calling attention to herself. In Christ, there was no hierarchy of man over woman. In Christ, cultural domination by men does not exist.

Paul also knew that order must be maintained under God's authority. So, wives are to voluntarily submit themselves to their husbands as to the Lord. This is a spiritual issue, not a matter of men getting what they want at the expense of women. Paul tells husbands to voluntarily submit as well. For men, this is extremely demanding. While in Christ there is no hierarchy, there is submission to Christ who is the head. In the home, Paul says order is appropriate.

It is hard to communicate the revolutionary aspects of the Spirit-filled life in marriage. In ancient cultures, domination on the part of the husband was assumed. In the Spirit, it is rejected. In Christ, the wife has equal standing, but she voluntarily submits, not because the culture demands it, but because it is the will of God. This, of course, does not mean that a wife is forced to do anything against the will of God. She is under the Lord first, and she voluntarily submits herself to her husband only after the primary relationship of the Lordship of Christ is lived out in the fullness of the Spirit.

Husbands, love your wives, just as Christ also loved the church and gave Himself for her, that He might sanctify and cleanse her with the washing of water by the word, that He might present her to Himself a glorious church, not having spot or wrinkle or any such thing, but that she should be holy and without blemish (vv. 25–27).

Paul revolutionizes the relationship of husbands towards wives in this section. Love, in all of its unconditional facets (Greek *agape*), is the demand put upon the husband. If you were a Greek living in Ephesus, your first response probably would be, "I have to do *what?*" There is a turning point in these verses. It tells of the radical nature of Spirit-filled living. The expectation of submission from one's wife was easy. That a husband would voluntarily submit to his wife through sacrificial love, thinking only of her benefit, was ridiculous in the ancient male-dominated culture. That a husband must totally give himself as Christ gave Himself for the church was beyond the imagination of an Ephesian husband.

The goal of Christ's giving of Himself was purity and wholeness for the church, to present the church in glorious fashion. Jesus did everything possible so that the church would have purity and redemption. So, husbands motivated by the Holy Spirit are to seek the same wholeness for their wives. This is radical.

The husband must submit to the Lord Jesus Christ so that he becomes the mirror of the person, character, and love of God through Jesus to his wife. Just as the love of Jesus attracts us, so the love of Jesus in a man will attract his wife to him.

The role of the husband as representing Christ in his home means this:

ACCENT ON APPLICATION
Christ and the Church Model the Marriage Relationship

The specific instructions that the apostle Paul gives to husbands and wives are a glimpse of the Bridegroom and bride—a heavenly model for every marriage on earth.

As a husband, how should I behave toward my wife? Look to Christ, the divine Bridegroom, in His relationship with the church: love her, sacrifice for her, listen to her concerns, take care of her; be as sensitive to her needs and her hurts as you are to those of your own body.

As a wife, how should I behave toward my husband? Look to the chosen bride, the church, in its relationship with Christ: respect him, acknowledge his calling as head of the family, respond to his leadership, listen to him, praise him, be unified in purpose and will with him; be a true helper (see Gen. 2:18).

No husband and wife can do this by mere willpower or resolve, but since you (including your marriage) are "His workmanship" (Eph. 2:8–10), God will bring this about.[35]

---

[35] Jack W. Hayford, general editor; consulting editors, Sam Middlebrook...[et.al.], *Spirit-filled Life Study Bible [computer file]*, electronic ed., Logos Library System, (Nashville: Thomas Nelson) 1997, © 1991, p. 1795.

Christ will function through a man to manifest God's saving purpose in the home and family. Anytime we say to Jesus, "I need to talk to you," He has time. Jesus always forgives. He is always patient; always accepts responsibility. This is how Jesus loves the church and this is how husbands are called to love their wives. This type of love begets a beautiful relationship and a voluntarily submissive wife.

So husbands ought to love their own wives as their own bodies; he who loves his wife loves himself. For no one ever hated his own flesh, but nourishes and cherishes it, just as the Lord does the church (vv. 28, 29).

If it wasn't enough to appeal to Christ's self-giving as an example, Paul provides another image to help husbands move from the domineering, controlling demeanor to become a compassionate, unconditionally loving man. Since the husband and wife are one flesh, which Paul refers to later, the husband ought to think about how he treats his own body and compare that to how he treats his wife. The truth is that a man cares for himself. Since his wife is part of him, he will care for her in the same way.

The final phrase, *just as the Lord does the church*, gives Paul an opportunity to change the focus from husband and wife relations to the church herself. Believers find the pattern of

relationships in the kingdom of God in the very nature of God's activity and character. So, it is imperative to look to Christ's relationship to the church for examples and patterns of behavior.

For we are members of His body, of His flesh and of His bones. "For this reason a man shall leave his father and mother and be joined to his wife, and the two shall become one flesh." This is a great mystery, but I speak concerning Christ and the church (vv. 30–32).

Our membership in Christ's body brings forth extraordinary benefits for us. Not the least of these is that we are His bride. We become the bride through the joining of the one new man, the church, with the Bridegroom, Christ. Paul's quotation from Genesis 2:24 is not meant to be a teaching on marriage, *per se*. It describes the relationship of Christ and the church as the pattern for marriage, not the other way around. Christ's ways of giving Himself to the church is the manner of marriage for Spirit-filled people.

The mystery spoken of here must be interpreted in light of the previous uses of the term. Earlier in Ephesians, the term related the idea of something that used to be hidden but now is revealed. Here it relates to the revelation that Genesis 2:24

ACCENT ON APPLICATION
Right Order in the Home

The disregard for parental authority that is so characteristic of our society has penetrated the life of the average believing home. This penetration of the world mindset into the homes of believers is not always the result of surrender to the spirit of the world. Frequently, it is simply the result of people not knowing the principles of right order in the home.

relates to the reality of Christ and the church and secondarily to earthly marriage. This, now being revealed in Christ, shows how a Spirit-filled relationship ought to be. The truth of the union of Christ and the church must be brought into the physical world through marriage. This communicates what God is like.

Children, obey your parents in the Lord, for this is right. "Honor your father and mother," which is the first commandment with promise: "that it may be well with you and you may live long on the earth." And you, fathers, do not provoke your children to wrath, but bring them up in the training and admonition of the Lord (vv. 1–4).

Paul's emphasis on husbands and wives leads to a second couplet: children and parents. The command for a child to obey would have been a given in first-century Ephesus. But Paul adds a twist. The motivation for obedience is not cultural. The new society of the people of God exhibits new motivations for behavior. The biblical reason for obedience springs from the command to honor parents. Obedience does not equal honor. A child can obey without honoring through hard heartedness. But Paul urges children to be in the Spirit and to listen to the Spirit's word from Deuteronomy 5:16. In almost the same way as a husband would care for his own body and therefore his wife, so a child would obey out of honor as a way of caring for himself. The promise of living well and long is linked to honoring the parents.

The promise is twofold: success in life and long life. This is a law that is woven into the fabric of the universe. People cannot dishonor their parents and realize fruitfulness or fullness in life. God desires children to have a life that is filled with all the benevolence, goodness, and blessing that God created humankind to enjoy. The child's experience of those blessings is dependent upon the parent developing a child that obeys his or her parents.

Paul's second admonition may seem odd to the twenty-first century reader. Paul only addresses fathers here. While we certainly can expand the understanding to parental authority in general, Paul specifically admonishes fathers. Paul urges them to not exasperate their children, provoking them to wrath. The Spirit-filled father knows how to provide encouragement, training, and godly formation in the home. This was a radical thought for a father of the first century. Then, fathers did little to raise children. They had business affairs to tend to. So, children were ignored, seen as nuisances, or bossed around.

To be honored, a parent ought to train a child in a way that engenders honor. You cannot demand it, but the training can be demanding. The Greek word translated *training* here has to do with discipline and correction. Not provoking children to wrath does not mean that they will like everything that they are asked to do as they are trained. To *provoke* means that something is done intentionally, insensitively, or ignorantly and becomes a provocation rather than an instruction. What this communicates is that there should be nothing inconsiderate, unbalanced, or cruel. We are not to provoke them to the type of anger that would not exist if a parent were dealing with a child sanely, sensitively, and scripturally.

The word *admonition* has to do with reasonableness. While children are being trained, they must be instructed as to why they are asked to do certain things. These reasons are not to be given merely in the light of social values, but in light of the Lord's standards. Training is done through deed and encompasses chastisement. Admonition is training by word and involves instruction, warning, and reproof.

The reason that training by action is mentioned first is that when we first deal with a child correctively and instructively they will not be able to understand the words that you speak. They will understand the things that you are doing before they can exchange in coherent speech. Training begins before instruction can be given in words understood by the child. This phrase *of the Lord* qualifies the way the training and admonition is to be given. If we miss any part of this verse, we are liable to confusion—a humanistic or legalist approach. Training by action, deed, or word of instruction should be in the Lord's way. We use the Bible as our textbook for understanding how to raise children. The Scripture is the way our heavenly Father teaches and instructs, the way He loves and leads, the way He punishes and chastises. God as Lawgiver gives explicit commands and detailed instructions, and describes the consequences of blessing or curse.

Bondservants, be obedient to those who are your masters according to the flesh, with fear and trembling, in sincerity of heart, as to Christ; not with eyeservice, as men-pleasers, but as bondservants of Christ, doing the will of God from the heart, with goodwill doing service, as to the Lord, and not to men, knowing that whatever good anyone does, he will receive the same from the Lord, whether he is a slave or free (vv. 5–8).

Paul does not condone slavery in these verses. He addresses a cultural reality within the church. He re-characterizes the slave-master relationship. Both are in Christ, just as Philemon and the slave Onesimus in Philemon 15–16. Paul is not out to change the cultural and social structures. He does obliterate slave-master distinctions in the church, however. In Christ, there is neither slave nor free, there is oneness in Him.

As the gospel spread, slaves became followers of Jesus. Many of them were bound to non-Christian masters. They too had to live in the Spirit. Yes, they had to obey their masters. Not to obey could lead to their death. But their obedience sprang from a new well. Their relationship with Christ, and their ultimate responsibility to Him, translated into a different kind of obedience. Yes, they obeyed, but with sincerity of heart. Their motivation changed. They were serving Christ. Their service to earthly masters reflected their service to their heavenly Master. God is a rewarder of those who do right, even to those slaves who obey in the context of the institution of slavery. God is not bound by culture.

ACCENT ON APPLICATION
The Believer's Obedience on the Job

Employee-employer relationships in some ways parallel the slave-master relationship of the first century. Of course, many differences exist as well. But the principles of what makes a good employee and a good employer emanate from this section. Both serve Christ as the Lord. Employees must fully comply with their employer's requests as much as it is in their power and insofar as the requests don't violate biblical standards. They must remember that they are not serving their employer; they are serving the Lord. Goodwill in every encounter rules the day. Employers must realize that they serve a master too, the Master in heaven. Both should live with the realization that in Christ there is no distinction between them. God is the great leveler of life.

And you, masters, do the same
things to them, giving up threaten-
ing, knowing that your own Master
also is in heaven, and there is no partiality with Him (v. 9).

As is the pattern, Paul now revolutionizes the cultural norm. Masters must behave entirely differently
as Spirit-filled people. When urged
to *do the same things to them* many
believing masters must have balked.
They were the ones in control,
weren't they? But mutual submission re-orients the relationship. The
entire social structure may not change,
but the manner of the household must
change. The God in whom there is
no partiality sees no distinction between slave and free. In the Lord,
there are no such class differences.
Masters who are Spirit-filled must
act accordingly. They may be regarded
as traitors in a society obsessed with
power, but the Spirit-directed life demands revolutionary behavior in the
midst of such evil.

QUESTIONS FOR PERSONAL REFLECTION AND GROUP DISCUSSION

Read Ephesians 5:15—6:9 and then answer the following questions.

1. What does it mean to redeem the time (v. 16)?

2. Why does Paul compare being drunk with wine with being filled with the Holy Spirit?

3. How does the structure of verses 18–21 help us understand this section?

4. How does verb tense help us to comprehend the meaning of the phrase *be filled with the Spirit*?

5. What does it mean to pray with supplication in the Spirit (v. 18)?

6. How is 5:22—6:9 a call for a radical reordering of life?

7. What do we learn about being a parent and an employee from 6:1–9?

Chapter 9

Ephesians 6:10–24

The Believer's Warfare and Victory

This section is the point of the entire letter. The church is fully competent in the heavenlies to bring decisive victory upon the earth. We do not have a simple metaphorical conflict of ideas. We are engaged in actual battle and have the resources to fight the battle. The church is fully gifted with all that is necessary for victory. It is overflowing Christ to the nations as His body, in partnership with Christ in His present kingdom, predestined to confound and overthrow the Adversary by the Spirit's power, and engaged in warfare to spread the kingdom of God everywhere.

The Reality of Spiritual Warfare

Ephesians 6:10–12

Finally, my brethren, be strong in the Lord and in the power of His might (v. 10).

This summons is for every believer. It points to the purpose and focus of the church of Jesus Christ—that is, to penetrate the darkness, drive it back, and advance the gospel. The power of the risen Christ resides in His body, the church. So, strength is found in the church focused on

Spirit-filled living. The tense of the verb *be strong* implies that we are to keep on being strong continually. Paul wants us to be reminded constantly of the need to bolster our courage.

Put on the whole armor of God, that you may be able to stand against the wiles of the devil (v. 11).

Here Paul's emphasis is to put the armor on now and leave it on. If the armor of God is on, and never removed, then God provides safety from the devil's schemes. The name *devil* means "slanderer" or "accuser," and his basic goal is to do everything that he can to berate and demean people so that they see themselves as less than significant under the will of the Living God. The word for *wiles* is the word from which we derive our word "method." The method of the adversary is geared to do anything possible to make our lives less than fulfilling.

For we do not wrestle against flesh and blood, but against principalities, against powers, against the rulers of the darkness of this age, against spiritual hosts of wickedness in the heavenly places (v. 12).

We wrestle in prayer to see the overthrow of those works of hell that manifest in this way. The arena of our conflict is not in the visible realm, although there are real challenges there. Heavenly places are the invisible realm of spiritual reality where spiritual conflict takes place. Behind the realm of the physical, there are larger realities. These are the real issue. Our struggles are not merely with things or people—spiritual struggles may manifest in those areas of our lives because there are spiritual powers behind them.

One of the church's greatest demands is to discern between the spiritual struggle and other social, personal, and political difficulties. Otherwise, individual believers and groups become too easily detoured, wrestling with human adversaries instead of prayerfully warring against the invisible works of hell behind the scenes. *Heavenly places* recalls earlier references to: (1) spiritual resources available to the church (1:3); (2) Christ's authority over evil (1:21); (3) the church's being seated together with her ascended Lord (2:6); and (4) the Father's will to display His wisdom through the church to the confounding of evil powers (3:10). On these grounds, this passage announces the church's corporate assignment to prayer-warfare: that evil will be driven back and the will of God advanced.[36]

---

[36] Jack W. Hayford, general editor; consulting editors, Sam Middlebrook… [et.al.], *Spirit-filled Life Study Bible [computer file]*, electronic ed., Logos Library System, (Nashville: Thomas Nelson) 1997, © 1991, p. 1796.

CHRIST'S VICTORY ON THE CROSS

The metaphor here is based on the armor and battle dress of the first-century Roman soldier. This shows the reader that he is engaged in an active battle. Though some suggest that the viewpoint of a continuous aggressive struggle minimizes the victory of the Cross, in fact it asserts that victory all the more. All spiritual warfare waged today is victorious only because of Christ's death on the Cross (Col. 2:15). Based on His victory, there are two distinct facets of a believer's spiritual life: The faith that positions itself against evil and the aggressive prayer-warfare that assails demonic strongholds.[37]

People who tilt the balance of power begin by recognizing that they are people of a dimension beyond the earthly plane. This dimension essentially influences everything else that goes on around us.

The Armor of God

Ephesians 6:13–17

Paul now provides specifics about the armor that protects us in the spiritual warfare. God protects His children in two ways: through supernatural enabling and the power that comes from Christ's own power in the heavenly realms. The church is enabled fully in the heavenly realms. Now is the time for action to take back the domains of darkness.

Therefore take up the whole armor of God, that you may be able to withstand in the evil day, and having done all, to stand (v. 13).

Because the battle rages in the heavenly realms, the church must put on the whole armor of God. The evil day is upon the church. The works of darkness already war against the light. The wrath of the devil seeks to destroy wherever there may be even a hint of wholeness left from God's creation. But where there is armor, there is protection. Only with the armor will the church be able to withstand the schemes of Satan.

After the armor is on, however, the command to stand firm remains. Paul does not see a day when there will be no battles. The return of Christ signals the final rest from battle. For now, the church is Christ's vehicle for advance against the spiritual powers of darkness.

---

37 Jack W. Hayford, general editor; consulting editors, Sam Middlebrook... [et.al.], *Spirit-filled Life Study Bible [computer file]*, electronic ed., Logos Library System, (Nashville: Thomas Nelson) 1997, © 1991, p. 1796.

WORD STUDY
STAND AGAINST

Stand against (Greek *anthistemi*)—This verb suggests vigorously opposing, bravely resisting, standing face-to-face against an adversary, standing your ground. Just as an antihistamine puts a block on histamine, *anthistemi* tells us that with the authority and spiritual weapons granted to us we can withstand evil forces.[38]

Stand therefore, having girded your waist with truth, having put on the breastplate of righteousness, and having shod your feet with the preparation of the gospel of peace (vv. 14, 15).

The believer stands ready for war with armor that may not have struck the average Roman soldier as effective.

But the battle is not an average battle. Since the battle is not against flesh and blood, the armor is not at all the same as a Roman soldier's —a leather belt, metal breastplate and helmet, etc. In our spiritual armor, truth is the belt bringing protection and allowed mobility. It tightens around an outer garment for better mobility. Truth holds things together.

The Roman's breastplate guarded the vital organs. Righteousness protects

ACCENT ON APPLICATION
Guidelines for Gaining Victory

Ephesians gives us insight into the nature of the spiritual warfare we face daily. Our combat is against spiritual forces, not men. Great are the protection and resources God has provided us to meet this enemy.

- 6:10–13—Stand in readiness for spiritual combat. Recognize that your demonic enemies are behind much of what comes against you to harm you.
- 6:14–17—Each day, consciously put on the spiritual armor God supplies. Learn and understand the nature of this divine protection.[39]

[38] Jack W. Hayford, general editor; consulting editors, Sam Middlebrook...[et.al.], *Spirit-filled Life Study Bible [computer file], electronic ed., Logos Library System*, (Nashville: Thomas Nelson) 1997, © 1991, pp. 1796–97.

[39] Jack W. Hayford, *Hayford's Bible Handbook [computer file], electronic ed., Logos Library System*, (Nashville: Thomas Nelson) 1997, © 1995, p. 385.

our eternal life. Only God's righteousness brings eternal life. Even God Himself put on the breastplate of righteousness (Is. 59:17). So, we believers walk as God walks. But, then again, the church is the body of Christ and we reflect how God is and what He does.

Our boots are the preparation of the gospel of peace. The church is ready and unmovable because she has the gospel's message that breaks through the darkness and brings peace. The Roman soldier's boots were designed to provide maximum stability and flexibility for marching. So, also, the church is ready to advance upon the powers of hell with the gospel of peace. What an irony that the weapon of war in the heavenlies is the gospel of peace on earth.

... above all, taking the shield of faith with which you will be able to quench all the fiery darts of the wicked one. And take the helmet of salvation, and the sword of the Spirit, which is the word of God (vv. 16, 17).

The shield and the helmet are meant for defensive purposes. A deep faith answers the call to believe in the power of Christ when all hell is breaking loose. And that is what is happening in the spiritual battle. Satan is the accuser, the father of lies, and the one to sow discord and malice. Satan will use every measure to create doubt in the believer. His malicious intent has no boundaries. But his advances are stopped by faith in the Son of God who proved His victory over the powers of darkness. No fiery darts will stick to the one whose faith is strong and vital. Fiery darts of the wicked one are those devises intended to penetrate your defenses. These will often penetrate your mind to create

THE ISSUES OF SPIRITUAL WARFARE

1. Spiritual warfare does not cultivate excitability or an elitist posture, but a discerning humility (2 Cor. 2:11) and a pursuit of effective action (2 Cor. 4:7).
2. Spiritual warfare emphasizes the authority of Christ and the victory of His Cross (Col. 2: 14, 15). This honors Jesus' commission on the grounds of His coronation.
3. Spiritual warfare is not a soul-wearying preoccupation. Also, a believer must not develop a fondness for it. Instead, we rest in the resources of Calvary's triumph by wearing the full armor of God. Then we can engage in a biblical confrontation of evil's subtle strategies.

PRAYER AND SUPPLICATION IN THE SPIRIT

The Holy Spirit, as contractor, anointed the Old Testament prophets Isaiah and Joel to prophesy of the day when He would be outpoured and His gifts would be exercised (Joel 2:28–32; Acts 2:17–21). In Isaiah 28:11–12, God told Judah that He would teach them in a manner they did not like and that He would give them knowledge through the language of foreigners as a sign of their unbelief. Centuries later the apostle Paul expanded the intent of this passage by attaching it to the gift of speaking in tongues as a manifestation or sign to unbelievers (1 Cor. 14:21, 22). This sign could be in languages either known or unknown to human beings (compare 1 Cor. 14 with Acts 2:1–11; 10:45–46).

In all these respects, we see the Holy Spirit as one who operates in the church as a definite personality—a Person given as a gift to the church to assure that the continued ministry of the resurrected Christ is expressed and verified.[40]

First, speaking in tongues is a private affair for self-edification (1 Cor. 14:2–4). Thus, the believer practices glossolalia devotionally in his most intimate and intercessory moments of communication with God as the Holy Spirit moves upon him. This devotional application may also be practiced by corporate agreement, in gatherings where no unbelievers or uninformed people are present (1 Cor. 14:23).

In line with this understanding, the following reasons are put forward for speaking with tongues:

1. Speaking with tongues as the Holy Spirit gives utterance is the unique spiritual gift identified with the church of Jesus Christ. All other gifts, miracles, and spiritual manifestations were in evidence during Old Testament times, before the Day of Pentecost. This new phenomenon became uniquely identified with the church and was ordained by God for the church (1 Cor. 12:28; 14:21).
2. Speaking with tongues is a specific fulfillment of prophecies by Isaiah and Jesus. (Compare Is. 28:11 with 1 Cor. 14:21, and Mark 16:17 with Acts 2:4; 10:46; 19:6; and 1 Cor. 14:5, 14–18, 39.)
3. Speaking with tongues is a proof of the resurrection and glorification of Jesus Christ (John 16:7; Acts 2:26).

---

[40] Jack W. Hayford, *Hayford's Bible Handbook [computer file]*, electronic ed., Logos Library System, (Nashville: Thomas Nelson) 1997, © 1995, pp. 642–43.

4. Speaking with tongues is an evidence of the baptism in or infilling of the Holy Spirit (Acts 2:4; 10:45–46; 19:6).

5. Speaking with tongues is a spiritual gift for self-edification (1 Cor. 14:4; Jude 20).

6. Speaking with tongues is a spiritual gift for spiritual edification of the church when accompanied by interpretation (1 Cor. 14:5).

7. Speaking with tongues is a spiritual gift for communication with God in private worship (1 Cor. 14:15).

8. Speaking with tongues is a means by which the Holy Spirit intercedes through us in prayer (Rom. 8:26; 1 Cor. 14:14; Eph. 6:18).

9. Speaking with tongues is a spiritual means for rejoicing (1 Cor. 14:15; Eph. 5:18–19).

10. Paul's application of Isaiah's prophecy seems to indicate that speaking with tongues is also intended as a means of rest or refreshment (Is. 28:12; 1 Cor. 14:21).

11. Speaking with tongues confirms the Word of God when it is preached (Mark 16:17, 20; 1 Cor. 14:22).[41]

doubt or error. Of course, being filled with the Spirit of God ensures richness of faith and, therefore, a strong shield.

The helmet protects our head. A full understanding of salvation, with all its victorious attributes, provides maximum safety for the mind of the believer. Knowing one is saved from the wrath of God and transferred into the kingdom of God brings extraordinary confidence and peace.

Our offensive weapon is God's Word. It is described as the sword of the Spirit, which is the Word of God. The Holy Spirit's primary vehicle for warfare is God's Word. When God speaks, actions occur. His Word never returns empty. Every time God speaks, the realm of darkness parts. Satan is powerless to prevent God's righteousness and grace from being realized through His Word.

The shield of faith and the sword of the Spirit go hand in hand. One is defensive, the other is offensive. The shield and the sword both have the same fountainhead—the Word. The sword is the cutting edge of the word of authority against the works of darkness. The shield is kept in place by the

41 Jack W. Hayford, *Hayford's Bible Handbook [computer file], electronic ed., Logos Library System,* (Nashville: Thomas Nelson) 1997, © 1995, p. 643.

resource of the Word of God (Rom. 10:17).

The Way of Spiritual Warfare

Ephesians 6:18–20

The armor protects, but the people of God must advance. In this section, Paul gives the strategy for battle. He delivers marching orders for the church. Nothing can stop the advance of the church when these orders are followed.

> Praying always with all prayer and supplication in the Spirit, being watchful to this end with all perseverance and supplication for all the saints (v. 18).

The method of our prayer should be that we pray always and we are enabled to do this by the power of the Holy Spirit. The main way that spiritual warfare occurs is praying in the Spirit with the Word of God as our resource. As we pray in the Spirit, we are engaging in spiritual warfare. God provides powerful prayer moved by His Spirit. Paul refers to the Spirit-motivated language of prayer—speaking in tongues for Spirit-originated assault upon the powers of hell.

Paul also asks for supplication for all the saints. This presupposes that believers know what to request of God. Believers must become knowledgeable of the needs of others in order to pray effectively.

> And for me, that utterance may be given to me, that I may open my mouth boldly to make known the mystery of the gospel, for which I am an ambassador in chains; that in it I may speak boldly, as I ought to speak (vv. 19, 20).

Paul was imprisoned at the time he wrote this letter. So, he asked the believers to pray for him. He desired that there might be a penetration by the gospel of the center of the Roman Empire. Because of the intercession, people of esteem within this great imperial power were touched by the gospel.

Concluding Remarks

Ephesians 6:21–24

> But that you also may know my affairs and how I am doing, Tychicus, a beloved brother and faithful minister in the Lord, will make all things known to you; whom I have sent to you for this very purpose, that you may know our affairs, and that he may comfort your hearts. Peace to the brethren, and love with faith, from God the Father and the Lord Jesus Christ. Grace be with all those who love our Lord Jesus Christ in sincerity. Amen (vv. 21–24).

Paul concludes this powerful letter with the introduction of Tychicus, who probably carried Paul's letter to the Ephesian church. There should be no question of the credentials of Tychicus, Paul says, since he has already proven himself as a faithful minister in the Lord. The Ephesian believers were obviously very concerned for Paul, and Tychicus was to fill them in with details about Paul's situation.

In closing, Paul wishes them to have peace, love with faith, and grace. In light of the warfare that was going on, Paul communicates that all is well for the believer who rests in the Lord. As people who have experienced love from the Father, they are to love one another with the love that faith in Christ provides. And, finally, Paul asks grace to rain down upon all who love Jesus. God is constantly giving grace to those who rest in the arms of Jesus.

QUESTIONS FOR PERSONAL REFLECTION AND GROUP DISCUSSION

Read Ephesians 6:10–24 and then answer the following questions.

1. Explain each of the elements that constitute the armor of God in verses 11–17.

2. How does the idea that we do not wrestle against flesh and blood conflict with your concept of fighting the world system?

3. What does the word *withstand* mean in the context of this section?

4. What does it mean to pray with supplication in the Spirit (v. 18)?

5. Paul requested that the Ephesians pray for him. How is this an example to us (vv.19–20)?

6. Why did Paul send Tychicus to the Ephesian church? What kind of an example is this for us?

7. How has an overall understanding of this epistle changed your understanding of the place of the church in God's plan for the world?

THE EPISTLE TO THE
COLOSSIANS

CONTENTS

INTRODUCTION

Colossians is one of four shorter epistles written by Paul while he was in prison in Rome. The others are Philippians, Ephesians, and Philemon. The Epistle to the Colossians focuses on the person and work of Jesus Christ. It reaches heights of expression that rival anything said of Christ elsewhere in Scripture. Colossians shares many similarities in style and content with Ephesians and was probably written as a companion to the brief letter to Philemon (compare Col. 4:7–13 and Philem. 12, 24).

Paul had never visited Colosse, a small town in the province of Asia, about 100 miles east of Ephesus. The Colossian church was an outgrowth of his three-year ministry in Ephesus about A.D. 52–55 (*see* Acts 19:10; 20:31). Epaphras, a native of the town and probably one of the apostle's converts, was likely the church's founder and leader (Col. 1:7, 8; 4:12, 13). The church apparently met in Philemon's home (Philem. 2).

Conservative scholars believe Paul wrote this letter during his first Roman imprisonment, around A.D. 61. Tychicus delivered the letters to the Colossians, to Philemon, and to the Ephesians to their respective destinations.

Sometime during Paul's imprisonment, Epaphras solicited his help in dealing with false teaching that threatened the church at Colosse (2:8, 9). This heresy was apparently a blend of pagan-occultism, Jewish legalism, and Christianity. The error resembles an early form of Gnosticism, which taught that Jesus was not fully God and fully man, but merely one of the semi-divine beings that bridged the chasm between God and the world. Therefore, these Gnostics said that Christ lacked the authority and ability to meet the needs of the Colossians. Enlightened believers could, they said, achieve spiritual fullness through special knowledge and rigorous self-discipline. Paul unmasks these false

COLOSSE

COLOSSE—a city in the Roman province of Asia (western Turkey), situated in the Lycus River Valley about 160 kilometers (100 miles) east of Ephesus. The apostle Paul wrote a letter to the church at Colosse (Col. 1:2; Colossae, NASB, REV, NRSV). The Christian community at Colosse apparently grew up under the leadership of Epaphras (Col. 1:7; 4:12) and Archippus (Col. 4:17; Philem. 2). Philemon and Onesimus lived at Colosse (Col. 4:9).

Colosse formed a triangle with two other cities of the Lycus Valley, Hierapolis and Laodicea, both of which are mentioned in the New Testament. As early as the fifth century B.C., Colosse was known as a prosperous city; but by the beginning of the Christian era it was eclipsed by its two neighbors. Thereafter its reputation declined to that of a small town.[1]

teachings as "empty deceit... of men" (2:8), having the "appearance of wisdom" (2:23), but useless in fact. He declares that the addition of such teachings dilutes rather than strengthens the faith (2:20).

With an urgency heightened by the repatriation of a runaway slave named Onesimus to his master at Colosse, Paul wrote this epistle with a fourfold purpose: (1) to expose and rebut the Gnostic heresy; (2) to instruct the Colossians in the truth and alert them to the danger of returning to pagan vices; (3) to express personal interest in the believers; and (4) to inspire them to promote mutual love and harmony.

No other book of the New Testament sets forth more fully or defends more thoroughly the universal lordship of Christ. Combative in tone and abrupt in style, Colossians bears a close resemblance to Ephesians in language and subject matter. Over seventy of the 155 verses in Ephesians contain expressions echoed in Colossians. On the other hand, Colossians has twenty-eight words found nowhere else in Paul's writings and thirty-four found nowhere else in the New Testament.

The false teachers at Colosse undercut the major doctrines of Christianity, not the least of which are the deity, absolute lordship, and sufficiency of Christ. Colossians sets forth Christ as the supreme Lord in whose sufficiency the believers can find completeness (1:15–20). The first two

---

[1] Ronald F. Youngblood, general editor; F. F. Bruce and R. K. Harrison, consulting editors, *Nelson's New Illustrated Bible Dictionary*: An authoritative one-volume reference work on the Bible with full color illustrations [computer file], electronic edition of the revised edition of *Nelson's Illustrated Bible Dictionary*, Logos Library System, (Nashville: Thomas Nelson) 1997, © 1995, p.288–89.

Authorship, Timing, and Historical Setting of Colossians

Authorship and Date. Colossians was written by Paul (and Timothy, 1:1) to a Christian community (perhaps "house churches," 1:2; 4:15) that he had not visited (2:1). Paul had established a resident ministry in Ephesus, 100 miles west of Colosse. For more than two years the influence of his ministry reached "all who dwelt in Asia" (Acts 19:10). Epaphras must have heard Paul in Ephesus and then carried the gospel to Colosse (1:7–8; 4:12–13).

Paul wrote the epistle from prison (4:3, 10, 18), but he did not indicate where he was imprisoned. Caesarea and Ephesus have been suggested, but the most probable place is Rome (Acts 28:30). This would date the epistle in the late 50s or early 60s.

Historical Setting. False teaching had taken root in Colosse. This teaching combined Jewish observances (2:16) and pagan speculation (2:8); it is possible that this resulted in an early form of Gnosticism. This teaching pretended to add to or improve upon the gospel that, indirectly at least, had come from Paul. Some of the additions Paul mentions are feasts and observances, some of them related to astrology (2:16), plus a list of rules (2:20). These practices were then included within a philosophy in which angels played a leading role (2:18); Paul calls this philosophy "the basic principles of the world" (2:8).

Theological Contribution. Paul unmasks the false teaching as "empty deceit ... of men" (2:8), having the "appearance of wisdom" (2:23), but useless in fact. He declares that the addition of such things dilutes rather than strengthens the faith (2:20).

But Paul does more than denounce false teaching. The best corrective is a firm grip on who Jesus Christ is and what He did for our salvation. In Christ "are hidden all the treasures of wisdom and knowledge" (2:3), and "in Him all fullness" dwells (1:19). In fact, "He is the image of the invisible God" (1:15). He has stripped every power opposed to Him (2:15), wiped out every accusation against us (2:14), and actually "reconciled all things to Himself" (1:20). He is not only head of the church (1:18); but He stands before all time and above every power, and at the end of all history (1:16).

This beautiful epistle on the majesty of Jesus Christ speaks to us today as much as to the Colossians. It reminds us that Jesus Christ is sufficient for every need and is still the most powerful force in the world.[2]

---

2   Ronald F. Youngblood, general editor; F. F. Bruce and R. K. Harrison, consulting editors, *Nelson's New Illustrated Bible Dictionary: An authoritative one-volume reference work on the Bible with full color illustrations* [computer file], electronic edition of the revised edition of *Nelson's Illustrated Bible Dictionary*, Logos Library System, (Nashville: Thomas Nelson) 1997, © 1995, pp. 289-90.

GNOSTICISM AND COLOSSIANS

While Gnosticism as a religious movement didn't really find favor and large numbers of adherents until the second century A.D., many scholars believe that Paul combats an early form of Gnosticism in Colossians. The Gnostics accepted the Greek idea of a radical dualism between God (spirit) and the world (matter). According to their worldview, the created order was evil, inferior, and opposed to the good. God may have created the first order, but each successive order was the work of anti-gods, archons, or a demiurge (a subordinate deity).

The Gnostics believed that the earth is surrounded by a number of cosmic spheres (usually seven) that separate human beings from God. These spheres are ruled by archons (spiritual principalities and powers) who guard their spheres by barring the souls who are seeking to ascend from the realm of darkness and captivity that is below to the realm of light that is above.

The Gnostics also taught that every human being is composed of body, soul, and spirit. Since the body and the soul are part of people's earthly existence, they are evil. Enclosed in the soul, however, is the spirit, the only divine part of this triad. This "spirit" is asleep and ignorant; it needs to be awakened and liberated by knowledge.

According to the Gnostics, the aim of salvation is for the spirit to be awakened by knowledge so the inner person can be released from the earthly dungeon and return to the realm of light where the soul becomes reunited with God. As the soul ascends, however, it needs to penetrate the cosmic spheres that separate it from its heavenly destiny. This, too, is accomplished by knowledge. One must understand certain formulas that are revealed only to the initiated.

Ethical behavior among the Gnostics varied considerably. Some sought to separate themselves from all evil matter in order to avoid contamination. Paul may be opposing such a view in 1 Timothy 4:1–5. For other Gnostics, ethical life took the form of libertinism. For them knowledge meant freedom to participate in all sorts of activities. Many reasoned that since they had received divine knowledge and were truly informed as to their divine nature, it did not matter how they lived.

Such an attitude is a misunderstanding of the gospel. Paul, on a number of occasions, reminded his readers that they were saved from sin to holiness. They were not to have an attitude of indifference toward the law. They had died to sin in their baptism into Christ (Rom. 6:1–11) and so were to walk "in newness of life." John reminded the Christians that once they had been saved they were not to continue living in sin (1 John 3:4–10).

These Gnostic teachings also had a disruptive effect on fellowship in the church. Those who were "enlightened" thought of themselves as being superior to those who did not have such knowledge. Divisions arose between the spiritual and the fleshly. This attitude of superiority is severely condemned in the New Testament. Christians are "one body" (1 Cor. 12) who should love one another (1 Cor. 13; 1 John). Spiritual gifts are for the Christian community rather than individual use; they should promote humility rather than pride (1 Cor. 12—14; Eph. 4:11–16).[3]

chapters present and defend this truth; the latter two unfold its practical implications.

Jesus Christ's supremacy hinges upon His uniqueness as God's eternal, beloved Son and heir (1:13, 15). In Him dwells the totality of divine attributes, essence, and power (1:19; 2:9). He is the exact revelation and representation of the Father, and has priority in time and primacy in rank over all creation (1:15). His sufficiency depends upon His superiority. Paul's conviction of Christ's absolute sovereignty gave impulse to his missionary activity (1:27–29).

Paul declares Christ's lordship in three primary ways, at the same time he proclaims His adequacy. First, Christ is Lord over all creation. His creative authority encompasses the whole material and spiritual universe (1:16). Since this includes the angels and planets (1:16; 2:10), Christ deserves to be worshiped instead of the angels (2:18). Further, there is no reason to fear demonic spirit-powers or to seek superstitiously for protection from them, because Christ has neutralized their power on the Cross (2:15) and shares this triumphant resurrection power with the believers (2:20). As the sovereign and sufficient potentate, Christ is not only Creator of the universe but also its sustainer (1:17), its uniting principle, and its goal (1:16).

Second, Jesus Christ is preeminent in the church as its Creator and Savior (1:18). He is its life and leader, and the church submits to Him alone. The

---

3   Ronald F. Youngblood, general editor; F. F. Bruce and R. K. Harrison, consulting editors, *Nelson's New Illustrated Bible Dictionary: An authoritative one-volume reference work on the Bible with full color illustrations* [computer file], electronic edition of the revised edition of *Nelson's Illustrated Bible Dictionary*, Logos Library System, (Nashville: Thomas Nelson) 1997, © 1995, pp. 500-01.

BIBLE CHARACTERS
The Role of Timothy in Paul's Ministry

Timothy first appears in Paul's second missionary journey when the apostle revisited Lystra (Acts 16:1–3). Timothy was the son of a Gentile father and a Jewish-Christian mother named Eunice, and the grandson of Lois (Acts 16:1; 2 Tim. 1:5). Timothy may have been converted under Paul's ministry, because the apostle refers to him as his "beloved and faithful son in the Lord" (1 Cor. 4:17) and as his "true son in the faith" (1 Tim. 1:2). Timothy was held in high regard in Lystra and Iconium, and Paul desired to take him along as a traveling companion (Acts 16:3).

During Paul's third missionary journey, Timothy was active in the evangelizing of Corinth, although he had little success. When news of disturbances in the church in Corinth reached Paul at Ephesus, he sent Timothy, perhaps along with Erastus (Acts 19:22), to resolve the difficulties. The mission failed, perhaps because of fear on Timothy's part (1 Cor. 16:10–11). Paul then sent the more forceful Titus, who was able to calm the situation at Corinth (2 Cor. 7). Later in the third journey, Timothy is listed as one of the group that accompanied Paul along the coast of Asia Minor on his way to Jerusalem (Acts 20:4–5).

Timothy's strongest traits were his sensitivity, affection, and loyalty. Paul commends him to the Philippians, for example, as one of proven character, faithful to Paul like a son to a father, and without rival in his concern for the Philippians (Phil. 2:19–23; also 2 Tim. 1:4; 3:10). Paul's warnings, however, to "be strong" (2 Tim. 2:1) suggest that Timothy suffered from fearfulness (1 Cor. 16:10–11; 2 Tim. 1:7) and perhaps youthful lusts (2 Tim. 2:22). But in spite of his weaknesses, Paul was closer to Timothy than to any of his other associates.

Writing about A.D. 325, Eusebius reported that Timothy was the first bishop of Ephesus. In 356, Constantius transferred what was thought to be Timothy's remains from Ephesus to Constantinople (modern Istanbul) and buried them in the Church of the Apostles, which had been built by the Emperor Constantine.[4]

Colossians must remain rooted in Him (2:6, 7) rather than become enchanted with empty speculation and traditions (2:8, 16–18).

---

[4] Ronald F. Youngblood, general editor; F. F. Bruce and R. K. Harrison, consulting editors, *Nelson's New Illustrated Bible Dictionary*: An authoritative one-volume reference work on the Bible with full color illustrations [computer file], electronic edition of the revised edition of *Nelson's Illustrated Bible Dictionary*, Logos Library System, (Nashville: Thomas Nelson) 1997, © 1995, pp. 1253-54.

Third, Jesus Christ is supreme in salvation (3:11). In Him, all man-made distinctions fade and barriers fall. He has made all Christians into one family in which all members are equal in forgiveness and adoption; and He is all that matters, first and last. Therefore, contrary to the Gnostic heresy, there are no special qualifications or requirements for experiencing God's favor (2:8–20).

Chapters 3 and 4 deal with the practical implications of Christ in the Colossians' daily life. Paul's use of the word *Lord* nine times in 3:1—4:18 indicates that Christ's supremacy pervades every aspect of the believers' relationships and activities.

Because ours is an age of religious pluralism and syncretism (that is, a diluting of truth for the sake of unity), Christ's lordship is deemed irrelevant by many who believe one religion is as good as another. His preeminence is denied by others who place the Christian stamp upon a fusion of beliefs from several religions. Usually hailed as an advance beyond apostolic Christianity, this religious blend promises self-fulfillment and freedom without surrender to Christ.

"Jesus is Lord" is the church's earliest confession. It remains the abiding test of authentic Christianity. Neither the church nor the individual believer can afford to compromise Christ's deity. In His sovereignty lies His sufficiency.

THE SAINTS IN CHRIST

Saints are people who have been separated from the world and consecrated to the worship and service of God. Followers of the Lord are referred to by this word throughout the Bible, although its meaning is developed fully in the New Testament. Consecration (to be set apart) and purity are the basic meanings of the word *saint*. Believers are called saints (Rom. 1:7) and "saints in Christ Jesus" (Phil. 1:1) because they belong to the One who provides their sanctification.

When Christ returns, the saints will be clothed in their righteous acts (Rev. 19:8) because they will have continued to live in faith through God's power (1 Sam. 2:9) and Christ's praying for them (Rom. 8:27). The saints are also those to whom the privilege of revelation (Col. 1:26; Jude 3) and the task of ministry (Eph. 4:12) are committed.[5]

---

[5] Ronald F. Youngblood, general editor; F. F. Bruce and R. K. Harrison, consulting editors, *Nelson's New Illustrated Bible Dictionary*: An authoritative one-volume reference work on the Bible with full color illustrations [computer file], electronic edition of the revised edition of *Nelson's Illustrated Bible Dictionary*, Logos Library System, (Nashville: Thomas Nelson) 1997, © 1995, p. 1113.

He will be Lord of everything or not Lord at all.[6]

Colossians shows that our acceptance before God, and thereby our authority under Him, result from our finding both pardon and position in Christ. *In Christ* is the grand New Testament expression that declares both our place of secure refuge and our platform of confident authority. To be in Christ is to be placed in the Anointed One who is the Messiah established as King of God's kingdom. In Christ, each believer is a joint-heir with Christ (Rom. 8:16–17), possibly the most amazing proposition among all of redemption's provisions. It is a grand thing to be completely forgiven and acquitted of all past sin. It is also a grand thing to be promised the future marvel of eternal life in the presence of God. But between these, consider that God has enabled us presently to share equally in the abounding resources of Christ's life, power, and dominion!

Our position in Christ grants us victory and authority over hell's powers. Colossians reveals how the health and continuing life of the church is found as we glory in the Cross (2:8–10; 3:1–4):[7]

1. Christ's dominion throughout the universe, which is His by right of His role as Creator and sustainer of all things (1:15–17), is shared with humankind through what He did on the Cross (1:18–20). Christ's sacrifice on the Cross was the price of this restored dominion.

2. Christ's dominion over all the works and workers of darkness (the principalities and powers) is ours for one reason alone: Jesus broke their power and gained the victory on the Cross. He invites us to share in this through the blood of His Cross.

---

[6] Jack W. Hayford, *Hayford's Bible Handbook* [computer file], electronic ed., Logos Library System, (Nashville: Thomas Nelson) 1997, © 1995, p. 395.

[7] Jack W. Hayford, *Hayford's Bible Handbook* [computer file], electronic ed., Logos Library System, (Nashville: Thomas Nelson) 1997, © 1995, p. 392.

Opening Greeting

Colossians 1:1–2

Paul, an apostle of Jesus Christ by the will of God, and Timothy our brother, to the saints and faithful brethren in Christ who are in Colosse: Grace to you and peace from God our Father and the Lord Jesus Christ (vv. 1, 2).

This brief introduction, which is among the shortest of all of Paul's epistles, is Paul's standard greeting and blessing. Yet, the apostle fills this formal opening with purpose. In other words, he said more than, "Dear Colossians, this is Paul." Instead, He reminded the Colossians that his apostleship is by God's will. In other words, Paul's apostleship was not his own choice, though he lives it out with vigor, knowing God's purpose for his life. As a Jew, Paul probably would not have chosen the path of apostle to the Gentiles, but God gave him the unique and very difficult task of ministering to people who were ethnically totally different than he.

Timothy, who traveled with Paul on his second missionary journey, was positioned in Macedonia for ministry with Silas. He then joined Paul for further work in Athens (Acts 16:1; 17:14; 18:5). Timothy was a companion of Paul in Rome, although he was probably not imprisoned with him. He is called a brother in Christ, indicating the close connection and fellowship that Paul had with him. This also indicated that the Colossian believers should have the same connection with Timothy.

Paul addressed the Book of Colossians to the saints and faithful brethren in Colosse. He used this form of address elsewhere only in Ephesians. He often used the term *saints* to refer to his readers. But here he adds the term *faithful*. Often, the apostle refers to God as faithful (1 Thess. 5:24; 2 Thess. 3:3; 1 Cor. 1:9). So, this is high praise for these followers of Jesus. He certainly views them as being set aside for God, which is the meaning of the designation *saint*. Paul obviously thinks highly of the Colossians even though they are struggling with people who wish to dissuade them from following the pure message of freedom in Christ.

Grace and peace, common companions in his greetings, form a beautiful dual emphasis for believers. Grace in Christ brings peace with God. Believers share this grace with each other and this creates peace in the church. The Father and the Son are the authors of such grace and peace. Verse 8 introduces the Holy Spirit, completing Paul's typical trinitarian tone.

Grace is one of Paul's favorite concepts. This is God's favor that has been freely given to us. We have done nothing to earn it. Grace is often defined as unmerited favor; it is a disposition of God towards us that we had nothing to do with. The Holy Spirit operates from the posture of grace (Acts 11:23). Paul pronounced an invocation of God's blessing by the power of the Spirit when he wrote, "Grace to you." This expresses one of the most important truths in the New Testament and reflects the early church's desire to see an ongoing work of the Holy Spirit in the lives of the saints.

Most people regard peace as the absence of conflict. This is not so with Paul. For him, peace marks the presence of God, for in His presence there is peace, harmony, and unity. The concept of peace describes the state where everything comes into full integration in the kingdom of God, whether it is a human personality, a home, or a society. This is what Paul wants the Colossian believers to experience by the power of the Holy Spirit.

Chapter 1

Colossians 1:3—2:5

PAUL'S LIFE GIVEN FOR THE
COLOSSIAN BELIEVERS

Paul's Life of Prayer

Colossians 1:3–14

The apostle Paul lived a life of thanksgiving and prayer. We find abundant evidence for this in all of his letters, especially Colossians. His life focused on others, not on himself. This lifestyle characterized Paul and his ministry. As the greeting indicates, this section highlights the role of the triune God in believers' lives. It gives special attention to God the Father as the originator of the blessings received by the Colossian believers. As in most of Paul's letters, the apostle here is *theocentric*, that is, centered on God the Father. God the Father is, of course, at work in Christ and through the Holy Spirit. But the Father receives the attention and praise in this section. Later, Paul shifts into praise of the Son of God (vv. 15–23).

We give thanks to the God and Father of our Lord Jesus Christ, praying always for you, since we heard of your faith in Christ Jesus and of your love for all the saints (vv. 3, 4).

Three elements make up verse 3. First, Paul mentions that he and Timothy give thanks. The Greek word

WORD STUDY
THANKSGIVING

Thanksgiving—*the aspect of praise that gives thanks to God for what He does for us.* Ideally, thanksgiving should spring from a grateful heart; but it is required of all believers, regardless of circumstance (1 Thess. 5:18). We are called to be grateful to God for all things (Eph. 5:20; Col. 3:17; 1 Thess. 5:18), especially for His gift of our Savior and our salvation (Rom. 7:25; Col. 1:3–5; 1 Thess. 1:2–7; 2:13). Thank God in anticipation of answered prayer (Phil. 4:6), knowing that His answers are promised to fulfill His perfect will for our lives (Rom. 8:28–29).[8]

here is *eucharistoumen* from which we get the word Eucharist. Many believers use this term for the Lord's Supper because the time of remembrance in communion centers on thanksgiving to God for the gift of Christ. Secondly, as noted above, praise is given to the Father. Finally, Paul's prayer is seen. He always prays for the Colossians. Certainly Paul does not spend every waking moment in prayer for the Colossian believers, but he does regularly lift up their needs to the Father. He is a praying leader.

Because of the hope which is laid up for you in heaven, of which you heard before in the word of the truth of the gospel, which has come to you, as it has also in all the world, and is bringing forth fruit, as it is also among you since the day you heard and knew the grace of God in truth (vv. 5, 6).

Paul's confidence in the Colossian believers rests not only upon their faith, but also their hope. God is committed to accomplish His promise for all believers. The message of Christ in the Gospels includes the expectation of a future with Christ in heaven. Paul told the Corinthians, "If in this life only we have hope in Christ, we are of all men the most pitiable" (1 Cor. 15:19). The apostle was all too familiar with the difficulties of a walk with Christ. True, blessings flow from the Father to His children, but the Christian life can be full of hardship and testing. The effectiveness of a believer's life is not measured in ease of life, but in its fruit.

Paul is pleased to see the Colossians' faith, hope, and fruitfulness. Just as a

---

[8] Jack W. Hayford, *Hayford's Bible Handbook* [computer file], electronic ed., Logos Library System, (Nashville: Thomas Nelson) 1997, © 1995, p. 779.

tree properly rooted and growing in good soil brings forth appropriate fruit, so also do followers of Christ. In fact, for the Colossians, their fruitfulness was immediately evident. The Colossians not only heard the gospel of grace and truth, but they also knew it. The Greek word for "knew" is *epiginosko*. This connotes more that simple intellectual knowing. It indicates an experiential knowledge of the gospel.

Paul here combines grace and truth in connection with the gospel. Jesus is full of grace and truth (John 1:14). The very essence of God is the perfect combination of grace and truth.

As you also learned from Epaphras, our dear fellow servant, who is a faithful minister of Christ on your behalf, who also declared to us your love in the Spirit (vv. 7, 8).

Epaphras obviously performed special service to the Colossian church. He is described as a teacher from whom the believers heard the grace and truth of Christ. In addition, he is a faithful minister. We must not think that he was a minister in the twenty-first century sense. Epaphras did not perform the services of a professional pastor. The word *minister* is a translation of the Greek word *diakonos* that often was translated *servant*. In fact, he is Paul's fellow servant for the Colossians. There

ACCENT ON APPLICATION
Spiritual Leaders Pray and Teach

Spiritual leaders must pray for their people as well as teach them. Paul prayed that his fellow believers would know the strength of the Spirit in their inner being, just as a storm-tossed ship on which the apostle once sailed was strengthened inside by braces and girded outside by cables (Acts 27:17). Knowing that the strength of Christianity is not outward laws but inward character, Paul prayed that Christ might enter the believers through the open door of faith, dwell in their hearts, and imprint His nature upon their minds, wills, and emotions. When Christ enters, He becomes our life—the very soil in which we take root and blossom, the ground in which our lives are founded. Prayer begets prayer, for the believer in whom Christ's love brings the fullness of God learns to ask and expect great things from Him! [9]

---

9   Jack W. Hayford, general editor; consulting editors, Sam Middlebrook... [et.al.], *Spirit-filled Life Study Bible* [computer file], electronic ed., Logos Library System, (Nashville: Thomas Nelson) 1997, © 1991, p. 1791.

ACCENT ON APPLICATION
Christian Fruitfulness

The truth of God and the work of the Holy Spirit in a Christian's life cause growth and fruitfulness. John 15 states that a Christian is to be bear fruit in his or her life in Christ. There is no exception: "By this my Father is glorified, that you bear much fruit; so you will be My disciples" (John 15:8). This fruit-bearing, however, is a function of simply being attached to the true vine, Christ; it is not born of human effort, but of a faithful relationship with Christ (John 15:4–5).[10]

is no ecclesiastical hierarchy inherent in the word *minister.*

Paul reports to the Colossians the great news he heard from Epaphras. The Colossians embraced faith, hope, and, as Epaphras reported, love in the Spirit. The Holy Spirit was so evident in the life of the congregation that love and fruitfulness became part of their reputation.

For this reason we also, since the day we heard it, do not cease to pray for you, and to ask that you may be filled with the knowledge of His will in all wisdom and spiritual understanding (v. 9).

This beautiful report of the faith, hope, and love of the Colossian believers provoked Paul to pray for these saints. This gives us insight into Paul's prayer life. His first request for the Colossians is that they experience the fullness of the knowledge of God's will in all wisdom and spiritual understanding. The word *epignosis* is again used to describe an experiential as well as intellectual understanding of God's will. Simple intellectual knowledge will not do, so Paul prayed for the depth of their experience of God to increase.

The apostle desired that the Colossians would know God's will in all wisdom and spiritual understanding. Wisdom enables believers to live in a way that is tuned in to God's way. Such spiritual wisdom contrasts with the worldly Gnostic wisdom that was being offered to the Colossians. It implies a deep understanding of the true nature of things from God's point of view. The world's wisdom focuses upon the outward appearance of knowledge and special insights that thrill the senses, whether in intellectual pride or sensual lust. God's wisdom is focused on Christ in whom is found true insight, true knowledge

---

[10] Jack W. Hayford, *Hayford's Bible Handbook* [computer file], electronic ed., Logos Library System, (Nashville: Thomas Nelson) 1997, © 1995, p. 395.

about the nature of life, both here and in the hereafter.

The phrase translated *spiritual understanding* (Greek, *sunesei pneumatike*) is probably better understood as *understanding from the Spirit*. True understanding only comes from the Holy Spirit (1 Cor. 2:12–13). So, Paul prays on behalf of these Colossian believers, asking that they would embrace the fullness of the experience of the Holy Spirit so that they may gain insight into God's will. The grammar of Colossians 1:9 indicates that both wisdom and understanding come from the Holy Spirit. Such an understanding puts the emphasis first on the Holy Spirit and secondly on understanding. Many pursue intellectual understanding as the only way to grow spiritually. But when believers seek understanding that comes from the Holy Spirit, which may or may not have intellectual pursuit as its source, powerful movement by God in believers' lives results.

That you may walk worthy of the

CROSS REFERENCE
1 Corinthians 1:21–23, 30

"For since, in the wisdom of God, the world through wisdom did not know God, it pleased God through the foolishness of the message preached to save those who believe. For Jews request a sign, and Greeks seek after wisdom; but we preach Christ crucified, to the Jews a stumbling block and to the Greeks foolishness... But of Him you are in Christ, who became for us wisdom from God—and righteousness and sanctification and redemption."

True wisdom is not found in the arguments of the philosophers or the scholars of this present age. God reveals true wisdom through Christ alone, though people may regard such wisdom as foolishness. Rational thought alone will not bring people to understand the truth in Christ. Knowledge of the gospel is not anti-intellectual. The message of the gospel is grounded in God's revelation of Himself in the arena of history through His Son, Jesus Christ. So, intelligent people can look at history and discern the truth about Jesus. Paul himself once regarded the gospel as foolishness. Then the revelation of the risen Christ was given to him on the road to Damascus. His understanding of the historical reality of Christ's resurrection then became a foundation stone of the truth. Belief in the risen Christ is not foolish. In fact, belief in Christ's work on the Cross and His vindication by the Resurrection confirms the reality and rationality of belief. But pure rationalism without revelation does not equal true wisdom.

WORD STUDY
WALK

Walk—*to move at a pace slower than a run; one's conduct of life.* The literal sense predominates in the Old Testament, but the figurative meaning of the word does occur (Gen. 5:24; 6:9; Eccl. 11:9). In the New Testament the word usually is used literally in the Gospels, while it is usually used figuratively in Paul and John's letters.

The figurative sense has decidedly spiritual overtones. One either walks (conducts his life) as a Christian or as a non-Christian (Rom. 8:4; Eph. 2:2, 10; 1 John 1:6–7). The believer can walk "in darkness" or "in the light," and constantly is urged to choose the latter; only such a path is "worthy of the calling with which you were called" (Eph. 4:1).[11]

Lord, fully pleasing Him, being fruitful in every good work and increasing in the knowledge of God (v. 10).

The purpose of knowing God's will through the Spirit is that people may walk worthy of the Lord. *Walk* is Paul's favorite word to describe the Christian life (Rom. 6:4; Gal. 5:16; Eph. 5:8). People do not put on a show in order to display their faith. Instead, they walk with God. Their speech must match their walk or the word *hypocrite* may soon apply to them. We are fully pleasing Him when our walk matches our words. The working of God's Spirit in salvation and sanctification energizes the Christian walk.

A person's life totally changes when it is infused by the insight and wisdom given by the Holy Spirit. Paul later describes the lifestyle of obedience to the revelation of the Spirit. Ultimately the key to Christian fruitfulness is found in humble submission to the Spirit's work.

Strengthened with all might, according to His glorious power, for all patience and longsuffering with joy; giving thanks to the Father who has qualified us to be partakers of the inheritance of the saints in the light (vv. 11, 12).

It is easy to be excited at the prospect of receiving the strength of all

---

11 Ronald F. Youngblood, general editor; F. F. Bruce and R. K. Harrison, consulting editors, *Nelson's New Illustrated Bible Dictionary: An authoritative one-volume reference work on the Bible with full color illustrations* [computer file], electronic edition of the revised edition of *Nelson's Illustrated Bible Dictionary*, Logos Library System, (Nashville: Thomas Nelson) 1997, © 1995, p. 1300.

God's glorious power. Believer's hearts are thrilled by the empowerment to live by God's strength. The word translated "strengthened" is *dynamoo* from which are derived words such as *dynamic, dynasty,* and *dynamite.* Believers are empowered by God's own dynamo. Sometimes, such empowerment is seen in dramatic or supernatural works (1 Corinthians 12—14). Here it is necessary for a Christian life of joyful patience and longsuffering.

The word *patience* (Greek, *hupomone*) usually is used in reference to dealing with things that are inanimate. Thus, in Romans 12:12 people are patient in tribulation. *Longsuffering* (Greek, *makrothumia*) is evident when a believer relates to other people. Some teachers call this *long-term people-patience. Sometimes this* term is used in reference to patience in the midst of suffering at the hands of people who wish to do evil to the people of God.

We are to exercise patience toward the ungodly just as God does. Such patience leads people to repentance (Rom. 2:4) and is demonstrated when infractions are graciously handled time after time. But Paul is not advocating being a doormat. He wants us to express Christ, who did not give evil for evil.

Whatever difficulty may face them, believers are to give thanks (Greek, *eucharistountes*) to the Father, just as Paul gives thanks to God for the

---

WORD STUDY
DARKNESS

Darkness—*the absence of light.* Darkness existed before the light of creation (Gen. 1:2). Since darkness was associated with the chaos that existed before the creation, it came to be associated with evil, bad luck, or affliction (Job 17:12; 21:17). Darkness was also equated with death. In Sheol, the land of the dead, there is only darkness (Job 10:21–22; 38:17). Darkness symbolizes human ignorance of God's will and, thus, is associated with sin (Job 24:13–17).

Darkness also describes the condition of those who have not yet seen the light concerning Jesus (John 1:4–5; 12:35; Eph. 5:14) and those who deliberately turn away from the light (John 3:19–20). Hating the light will bring condemnation (Col. 1:13; 2 Pet. 2:17). Living in extreme darkness describes those who at the end of time have not repented (Rev. 16:10; 18:23).[12]

---

12 Ronald F. Youngblood, general editor; F. F. Bruce and R. K. Harrison, consulting editors, *Nelson's New Illustrated Bible Dictionary:* An authoritative one-volume reference work on the Bible with full color illustrations [computer file], electronic edition of the revised edition of *Nelson's Illustrated Bible Dictionary,* Logos Library System, (Nashville: Thomas Nelson) 1997, © 1995, p. 331.

THE PEOPLE OF THE KINGDOM

The transfer of a believer from Satan's authority to Christ's is described as the movement from one kingdom to another (Col. 1:13). Furthermore, Christ's redemption brings us to a place of completeness; of spiritual adequacy, authority; the ability to live victoriously over the invisible powers of darkness (vv. 14–16; 2:6–10). This becomes functionally true, as opposed to merely theoretically so, when we live and love as citizens of the heavenly kingdom (Phil. 3:20), utilize the kingdom's currency, which is of irresistible value (Acts 3:6), operate as ambassadors authorized to offer the kingdom's peace and reconciliation to the world (2 Cor. 5:20), and serve as the kingdom's militia, girded for prayerful conflict against the world's dark powers (Eph. 6:10–20). The image of a transfer of kingdoms is more than poetic. It is practically applicable to all our living.[13]

Colossian believers themselves. We should give thanks not because of our circumstances but because of the fact that God, by His gracious choice, has qualified us to be partakers of the inheritance of the saints in the light. This inheritance is characterized by a life lived in God's light. This is kingdom living and is guaranteed to the children of the King.

He has delivered us from the power of darkness and conveyed us into the kingdom of the Son of His love, in whom we have redemption through His blood, the forgiveness of sins (vv. 13, 14).

Believers have been delivered from the power of darkness. Here Paul contrasts the inheritance of the children of the light in verse 12 with the power of darkness of our pre-Christian life. God frees the follower of Christ from the companions of darkness such as death, danger, sickness, and the futility that follows the unbeliever. Because believers are part of the kingdom of the Son of His love, God gives us a portion of this experience in this world through the reign of Christ in the church by the Holy Spirit. In addition, believers enjoy the assurance of the completed redemption and the joy of the forgiveness of sins.

---

[13] Jack W. Hayford, general editor; consulting editors, Sam Middlebrook. . . [et.al.], *Spirit-filled Life Study Bible* [computer file], electronic ed., Logos Library System, (Nashville: Thomas Nelson) 1997, © 1991, p. 1813.

THE BLOOD OF CHRIST

From the Garden of Eden to the garden in heaven's paradise, blood sacrifice is the testimony of God's grace. Initially, fallen man was clothed with skins of animals sacrificed by God Himself (Gen. 3:21). Finally, the blood of the Lamb was shed to clothe every believing member of mankind. Thus, God will gather to Himself "those who have made a covenant with Me by sacrifice" (Ps. 50:5). Forever they shall sing the song of the redeemed: "To Him who loved us and washed us from our sins in His own blood" (Rev. 1:5).

"For the life of the flesh is in the blood, and I have given it to you upon the altar to make atonement for your souls; for it is the blood that makes atonement for the soul" (Lev. 17:11). This is the Bible's clearest statement of the necessity of blood as it relates to sacrificial offerings: life is in the blood. Life and blood were given upon the altar for the purpose of reconciliation with God. Apart from the shedding of blood, giving a life in sacrifice, there is no atonement. This ordinance is reaffirmed in the New Covenant (Heb. 9:22). The New Covenant in Christ's blood fulfilled the requirements of the old covenant for redemption. The blood of Christ surpasses the blood sacrifices of the old covenant and eternally satisfies the requirements of the holy God (Heb. 9:12).

A right relationship with God is found through the blood of Christ (Rom. 3:25). God presented Jesus as the sacrifice for reconciliation for mankind. Fellowship with the holy God could only be realized through Christ's atoning death for the sins that separated mankind from God and His covenant promises. The shed blood of Christ ultimately satisfied the requirements of God's justice. God's judgment was fully put upon Christ, the blameless sacrifice, for all sins of humanity both past and present. Through faith in the blood of Christ, mankind is justified in God's eyes. The blood of Christ is the bond that joins people to God and entitles them to God's covenant provisions. The blood of Christ is forever the only means of attaining a right relationship with the holy God.[14]

---

14 Jack W. Hayford, *Hayford's Bible Handbook* [computer file], electronic ed., Logos Library System, (Nashville: Thomas Nelson) 1997, © 1995, pp. 562-63.

QUESTIONS FOR PERSONAL REFLECTION AND GROUP DISCUSSION

Read Colossians 1:3–14 and then answer the following questions.

1. Why is Paul moved to pray for the Colossians in verses 3–8?

2. How is Epaphras a good example of a servant of Christ?

3. What is on Paul's prayer list for the Colossians in verses 9–11?

4. How should we understand the word *knowledge* in verses 9, 10?

5. How can we describe the essential elements of transference from the kingdom of darkness to the kingdom of light in verses 13–14?

Paul's Life of Praise

Colossians 1:15–23

In all the New Testament, the most highly focused praise of Jesus Christ is found in Colossians 1:15–23. In fact, many think that these verses were an early Christian hymn that Paul borrows for his own use. Here we have great lessons in Christology (the study of the person of Christ). These lessons help believers to understand that the praiseworthy Christ does not leave them unchanged. Instead, they must grapple with the demands upon their lives in light of the dramatic actions of the Son of God in all of His glory.

He is the image of the invisible God, the firstborn over all creation (v. 15).

The Holy Spirit begins with a description of Christ. In Genesis 1:26–27 humankind is created in the image of God. However, here Christ is the image of God. Ancient Israel was forbidden to create for themselves idols or images of created things. Here Jesus is the image of God present on earth. All of what God is, Christ is as well. The image is the imprint of God Himself. Christ is the exact representation and revelation of God (Heb. 1:3).

Jesus is also the Firstborn over all creation. We must be careful here. Though he is the Firstborn, this does not mean that Jesus is the first of all created things. John 1:1–3 says that everything that has been created was created through Christ, the Word of God. He existed before there was a creation. This phrase from Colossians points to the exalted status of the Son of God. The firstborn in any family has special honor. In ancient Israel, the leadership of the family and a double portion of the father's inheritance were given to the firstborn son. Jesus, the Son of God, enjoys this special honor. He is preeminent in the kingdom of God. Even the Spirit of God glorifies Christ (John 16:14).

For by Him all things were created that are in heaven and that are on earth, visible and invisible, whether thrones or dominions or principalities or powers. All things were created through Him and for Him (v. 16).

Paul now clarifies the exalted position Jesus has as creator of all things. Christ created everything that exists, both in the heavenly realm and in the earthly realm. The Colossian believers were tempted to seek after Gnostic angelic realities, lessening the importance of Christ. So, Paul boldly places Jesus far above everything. Nothing exists within creation that is higher than Christ. No power or authority can trump the power of the Son of God. Indeed,

THE IMAGE OF GOD

The term *image of God* describes the characteristics of humanity that distinguish us from the rest of God's creatures.

This expression appears in Genesis 1:26–27; 9:6, and 1 Corinthians 11:7. Some also see allusions to this image in Romans 8:29, 1 Corinthians 15:49, 2 Corinthians 3:18, Ephesians 4:24, Colossians 3:10, and Psalm 8:5. Jesus is the image of the invisible God (Col. 1:15) and the express image of God's person (Heb. 1:3).

One understanding of the image of God is that it refers to qualities or attributes such as human reason, will, or personality. Others believe the image is something present when a person is in a relationship to God, and in fact, is that relationship. The image is living, like a reflection in a mirror rather than like a photo. Still others believe the image is something a person does. Immediately after God made people in His image, He gave them authority over the whole earth (Gen. 1:28). According to this view, this active tending and caring for God's creation expresses the image of God in humanity.

The Bible does not indicate exactly what the image of God in humankind is. It may involve all of the above ideas. Still, it is evident that human beings alone have personal, conscious fellowship with God (Gen. 1:29–30; 2:15–16; 3:8). Man was to take God's place in ruling over and developing the creation (Gen. 1:26, 28). These things are possible only because of certain qualities that are only found in human beings (Ps. 139:14).

To be created in the image of God means that we humans have the ability and the privilege of knowing, serving, and loving God, and that we are most fully human when fulfilling our spiritual potential. Every human life is precious to God, and this fact should control the way we treat the people with whom we share the world.[15]

all creation should glorify the Son, since all things were created through and for Him. Still, the powers of darkness seek to pull people away from allegiance to the King at every turn.

And He is before all things, and in Him all things consist (v. 17).

Christ is before (Greek, *pro*) all things.

[15] Ronald F. Youngblood, general editor; F. F. Bruce and R. K. Harrison, consulting editors, *Nelson's New Illustrated Bible Dictionary: An authoritative one-volume reference work on the Bible with full color illustrations* [computer file], electronic edition of the revised edition of *Nelson's Illustrated Bible Dictionary*, Logos Library System, (Nashville: Thomas Nelson) 1997, © 1995, pp. 593-93.

The Organized Structure of the Angelic Realm

There is an organized structure in the angelic realm. Angels are profoundly influential in humanity's history and are involved according to their designated ranks. Though opinion differs as to the placement of angelic offices, it is clear that the angels are part of a highly organized world. For example, Daniel 10:13 shows that warring angels have a chief prince, Michael, who is also called an archangel, that is, one who rules over others. Seraphim and cherubim seem to be of a slightly lower rank, just ahead of ministering spirits (Heb. 1:14). However, it may also be that the seraphim and cherubim fill a leadership role in worship while Michael leads the warring angels. As to the dark angels, Ephesians 6:12 offers insight into the ranks of the evil angelic realm: principalities, powers, rulers of the darkness of this world, and spiritual wickedness in high places. From biblical information, we can see that the angelic realm is a distinct, structured society with levels of authority or power endowed to angelic beings according to God's creative order.[16]

There are two ways of understanding this phrase. The first is that Christ exists before other created things existed. John 1:1–14 clearly affirms such a concept. But it is also possible to conclude that Christ is before all things in superiority or preeminent among all things. Perhaps Paul intentionally built ambiguity into this phrase.

All things consist in Christ as well. All created things depend upon the creator not only for their initial existence, but also for their continuing existence. While the powers of darkness set themselves up against the Son of God, they depend on the Son for their continuing existence.

And He is the head of the body, the church, who is the beginning, the firstborn from the dead, that in all things He may have the preeminence (v. 18).

Paul highlights the supremacy of Christ in the church as well as in creation. Christ is not simply in the beginning. No, Christ is the beginning. Nothing can detract from Christ as the central focus in creation and within the church. In the context of a church like that in Colosse, which was challenged by teachings that diminished Christ, Paul was clear

---

16 Jack W. Hayford, general editor; consulting editors, Sam Middlebrook...[et.al.], *Spirit-filled Life Study Bible* [computer file], electronic ed., Logos Library System, (Nashville: Thomas Nelson) 1997, © 1991, p. 1814.

about Jesus' preeminence in all things.

Jesus was the firstborn from the dead. This means that He was the first person to resurrect from the dead. Note that in 1 Corinthians 15:23 Jesus is called the firstfruits of the resurrection. Paul also calls Jesus the firstborn of many brethren (Rom. 8:29). This indicates that we too, as Jesus' brothers, will resurrect from the dead. Jesus leads the way in our reconciliation and salvation, as well as in our resurrection and glorification.

In addition, the focus upon the church as the body of Christ is key. As in Ephesians the concept of "the church as Christ's body" must be seen as a prophetic truth, not only a poetic term. The church is that agency that presently incarnates the ministry of Jesus Christ. Her ministry not only is

to proclaim the merits and benefits of His saving and sanctifying work, but also reach with continual ministry in the power and love of His caring, healing, and delivering works. There is an incomplete definition that prevails in the church, concerning our mission (actually "unworthy," i.e., without full weight). It is born of a limited view of our role as "Christ's body," and advanced by a reticence born of misapplied "power" emphases concerning "Spirit-fullness."

For it pleased the Father that in Him all the fullness should dwell (v. 19).

This verse emphasizes that nothing is deficient in the Person of Christ. All that the Father is, the Son of God is also. Jesus is not a lesser God as some

WORD STUDY
PRINCIPALITY

Principality—a powerful ruler, or the rule of someone in authority. This word, often found in the plural, may refer to human rulers (Titus 3:1, KJV), demonic spirits (Rom. 8:38; Eph. 6:12; Col. 2:15), angels, and demons in general (Eph. 3:10; Col. 1:16), or any type of ruler other than God Himself, especially when used in the singular (Eph. 1:21; Col. 2:10). While Christians must often wrestle against evil principalities (Eph. 6:12), they can be victorious because Christ defeated all wicked spirits (Col. 2:15).[17]

---

[17] Ronald F. Youngblood, general editor; F. F. Bruce and R. K. Harrison, consulting editors, *Nelson's New Illustrated Bible Dictionary: An authoritative one-volume reference work on the Bible with full color illustrations* [computer file], electronic edition of the revised edition of *Nelson's Illustrated Bible Dictionary*, Logos Library System, (Nashville: Thomas Nelson) 1997, © 1995, p. 1030.

THE PREEMINENCE OF CHRIST (1:18)

CHRIST

In universal goverment	In reconciliation	In wisdom and knowledge	In personal observance	In Christian living
•The visible image of God (1:15) •The agent of creation (1:16) •The Sustainer (1:17) •The Head of the church (1:18)	•Pleases the father (1:19, 20) •Reconciles us through His death (1:21, 22) •Lives in us as our hope of glory (1:27)	•The sources of all the treasures (2:2, 3) •Worldly philosophy does not conform to Him (2:8)	•We are alive in Him (2:11–13) •No need for legalism and ritualism (2:16–23)	•He is our life (3:3) •We can avoid immorality and can bless others (3:5–14)

religious systems view Him. Because there is nothing lacking in Christ, we can seek complete restoration and fulfillment through Him and not, as some of the Colossians were advocating, through either ritualistic or esoteric means. Jesus is enough for all believers.

could pour forth anger and distress upon those who have spurned Him. These parties need to be reconciled. God does this through Christ and brings those who are far from God near. Through Christ's blood atonement, reconciliation, and forgiveness are accomplished.

And by Him to reconcile all things to Himself, by Him, whether things on earth or things in heaven, having made peace through the blood of His cross (v. 20).

To reconcile is to bring two estranged parties together. God's wrath justly rests upon the sinner (Rom. 1:18—3:20). Sinners have actively turned their backs to God in shameful ways. They have actively turned away from Him as ruler and authority over all creation to follow paths of their own choosing. God

And you, who once were alienated and enemies in your mind by wicked works, yet now He has reconciled in the body of His flesh through death, to present you holy, and blameless, and above reproach in His sight (vv. 21, 22).

In these two verses, Paul sums up the work of justification, atonement, reconciliation, and redemption, along with sanctification and glorification. Below we refer to Romans 3:25–28 for further insight into these themes. These verses read as follows:

Whom God set forth as a propitiation by His blood, through faith, to demonstrate His righteousness, because in His forbearance God had passed over the sins that were previously committed, to demonstrate at the present time His righteousness, that He might be just and the justifier of the one who has faith in Jesus. Where is boasting then? It is excluded. By what law? Of works? No, but by the law of faith. Therefore we conclude that a man is justified by faith apart from the deeds of the law.

All sin must be punished and paid for. God's wrath justly falls upon the sinful. He rightly punishes sin. It is part of God's justice in the economy of creation that sin receives its due.

In this verse, God takes action for the redemption of sinners. God's wrath fell upon Jesus because He is the propitiation for sin. Some have translated this word as *expiation*, pointing to the release or forgiveness of sin. But the idea of propitiation, which carries with it the thought of turning away the wrath of God, is ideally suited to the overall context of this letter. It is clear in 1:18—3:20 that wrath will rightly fall upon the sinner, whether Jew or Gentile. People sometimes struggle with the idea that God may capriciously, vindictively, or irrationally bring forth wrath. Pagan deities irrationally exercise wrath, but not the God of our Lord Jesus Christ.

There is no caprice, vindictiveness, or irrationality in God's wrath. In fact, logical, reasonable justice demands wrath. There can be no other way. The extraordinary truth is that Jesus took the wrath of God upon Himself. The man who knew no sin took on the sins of humanity and received the payment for those sins. The wrath of God came in full force upon the person of Jesus Christ at the Cross. The payment is "by His blood, through faith." It is possible that the word *faith* here should to be translated *faithfulness.* Thus, the reference is to the faithfulness

WORD STUDY
FULLNESS

Fullness (Greek, *pleroma*)—*full number, full complement, full measure, copiousness, plenitude, that which has been completed.* The word describes a ship with a full cargo and crew, and a town with no empty houses. *Pleroma* strongly emphasizes fullness and completion.[18]

---

[18] Jack W. Hayford, *Hayford's Bible Handbook* [computer file], electronic ed., Logos Library System, (Nashville: Thomas Nelson) 1997, © 1995, p. 614.

BLOOD AND PEACE

Mankind was separated from God because of sin and had no acceptable offering to satisfy the demands of God's holy nature. God sent Christ to provide this acceptable sacrifice for sin. His death accomplished reconciliation and established a bond with those who receive Him. Leviticus 17:11 declares that sin cannot be forgiven without the shedding of blood. Because sin takes life away, life is required to repay sin's debts. Jesus Christ gave his perfect human life to satisfy all of mankind's sin debts and to restore a covenant of peace between God and man.[19]

of Jesus Christ to His Holy God and to the righteous demands of God's Law. He is able to offer Himself as the pure sacrifice for humanity because of His faithfulness.

The atoning work of Christ is the declaration of the righteousness of God. Sin's disastrous effects caused God to act. The public spectacle of the Cross of Jesus Christ, where sin is ultimately addressed, shows God's commitment to justice. Thus, Jesus Christ was put to death before the world, received the wrath of God destined for sinners, and so showcased the righteousness of God. Ultimately the sin problem was dealt with before all. Whether or not people embrace this remains to be seen. The divine judge will bring the required wrath nonetheless. The "wages of sin is death" (Rom. 6:23), but God has not required payment to this time. But a time is coming when God will bring forth all of humanity for judgment.

Until the time of Jesus' public sacrifice, sin was not yet dealt with. Judgment was in the future and still is. But for those who embrace the work of Christ, judgment has already come. Their judgment fell upon the perfect man who gave Himself for their sins. He was offered for justice's sake—God's justice. So, we either have the justice of God for sin meted out upon Jesus who died in our stead or we wait for it to come upon us personally.

God's forbearance, His patience, has allowed the deferral of ultimate justice for humanity. But one should not consider that His patience indicates a lack of commitment to justice. Patience with sinners is not the same as tolerance of sin. The Cross of Christ proves God's demand for justice. In the future, when everyone is presented at the throne of God, it will be clear that God's patience will not last forever.

---

[19] Jack W. Hayford, general editor; consulting editors, Sam Middlebrook... [et.al.], *Spirit-filled Life Study Bible* [computer file], electronic ed., Logos Library System, (Nashville: Thomas Nelson) 1997, © 1991, p. 1814.

WORD STUDY
FORGIVENESS

Forgiveness—*the act of excusing or pardoning another in spite of his slights, shortcomings, and errors.* As a theological term, forgiveness refers to God's pardoning or passing over the sins of human beings and His releasing them from the implications and effect of those deeds.

No religious book except the Bible teaches that God completely forgives sin (Ps. 51:1, 9; Is. 38:17; Heb. 10:17). The initiative comes from Him (John 3:16; Col. 2:13) because He is ready to forgive (Luke 15:11–32). He is a God of grace and pardon (Neh. 9:17; Dan. 9:9).

Sin deserves divine punishment because it is a violation of God's holy character (Gen. 2:17; Rom. 1:18–32; 1 Pet. 1:16), but His pardon is gracious (Ps. 130:4; Rom. 5:6–8). In order for God to forgive sin, two conditions are necessary. A life must be taken as a substitute for that of the sinner (Lev. 17:11, 14; Heb. 9:22), and the sinner must come to God's sacrifice in a spirit of repentance and faith (Mark 1:4; Acts 10:43; James 5:15).

Forgiveness in the New Testament is directly linked to Christ (Acts 5:31; Col. 1:14), His sacrificial death on the Cross (Rom. 4:24), and His resurrection (2 Cor. 5:15). He was the morally perfect sacrifice (Rom. 8:3), the final and ultimate fulfillment of all Old Testament sacrifices (Heb. 9:11—10:18). Since He bore the law's death penalty against sinners (Gal. 3:10-13), those who trust in His sacrifice are freed from that penalty. By faith, sinners are forgiven, that is, justified (Rom. 3:28; Gal. 3:8-9). Those who are forgiven sin's penalty are also freed to live beyond its controlling power in their lives (Rom. 6:1–23).

Christ's resurrection was more than proof of His deity or innocence; it was related in a special way to His forgiveness. Christ's resurrection was the act by which God demonstrated to all the incapability of sin to triumph over Christ or for the guilt He bore for us to continue to exist. It was God's declaration of the perfect righteousness of His Son, the Second Adam, representing us. The Resurrection declared God's acceptance of Christ's sacrifice (1 Tim. 3:16). Thus, in Him all who believe are acquitted and declared righteous. Further, Christ's resurrection was a necessary action for the forgiveness of man's sins (1 Cor. 15:12–28), for it not only verified His dominion over sin and death, but certified the same to all His redeemed. To be forgiven is to be identified with Christ in the full triumph of His crucifixion and resurrection.

Christ has the authority to forgive sins (Matt. 1:21; Heb. 9:11—10:18). This forgiveness is an essential part of the gospel message (Acts 2:38; 5:31). But blasphemy against the Holy Spirit (attributing to Satan a deed done by Jesus through the power of God's Spirit) is an unpardonable sin (Mark 3:28–29)—not because God cannot or will not forgive such a sin but because such a hard-hearted person has put himself beyond the possibility of repentance and faith.

God's forgiveness of us demands that we forgive others, because grace brings responsibility and obligation (Matt. 18:23–35; Luke 6:37). Jesus placed no limits on the extent to which Christians are to forgive their fellowmen (Matt. 18:22, 35; Luke 17:4). A ceaselessly forgiving spirit shows that we are truly living as followers of Jesus the Lord (Matt. 5:43–48; Mark 11:25).[21]

Although Old Testament believers were truly forgiven and received genuine atonement through animal sacrifice, the New Testament states that during the Old Testament period God's justice was not served: "For it is not possible that the blood of bulls and goats could take away sins" (Heb. 10:4). Atonement was possible "because in His forbearance God had passed over the sins that were previously committed" (Rom. 3:25). However, God's justice was served in the death of Jesus Christ as a substitute: "Not with the blood of goats and calves, but with His own blood He entered the Most Holy Place once for all, having obtained eternal redemption... And for this reason He is the Mediator of the new covenant" (Heb. 9:12, 15).[20]

We must remember that the present time Paul speaks of is not just the time of the first century. This is the present age (Greek, *kairos*). The new season, a fresh era arrived. The move of God in the New Covenant marks this era. The old is gone and God's righteousness is seen in all of its fullness. Here we see the justice that required the punishment for sin; we see the justice that allows the acquittal of individuals by the faithful work of Jesus Christ on their behalf; we see the

---

[20] Ronald F. Youngblood, general editor; F. F. Bruce and R. K. Harrison, consulting editors, *Nelson's New Illustrated Bible Dictionary: An authoritative one-volume reference work on the Bible with full color illustrations* [computer file], electronic edition of the revised edition of *Nelson's Illustrated Bible Dictionary*, Logos Library System, (Nashville: Thomas Nelson) 1997, © 1995, p. 139.

[21] Jack W. Hayford, *Hayford's Bible Handbook* [computer file], electronic ed., Logos Library System, (Nashville: Thomas Nelson) 1997, © 1995, p. 613.

WORD STUDY
REDEMPTION

Redemption—*deliverance by payment of a price.* In the New Testament, redemption refers to salvation's provision to buy back what has been lost. In the Old Testament, the word redemption refers to redemption by a kinsman (Lev. 25:24, 51–52; Ruth 4:6; Jer. 32:7–8), rescue or deliverance (Num. 3:49), and ransom (Ps. 111:9; 130:7). In the New Testament, it refers to loosing (Luke 2:38; 21:28; Rom. 3:24; Eph. 1:14; Heb. 9:12).

In the Old Testament, redemption was applied to the recovery of property, animals, persons, and the whole nation. These things typify the dimensions of recovery and release New Testament believers experience in life through the price Jesus paid. So, the Old Testament evidences New Testament promise—God's ability in Christ to redeem humanity from the slavery of sin (Ps. 130:7–8), from enemy oppressors (Deut. 15:15), and from the power of death (Job 19:25–26; Ps. 49:8–9).

The New Testament describes the exact cost of redemption: "the precious blood of Christ" (1 Pet. 1:19; Eph. 1:7), which believers are exhorted to remember as they pursue obedient service, faithful ministry, and personal holiness (1 Cor. 6:19–20; 1 Pet. 1:13–19).[22]

justice of God's righteous actions to bring redemption through the blood of Jesus, the perfect sacrifice, upon whom the wrath of God rests. We also see God as the justifier who both punishes based on His absolutely pure and perfect character and acquits based upon His absolutely pure and perfect character. The God of forgiveness and grace differs in no way from the God of wrath and ultimate punishment. In fact, the total righteousness of God is seen in both sides. To understand God one must embrace the God of grace and the God of righteous judgment, who is one and the same. Paul has already demonstrated with complete and convincing logic that God deals justly with humanity.

Those who have faith in Jesus understand God's just judgment as well as His just acquittal—God's justification. The faithfulness of Jesus brings this to pass. Romans 2:6–11 requires that God reward the absolute, total obedience of Jesus Christ with glory, honor, and immortality. Indeed, Jesus is the only one to whom God could

22 Jack W. Hayford, *Hayford's Bible Handbook* [computer file], electronic ed., Logos Library System, (Nashville: Thomas Nelson) 1997, © 1995, p. 740.

freely grant the promise of merited glory. Jesus' holy life provided the opportunity for a perfect, atoning death. If it were not for the perfection of Jesus' daily life on earth, His death would only have been for His own sin. But, because He had no sin, the wrath that fell on Jesus was for others; because He was God, He could be the justifier.

God the Father brought wrath upon Jesus who freely gave Himself for the redemption of humanity. At the Cross, Jesus' life of perfection became our life of perfection. We exchanged our daily sinfulness for the absolute perfection of Jesus' daily life. Jesus chose the death that would have rightly fallen upon both the religious and the irreligious. This atonement was a part of the divine plan, so the wrath that fell upon Him was not capricious or improper. Justice and mercy were linked inextricably in the atoning work of God through Christ. Thus, the benefits of Christ's holy life are to our benefit; Christ's redeeming death is to our benefit; the justice God requires regarding our sin has been fully met; the demand to keep the law perfectly is also met in Christ. His life is our life and His death is our death. This is ours by faith in Him.

WORD STUDY
ATONEMENT

Atonement—The Law required that sacrificial victims be free from defect. Buying them always involved some cost to the one offering the sacrifice. But an animal's death did not automatically make people right with God in some simple, mechanical way. The hostility between God and people because of sin is a personal matter. God for His part personally gave the means of atonement in the sacrificial system; men and women for their part personally are expected to recognize the seriousness of their sin (Lev. 16:29–30; Mic. 6:6–8). They must also identify themselves personally with the victim that dies: "Then he shall put his hand on the head of the burnt offering, and it will be accepted on his behalf to make atonement for him" (Lev. 1:4).

In the Old Testament, God Himself brought about atonement by graciously providing the appointed sacrifices. The priests represented Him in the atonement ritual, and the sinner received the benefits of being reconciled to God in forgiveness and harmony.[23]

---

[23] Jack W. Hayford, *Hayford's Bible Handbook* [computer file], electronic ed., Logos Library System, (Nashville: Thomas Nelson) 1997, © 1995, pp. 549-50.

So, we move from the Colossians' glorious salvation to Paul's hope for them.

If indeed you continue in the faith, grounded and steadfast, and are not moved away from the hope of the gospel which you heard, which was preached to every creature under heaven, of which I, Paul, became a minister (v. 23).

Paul was not worried about the Colossian believers, though the translation may imply doubt. He already had knowledge of their faith and hope and love. He simply pointed them to the importance of continuing to live in faith in the gospel that he preached.

Perhaps Paul saw the world at the end of history. He referred to the proclamation of the gospel as having already been accomplished—it was preached to every creature under heaven. Paul may also have been referring to the knowledge of the gospel in the heavenly realms since Christ was raised and ascended to the right hand of God the Father. Every creature in the heavenly places understands the glory and power of the gospel. Paul, as earthly representative of this gospel, encouraged the believers to stand firm in what is known in the heavenly realms but is not yet fully embraced on earth.

WORD STUDY
TIME

Time (Greek, *kairos*)—*Opportune time, set time, appointed time, due time, definitive time, seasonable time, proper time for action. Kairos describes kind, or quality, of time, whereas chronos denotes extent, or quantity, of time.*[24]

---

[24] Jack W. Hayford, general editor; consulting editors, Sam Middlebrook... [et.al.], *Spirit-filled Life Study Bible* [computer file], electronic ed., Logos Library System, (Nashville: Thomas Nelson) 1997, © 1991, p. 780.

QUESTIONS FOR PERSONAL REFLECTION AND GROUP DISCUSSION

Read Colossians 1:15–23 and then answer the following questions.

1. Why is it important for Paul to establish the supremacy of Christ through his praise in verses 15–18 in the context of the challenge faced by the Colossians?

2. What does *firstborn over all creation* mean (v. 15)?

3. What are the principalities and powers of verse 16?

4. Why is the blood of His Cross (v. 20) so important to the Christian? Explain the ramifications of blood sacrifice.

5. Why were the Colossians enemies of God? How did God reconcile these believers to Himself according to verses 21–23?

Paul's Life of Sacrifice

Colossians 1:24—2:5

The apostle moves on to his labors on behalf of the Colossian believers. His was a life of sacrifice on their behalf. Here we have a glimpse of the manner of life that characterizes an apostle. His life was full of hardship—but with a purpose. Paul intended to build up the believers and churches under his care. Paul grounded such edification in the truth of Christ and the gospel. There are no additions necessary for the gospel to be powerful and effective. Yet, some people were teaching the Colossians that the simple message was deficient. Paul opposed such teaching for the sake of the freedom of believers everywhere.

I now rejoice in my sufferings for you, and fill up in my flesh what is lacking in the afflictions of Christ, for the sake of His body, which is the church, of which I became a minister according to the stewardship from God which was given to me for you, to fulfill the word of God (vv. 24, 25).

Here we are reminded of Romans 8:18 where Paul declared, "I consider that the sufferings of this present time are not worthy to be compared with the glory which shall be revealed in us." Suffering for the sake of Jesus is part and parcel of the Christian walk. Paul expected that hardships would accompany his role as the apostle to the Gentiles. He counted this a privilege and realized that it would require cost and sacrifice for the body of Christ to expand. So, he gladly fulfilled his role, which was given him directly by Christ.

People have thought long and hard about what Paul meant when he wrote that his sufferings somehow filled up in his flesh what is lacking in the afflictions of Christ, for the sake of His body. In no way is Paul implying that there are deficiencies in the sacrifice of Christ. Nor does Paul anywhere suggest that Jesus is continuing to suffer. But Paul is aware that as part of Christ's body, the church, he took part in the sufferings of Christ through his ministry of the gospel. He probably meant that there remains a portion of suffering which God intends His body to suffer for the sake of the gospel. This is part of the plan of the ages. Atonement is complete in Christ's sacrifice.

Reconciliation and justification are complete at the Cross. But the spread of the gospel requires sufferings not unlike those of Jesus. "Paul neither sees Christ's vicarious suffering as deficient nor his own as having any redemptive value. Rather, to him Christ's sacrificial suffering is past, and his own suffering is a joyous privilege whereby he is identified with his Lord (Acts 9:16; Phil. 3:10).

WORD STUDY
SUFFERING

Suffering—The Bible makes it clear that some suffering is the result of evil action or sin in the world. This type of suffering came upon people after the Fall in the Garden of Eden (Gen. 3:16–19). But some suffering is not related to the past. It is forward-looking in that it serves to shape and refine God's children (1 Pet. 1:6–7; 5:10). The Book of Hebrews declares that Jesus learned obedience by the things He suffered (Heb. 5:8), and that He was perfected through suffering (Heb. 2:10). Suffering has the potential of demonstrating God's power (2 Cor. 12:7). Those who suffer are in a position to comfort others (2 Cor. 1:3–6).

Suffering also helps believers to identify with Christ, which is more than suffering for Christ. Through persecution and tortures, people have suffered for the sake of Christ and His kingdom (Phil. 1:29; 2 Thess. 1:5; 2 Tim. 3:12). To suffer with Christ, however, is another matter. Paul speaks of the "fellowship of His [Christ's] sufferings" (Phil. 3:10). Believers share in the suffering of Christ in the sense that through suffering they identify with Christ. To be a disciple involves suffering like the Master. Christ as Lord and His believers as disciples are bonded even further through the experience of suffering.

Another type of suffering is that endured for the sake of others. The prophet Isaiah portrayed the Suffering Servant as sin-bearer when he declared, "By His stripes we are healed" (Is. 53:5). Jesus announced repeatedly that His suffering was His mission (Matt. 17:12; Luke 24:46). Looking back to the Cross, Peter explained that "Christ also suffered once for sins, the just for the unjust, that He might bring us to God" (1 Pet. 3:18).[26]

His Lord is identified with His church (Acts 9:4), whose destiny is also suffering (Phil. 1:29)."[25]

The mystery which has been hidden

from ages and from generations, but now has been revealed to His saints (v. 26).

Paul called the gospel a mystery. Obviously, the gospel is no longer a

---

[25] *Spirit-Filled Life Study Bible*, p. 1815.

[26] Ronald F. Youngblood, general editor; F. F. Bruce and R. K. Harrison, consulting editors, *Nelson's New Illustrated Bible Dictionary*: An authoritative one-volume reference work on the Bible with full color illustrations [computer file], electronic edition of the revised edition of *Nelson's Illustrated Bible Dictionary*, Logos Library System, (Nashville: Thomas Nelson) 1997, © 1995, p. 1207.

mystery in the English sense of the word. The word *mystery* occurs four times in this book (1:26, 27; 2:2; 4:3). Until this word is demystified, it will be a hurdle for people new to the New Testament.

The gospel is a mystery, but this does not mean that it is a secret—just the opposite. It means that God has made known to us the full disclosure of His will. There is nothing mysterious about the will of God. It unfolds step by step, but He never leaves His children in the dark. The way we understand God's will is by walking with Him. There are no secrets in God's will because He has made it known. He wants His will to be revealed so that we can participate in it.

The beauty of this revelation resides within the body of Christ. The church is the witness to the completed revelation of the gospel of Jesus Christ. What was hidden is now fully known, first through the testimony of the resurrection of Christ, and then as the church spreads the gospel throughout the world.

THE MEANING OF MYSTERY

In the New Testament, *mystery* refers to a secret that is revealed by God to His servants through His Spirit. As such, it is an open secret. The word *mystery* occurs three times in the four gospels. Jesus told His disciples, "To you it has been given to know the mystery of the kingdom of God" (Matt. 13:11; Mark 4:11; Luke 8:10). Jesus explained the mystery of God's kingdom to His disciples. But to others, "All things come in parables" (Mark 4:11).

Most of the occurrences of the word mystery are in the Pauline Epistles. The mystery is the revelation of God's plan of salvation in Christ. The gospel itself is a mystery that was kept secret since the world began (Rom. 16:25). God revealed this mystery through the prophetic Scriptures (1 Cor. 2:7; Eph. 6:19; Col. 4:3).

Mystery also refers to the future resurrection of Christians (1 Cor. 15:51), the summing up of all things in Christ (Eph. 1:9), the inclusion of Gentiles in the church (Eph. 3:3–9), the future salvation of Israel (Rom. 11:25), the phenomenon of lawlessness (2 Thess. 2:7), and the godliness of Christ (1 Tim. 3:16).[27]

---

[27] Ronald F. Youngblood, general editor; F. F. Bruce and R. K. Harrison, consulting editors, *Nelson's New Illustrated Bible Dictionary*: An authoritative one-volume reference work on the Bible with full color illustrations [computer file], electronic edition of the revised edition of *Nelson's Illustrated Bible Dictionary*, Logos Library System, (Nashville: Thomas Nelson) 1997, © 1995, p. 872.

To them God willed to make known what are the riches of the glory of this mystery among the Gentiles: which is Christ in you, the hope of glory (v. 27).

God willed to make known to the saints what are the riches of the glory of the mystery among the Gentiles. God revealed to the Jews through prophecy that the divine plan includes the Gentiles. When the infant Jesus was presented in the temple, Simeon quoted Isaiah 42:6 to declare that Jesus would be a light to bring revelation to the Gentiles. The essence of this mystery, which is revealed to the Jews and the Gentiles is Christ in you, the hope of glory. The believer's hope for the future rests on the indwelling Christ. The "hope of glory" is really the hope of the final and future perfection that believers will share when Christ returns. It is the final reversal of the curse of humanity unto the total fulfillment of what men and women ought to be.

Him we preach, warning every man and teaching every man in all wisdom, that we may present every man perfect in Christ Jesus. To this end I also labor, striving according to His working which works in me mightily (vv. 28, 29).

Two aspects of the message of Paul are highlighted here. First, he practiced Christ-centered preaching. He did not get off track to follow the latest theories of spirituality. He knew that the truth rested upon a simple, yet world-changing reality of Christ reconciling the world to God. Secondly, Paul sought to present every man perfect in Christ Jesus. There are two ideas contained in the word *perfect* as it is used here. Once we are reconciled to God through faith in Christ, we are perfect in the eyes of God. Then, we grow to maturity through the working of Christ who resides in us as the Holy Spirit. Paul, in his role as an apostle, worked hard to bring both aspects into the reality of all the people under his care. He wanted people everywhere to give their lives to Christ. But he also wanted them to progress on to the maturity of love, devotion, and sanctification in Christ.

For I want you to know what a great conflict I have for you and those in Laodicea, and for as many as have not seen my face in the flesh (2:1).

This verse provides a glimpse into Paul's heart for his fellow believers both in Colosse and in Laodicea. His concern even extended to those he did not know personally. He labored to bring them to maturity in Christ.

That their hearts may be encouraged, being knit together in love, and

THE MEANING OF "IN CHRIST"

Paul most frequently uses the term *in Christ* to describe the Christian life. The Messiah (Christ) is the King. In Christ, a believer is within the circle of all that is represented by and contained in the King, including His salvation conquest and personal rule. The essential truth is that the Savior-King has come, and in Him the God has altered the limits that sin has heretofore placed on individuals. People no longer need be ruled by their flesh or controlled by the devil. Since they have been transferred into the kingdom of the Son, they know the joy of a relationship with God through the power of the Cross and can realize the reinstatement of their authority under God. Thereby, life in the kingdom brings a dual hope: eternity with Christ and the promise of grace to reign in life. *In Christ* designates the new life that is lived in the benefits and power of Jesus, "who has brought life and immortality to light through the gospel" (2 Tim. 1:10).[28]

attaining to all riches of the full assurance of understanding, to the knowledge of the mystery of God, both of the Father and of Christ, in whom are hidden all the treasures of wisdom and knowledge (vv. 2, 3).

Here is further definition to the idea of maturity in Christ. First, a maturing church receives the comfort of mutual edification through their knowledge of God in Christ. Paul worked to lift up the believers to new heights of encouragement. Second, maturity is seen when the believers are knit together in love. A maturing church purges malice and discord and grows in love, which is the fruit of the Holy Spirit. Finally, a maturing church increases in the understanding of the revelation of God the Father and Jesus Christ the Son. In them, one finds all the treasures of wisdom and knowledge. This is in contradiction to what some were saying in the Colossian community. They advocated Gnostic rituals and methods of gaining a secret wisdom. These were not focused on what had already been revealed in Christ. A maturing church does not go after extraneous or erroneous ideas.

Now this I say lest anyone should deceive you with persuasive words. For though I am absent in the flesh, yet I am with you in spirit, rejoicing to see your good order and the steadfastness of your faith in Christ (vv. 4, 5).

---

[28] Jack W. Hayford, general editor; consulting editors, Sam Middlebrook...[et.al.], *Spirit-filled Life Study Bible* [computer file], electronic ed., Logos Library System, (Nashville: Thomas Nelson) 1997, © 1991, p. 1815.

Paul turns to his main point. Christians must hang on to the message they know to be true, which is the message they have received from Paul. There are people who wish to derail the church from the simple and powerful preoccupation with Christ as the crucified and risen Lord sent from the Father. For example, persuasive, distracting ideas came to these Colossian believers from people with Gnostic influences. Paul urged them to stand firm in the faith.

Though the Colossians were apart from him physically, through the communion of the Holy Spirit, Paul was connected with them. The New King James translation renders the word *spirit* with a lower case *s*. This implies Paul's spirit. But Paul does not use the term *spirit* in this way without referring to the Holy Spirit. His connection with the Colossian followers of Jesus is a result of their fellowship in Christ by the Holy Spirit.

QUESTIONS FOR PERSONAL REFLECTION AND GROUP DISCUSSION

Read Colossians 1:24—2:5 and then answer the following questions.

1. What did Paul mean when he referred to his sufferings as filling up "what is lacking in the afflictions of Christ" (v. 24)?

2. What ideas are in Paul's mind when he uses the phrase *in Christ*?

3. Explain the term *mystery* as Paul uses it in verses 26–27.

4. What balance does Paul bring to Christian ministry as expressed in verse 29?

5. Why, in the context of the letter, is it important for Paul to declare that in Christ are hidden all the treasures of wisdom and knowledge (v. 3)?

Chapter 2

Colossians 2:6–7

PAUL'S THEME: PERSEVERE IN WHAT YOU HAVE RECEIVED

As you therefore have received Christ Jesus the Lord, so walk in Him, rooted and built up in Him and established in the faith, as you have been taught, abounding in it with thanksgiving (vv. 6, 7).

Paul praised God for the Colossian believers; he prayed for them; and, if we consider 1:15–20 a hymn about Christ, he even sang to God for them. He told about his labors for them to bring them to maturity, labors that cost Paul in sufferings and hardships. Now, beginning with the word *therefore*, the apostle gave the Colossians further direction.

Paul provided the believers with a powerful argument for remaining on the course that he set for them. He was very aware of those who wished to derail their faith through irrelevant issues. He exhorted them to walk in the manner they were taught. In addition, to do so with thanksgiving for the work of the apostle who imparted the gospel to them.

Chapter 3

Colossians 2:8–23

CHRIST AS SUPREME REVELATION

Christ Is Superior to Philosophy

Colossians 2:8–15

Christ is supreme. That is a simple statement. But there were some in Colosse who did not think this was sufficient. They wanted to add to the worship and teaching of Christ and thus move the believers from their steadfastness in the gospel. So, Paul warned the believers to beware of the danger of abandoning the simple, sufficient message of Christ.

Beware lest anyone cheat you through philosophy and empty deceit, according to the tradition of men, according to the basic principles of the world, and not according to Christ (v. 8).

Paul warns these dear brothers and sisters in Christ against following fine-sounding philosophical arguments that deny the truth that is in Jesus. He informed the Colossians that these deceitful ideas are according to the basic principles of the world. Demonic spirits wish to deceive believers into thinking that something must be added to the gospel message. These demonic spirits work through tradition, philosophy, sophisticated arguments, and fine rituals that corrupt the simple message of Christ.

WORD STUDY
PHILOSOPHY

Philosophy—*the love of wisdom* (from *philo* "to love," and *sophia* "wisdom"). The philosopher Pythagoras said that at the sporting events of ancient Greece there were three types of people: lovers of money (selling refreshments), lovers of fame (sports heroes), and lovers of wisdom (seekers of wisdom in sports and life in general). Everyone who lives by certain convictions is a philosopher. However, those called philosophers in a formal sense consciously seek well-founded convictions by which to live.

Teachers of philosophy give their lives to examining convictions by which people live in order to develop a consistent worldview and ways of life based on reliable evidence. The Bible warns against philosophies whose highest realities and concerns are atoms, energy, cosmic laws, or humanity—those founded on "the basic principles of the world, and not according to Christ" (Col. 2:8). Christians ought to beware that their minds not be taken captive by such philosophies as secular humanism, communist materialism, and capitalist materialism. These philosophies are best fought with spiritual weapons (2 Cor. 10:4–5).

Christian wisdom appears to be foolishness to the people of the world (1 Cor. 1:18). But it is wiser than the philosophy of this age, which comes to nothing (1 Cor. 1:25; 2:6). Christians "speak the wisdom of God" (1 Cor. 2:7), which is revealed through His Spirit (1 Cor. 2:10) and received by His Spirit (1 Cor. 2:12–14). In Christ, Christians have the highest and most complete wisdom (Col. 2:8–10).

The chief biblical example of how to help students of philosophy who do not accept biblical authority is found in Paul's ministry to the Epicurean and Stoic philosophers at Athens. Paul commended their zeal, quoted them favorably on a point of agreement, declared the truth about the living Lord of all, announced their accountability to Christ (not to Socrates, Plato, Aristotle, Epicurus, or Zeno), and called on them to repent and trust Jesus Christ (Acts 17:16–34).[29]

---

[29] Ronald F. Youngblood, general editor; F. F. Bruce and R. K. Harrison, consulting editors, *Nelson's New Illustrated Bible Dictionary: An authoritative one-volume reference work on the Bible with full color illustrations* [computer file], electronic edition of the revised edition of *Nelson's Illustrated Bible Dictionary*, Logos Library System, (Nashville: Thomas Nelson) 1997, © 1995, pp. 988–89.

WORD STUDY
CIRCUMCISION

Circumcision—*the surgical removal of the foreskin of the male sex organ.* This action served as a sign of God's covenant with His people.

Circumcision, as practiced in some parts of the ancient world, was performed at the beginning of puberty (about age twelve) as an initiation into manhood. In contrast, the Hebrews performed circumcision on infants. This rite had an important ethical meaning. It signified the Jews' responsibility as the holy people whom God had called as His special servants in the midst of a pagan world.

The Bible first mentions circumcision when God instructs Abraham to circumcise every male in his household (Gen. 17:11). After this, the ritual was to be performed on every male child on the eighth day after birth (Gen. 17:12), at the time that child was named (Luke 1:59; 2:21).

Circumcision of the Jewish male was a visible, physical sign of the covenant between the Lord and His people. Any male not circumcised was to be "cut off from his people" (Gen. 17:14) and regarded as a covenant-breaker (Ex. 12:48).

Moses and the prophets used the term *circumcised* as a symbol for purity of heart and readiness to hear and obey. Through Moses, the Lord challenged the Israelites to submit to "circumcision of the heart," a reference to their need for repentance. "If their uncircumcised hearts are humbled, and they accept their guilt," God declared, "then I will remember my covenant" (Lev. 26:41–42; also Deut. 10:16). Jeremiah characterized rebellious Israel as having uncircumcised ears (6:10) and being "uncircumcised in the heart" (9:26).

In the New Testament, devout Jews faithfully practiced circumcision as recognition of God's continuing covenant with Israel. Both John the Baptist (Luke 1:59) and Jesus (Luke 2:21) were circumcised.

A problem erupted in New Testament times because circumcision had become a badge of spiritual superiority. Some early Jewish believers in Jesus as the Messiah had difficulty relating to Gentile believers who had received Christ but were not circumcised. Gentile believers regarded their Jewish brethren as eccentric because of their dietary laws, Sabbath rules, and circumcision practices. Jewish believers tended to view their uncircumcised Gentile brothers as unenlightened and disobedient to the Law of Moses.

A crisis arose in the church at Antioch when some believers from Judea (known as Judaizers) taught the brethren, "Unless you are circumcised according to the custom of Moses, you cannot be saved" (Acts 15:1–2). In effect, the Judaizers insisted that a believer from a non-Jewish background, that is, a Gentile, must first become a Jew ceremonially by being circumcised before he could be admitted to the Christian brotherhood.

A council of apostles and elders was convened in Jerusalem to resolve the issue (Acts 15:6–29). Among those attending were Paul, Barnabas, Simon Peter, and James, pastor of the Jerusalem church. To insist on circumcision for the Gentiles, Peter argued, would amount to a burdensome yoke (Acts 15:10). This was the decision handed down by the council, and the church broke away from the binding legalism of Judaism.

Years later, reinforcing this decision, the apostle Paul wrote to the believers in Rome saying that Abraham, "the father of circumcision" (Rom. 4:12), was saved by faith rather than by circumcision (Rom. 4:9–12). He declared circumcision to be of no value unless accompanied by an obedient spirit (Rom. 2:25–26).

Paul also spoke of the "circumcision of Christ" (Col. 2:11), a reference to Christ's atoning death, which "condemned sin in the flesh" (Rom. 8:3) and nailed legalism "to the cross" (Col. 2:14). In essence, Paul declared that the new covenant of Christ's shed blood had provided forgiveness to both Jew and Gentile and had made circumcision totally unnecessary. All that ultimately matters for both Jew and Gentile, Paul declared, is a changed nature—a new creation that makes them one in Jesus Christ (Eph. 2:14–18).[30]

For in Him dwells all the fullness of the Godhead bodily; and you are complete in Him, who is the head of all principality and power (vv. 9, 10).

There is only one Lord. There is only one King. There is only one Messiah.

God the Father has invested everything in Him. Nothing is deficient in Christ. What God is, Christ is. If a person is found in Christ, he or she is absolutely and completely acceptable to the Father. Nothing additional is necessary. People may try to add elements of the world to the Christian message, but these must be rejected. This King is over

---

30 Jack W. Hayford, *Hayford's Bible Handbook* [computer file], electronic ed., Logos Library System, (Nashville: Thomas Nelson) 1997, © 1995, pp. 572–73.

all other authorities, even the demonic authorities that wish to corrupt the simple gospel message.

In Him you were also circumcised with the circumcision made without hands, by putting off the body of the sins of the flesh, by the circumcision of Christ, buried with Him in baptism, in which you also were raised with Him through faith in the working of God, who raised Him from the dead (vv. 11, 12).

Two concepts occupy Paul's mind. The first is circumcision. The second is baptism. Both are significant signs in their respective covenant contexts. Circumcision was important for the Jews under the old covenant regarding their relationship with God. So, also, baptism as a sign of the New Covenant is of great importance in Paul's gospel.

The New Covenant comes with a new marker, a new sign: baptism. This sign points to the inward reality of a changed heart through the work of Jesus Christ. When believers seek baptism,

CROSS REFERENCE
Romans 2:28, 29

"For he is not a Jew who is one outwardly, nor is circumcision that which is outward in the flesh; but he is a Jew who is one inwardly; and circumcision is that of the heart, in the Spirit, not in the letter; whose praise is not from men but from God."

In these verses, Paul travels to the heart of the matter. Outward manifestations are irrelevant in the New Covenant. The essence of the New Covenant is found in the inward realities of God Himself. It is no longer important whether one is circumcised or not. That is part of the Old Covenant, which is passing away. The New Covenant, found in Jeremiah 31 and Ezekiel 36, speaks of a new work by God who, by His Spirit, brings His purifying work to humanity through direct working on the heart. In words echoing these beautiful Old Testament texts, the Holy Spirit presents Himself here as the essential element in righteousness. The outflow that is pleasing to God requires an inward reality that is the work of God Himself by His Spirit. This is the true circumcision. Rather than boasting in God (2:17), as the Jews did because of circumcision, now all people redeemed and renewed by the Holy Spirit find that God brings praises to them! What a concept. God totally accepts those who have such an inward circumcision and He commends them. There is no condemnation here, just commendation.

THE OLD AND NEW COVENANTS COMPARED

Note the dramatic comparison of the old covenant with the New Covenant in 2 Corinthians 3. The benefits and characteristics of the old covenant are contrasted with those of the New Covenant:

Characteristics of the Old Covenant
- Of the letter (2 Cor. 3:6)
- Which kills (2 Cor. 3:6)
- Written on stone (2 Cor. 3:3, 7)
- Came with glory, though fading (2 Cor. 3:7)
- Brought condemnation (2 Cor. 3:9)
- Temporary (2 Cor. 3:11)

Characteristics of the New Covenant
- Of the Spirit (2 Cor. 3:6)
- Which brings life (2 Cor. 3:6)
- Written on hearts (2 Cor. 3:3)
- Came with surpassing glory (2 Cor. 3:8, 10)
- Brought righteousness (2 Cor. 3:9)
- Permanent (2 Cor. 3:11)

they are declaring for all to see that their allegiance is now with Christ as Lord and master of their lives. Baptism by immersion dramatically symbolizes the work of Christ as it is applied to us. When people enter the waters of baptism, they do so upon declaring their own sinfulness and faith in the Lord Jesus. They proclaim verbally that Christ's work is now applied to them. When people enter the water, their bodily action symbolizes their lives reclining in death. Yet, it is not their own deaths that they embrace, but Christ's death on their behalf. As people are raised up out of the waters of baptism, they have an altogether different look about them. Their appearance has changed visibly, thus corresponding to the change that occurs spiritually when they embraced Christ by faith. Jesus' death is theirs. Jesus' resurrected life is also theirs. That resurrected life, the life that has died to sin just as Christ died to sin once and for all, is the way of the normal Christian life.

And you, being dead in your trespasses and the uncircumcision of your flesh, He has made alive together with Him, having forgiven you all trespasses (v. 13).

Here Paul refers to the glorious truth of the New Covenant. People who were far off have been brought near to God in Christ. People who had no right to claim a relationship with the Living God now live in close relationship with Him through Christ. Paul emphasizes the sorry state of people before God invaded their lives through grace. The word order of this verse spotlights the trespasses and sins that bound the believers before coming to Christ. The pervading influence of evil overshadows any freedom of choice that may be claimed by people who do not know Christ. Yet it is these people, even with such evil influences and tendencies, that God made alive. God forgave such sins and brought freedom.

Having wiped out the handwriting of requirements that was against us, which was contrary to us. And He has taken it out of the way, having nailed it to the cross (v. 14)

Paul used similar words in Ephesians 2:15 to describe the enmity unbelievers had with God due to their

Cross Reference
Romans 7:6

"But now we have been delivered from the law, having died to what we were held by, so that we should serve in the newness of the Spirit and not in the oldness of the letter."

The word "delivered" here in Romans 7:6 (Greek *katargeo*) is the same as that used in the illustration of the woman who is released from the law of the husband in Romans 7:2. This is the end of the illustration and its point is made here. The law-oriented life, which brought the perpetuation of sin for the sinner and bore deadly fruit, is terminated. This stranglehold that the law had over the sinner is abolished. Freedom is declared due to the death of Christ. He has freed us from that which dominated us. But this freedom is now to be lived out in the newness of the Spirit and apart from the law. The oldness of the letter, which is another way of saying "law-orientation," cannot be the way of true life. Life, in the pattern of the Resurrected One is to be lived by the Holy Spirit. No other way bears living fruit. Religious traditions and legality are totally incompatible with a life lived by the Holy Spirit. Paul will further explain such a life in Romans 8.

CONFLICT AND THE KINGDOM

Jesus Christ's triumph over sin and evil powers was accomplished in "it"—that is, in the Cross. Colossians 2:15, with others (Eph. 2:13–16; Gal. 3:13, 14; 2 Cor. 5:14–17; Rom. 5:6–15; and Rev. 12:10, 11), firmly establishes Jesus' suffering, shed blood, sacrificial death, and resurrection as the only adequate and available grounds for ransom from sin, reconciliation to God, redemption from slavery to the Law, and restoration. The Cross is the sole hope and means for full reinstatement to a right relationship with God. By it, we "reign in life" (Rom. 5:17).

To avoid presumption or imbalance regarding the message and ministry of the present power of the kingdom of God, we must focus on and regularly review two points: the source and the grounds for the delegation of such authority and power. God's sovereign authority and almighty power is the source from which mankind derives any ability to share in the exercise of God's kingdom power. But even more important, seeing sinful, fallen man had lost all claim to his early privilege of rule under God, let us remember the grounds upon which all kingdom privilege or power may be restored and by which such spiritual ministry with authority may be exercised.[31]

sins. The enmity is the stress or hostility that came through the transgressing of the Law of the commandments. This Christ abolished through His own flesh, that is, the atoning death on the Cross. As the perfect man who adhered to every demand of the Law of God, He could make atonement for those who sinned. Christ also abolished the legal demand that one must conform to the ordinances to be considered innocent before God.

Only through Christ does one find the fulfillment of the Law. Christ's holy life becomes the believer's through faith in Him. In the same way, the atoning death becomes the believer's as signified in baptism. Thus, the distinctions between the Jews and Gentiles based on law-keeping are abolished, obliterated in Christ. Those who are in Christ are indistinguishable no matter their ethnic, gender, or class distinctions. The Cross is the answer to any demand of obedience upon a believer in Christ. Nothing can be added to Christ's obedience that will make it more perfect to God the Father.

Having disarmed principalities and powers, He made a public spectacle

---

[31] Jack W. Hayford, general editor; consulting editors, Sam Middlebrook... [et.al.], *Spirit-filled Life Study Bible* [computer file], electronic ed., Logos Library System, (Nashville: Thomas Nelson) 1997, © 1991, p. 1816.

of them, triumphing over them in it (v. 15).

God answered every demand in Christ. Through Christ's resurrection from the dead, God declared to all that Jesus is both Lord and Christ (Acts 2:36). Christ alone is master; He alone is king. Our allegiance is to Him and not to manmade regulations or to demonic demands.

Christ Is Superior to Legalistic Practices

Colossians 2:16, 17

So let no one judge you in food or in drink, or regarding a festival or a new moon or sabbaths, which are a shadow of things to come, but the substance is of Christ (vv. 16, 17).

Some within the Colossian Christian community were advocating adherence to Jewish legalistic demands. Paul here provides a strong prohibition against yielding to such demands. In fact, Paul urges these believers to ignore the judgments of those who think that in following these legalistic requirements they will find holiness. These regulations mostly related to Jewish practices and may have had great ethnic importance. But in Christ, such importance is wiped out. Paul declares these things *a shadow of things to come.* Shadows give way to substance. Christ is the substance.

Christ Is Superior to Angels

Colossians 2:18, 19

Let no one cheat you of your reward,

THE NEW MOON

The references in the Bible to the new moon celebration include Exodus 40:2, 17; Numbers 10:10; 28:1–10, 11–15; and Psalm 104:19. The law specified that two bullocks, one ram, seven lambs, and one kid were to be offered in connection with this celebration. Grain mixed with oil accompanied the offerings; a trumpet blast introduced this feast. The sins committed and not expiated during the previous month were covered by the offerings of the new moon festival.[32]

---

[32] Ronald F. Youngblood, general editor; F. F. Bruce and R. K. Harrison, consulting editors, *Nelson's New Illustrated Bible Dictionary: An authoritative one-volume reference work on the Bible with full color illustrations* [computer file], electronic edition of the revised edition of *Nelson's Illustrated Bible Dictionary*, Logos Library System, (Nashville: Thomas Nelson) 1997, © 1995, p. 447.

taking delight in false humility and worship of angels, intruding into those things which he has not seen, vainly puffed up by his fleshly mind, and not holding fast to the Head, from whom all the body, nourished and knit together by joints and ligaments, grows with the increase that is from God (vv. 18, 19).

Paul moves from those who take pride in Jewish legalistic practices to those who emphasize esoteric experiences of a spiritual nature. Some were advocating a connection to the heavenly realm through angels. We are not told exactly how this occurred. But the net effect was to dilute one's attention from Christ.

Some believers in the Colossian church were preoccupied with personal spirituality and spiritual powers. The cheating mentioned in 2:18 does not refer to an absence of spiritual experience but the deceiving nature of false humility and the worship of angels. Our preoccupation must be with Jesus Christ only. Our appeal is to the Holy Spirit, who makes available every gift necessary for our lives and for the liberating work of Christ in the world. The pursuit of angels or demons or other spiritual powers leads to deception and spiritual bondage.[33]

Paul desperately wants the believers to focus on Christ, who is the head of the church. It is in Him that true growth and maturity develops. Such maturity is from God and not from ritualistic or esoteric spiritual explorations.

Christ Is Superior to Asceticism

Colossians 2:20–23

Therefore, if you died with Christ from the basic principles of the world, why, as though living in the world, do you subject yourselves to regulations—"Do not touch, do not taste, do not handle," which all concern things which perish with the using—according to the commandments and doctrines of men? These things indeed have an appearance of wisdom in self-imposed religion, false humility, and neglect of the body, but are of no value against the indulgence of the flesh (vv. 20–23).

Here Paul provides the conclusion to his argument in this chapter. He declares that the focus on outward behaviors such as eating, drinking, or touching is irrelevant. Yet, in observance of these regulations a person may find a certain satisfaction. But this is not the satisfaction given by the Holy Spirit. It is the satisfaction of the flesh because eating, drinking, and

---

[33] Jack W. Hayford, *Hayford's Bible Handbook* [computer file], electronic ed., Logos Library System, (Nashville: Thomas Nelson) 1997, © 1995, p. 396.

touching are fleshly in nature. In fact, while such observances have an air of godliness, they actually have no value in fighting the flesh. One might argue from Romans chapter 7 that they actually promote sin rather than hindering it.

The believer has died with Christ from the basic principles of the world. These outward regulations come from demonic powers that wish to ruin a believer's walk with Christ. So, Paul urged the Colossian believers to reject such externals and cling to Christ.

QUESTIONS FOR PERSONAL REFLECTION AND GROUP DISCUSSION

Read Colossians 2:8–23 and then answer the following questions.

1. Why are the philosophies and traditions of those in Colosse against the revelation of Christ according to verse 8? How does that relate to today?

2. In Christ *all the fullness of the Godhead* dwells (v. 9). Why is this an important concept?

3. Why are legalistic practices so dangerous for the believer?

4. Why is it so easy to look at outward appearances, behaviors, and rituals and forget the truth of the gospel?

5. How should believers view ascetic practices that some espouse as the key to spiritual knowledge according to verses 20–23?

Chapter 4

Colossians 3:1—4:6

CHRIST AS SUPREME LORD OF DAILY LIVING

Supremacy of Christ in Daily Living

Colossians 3:1–8

To this point in his epistle to the Colossians, Paul has addressed the issue of erroneous spiritual teachings. Now he explains the believer's reality of identification with Christ, which is to be lived out in daily living. God has made our identity with Christ sure through His glorification and by our faith in Him. We can live in a manner consistent with that reality by embracing the resurrected Christ.

If then you were raised with Christ, seek those things which are above,

where Christ is, sitting at the right hand of God (v. 1).

The Colossian believers had identified themselves with Christ through baptism (2:11–12). They identified with the death and resurrection of Christ through belief in Him. Because this is the truth in the heavenly realms, the believers could apply these realities to daily living. The first step in such a life is to seek those things that are above. The verb *to seek* (Greek, *zeteite*) can be translated *to aim at*. Jesus lives with all perfection and power in the heavenly realms. Believers can embrace a power-filled lifestyle and advance in both personal maturity and ministerial effectiveness by aiming their life at Christ.

CROSS REFERENCE
Philippians 2:5

"Let this mind be in you which was also in Christ Jesus."

In Philippians 2:5–11, Paul uses the example of Christ to enforce an appeal for unselfishness. As Christ willingly laid aside His heavenly glory to come to Earth and die, we should be willing to look beyond our own interests for ("not only . . . but also," v. 4) the sake of others. Although his purpose is to strengthen his exhortation rather than to establish doctrine, Paul here presents one of the greatest statements in the NT concerning the Person and work of Jesus Christ.[34]

Set your mind on things above, not on things on the earth. For you died, and your life is hidden with Christ in God (vv. 2, 3).

The reality of the believer's position of resurrection in Christ is established. So, the mind must demonstrate concurrence with this reality by focusing on spiritual realities rather than on earthly ones. Believers, in fixing their minds on spiritual realities, disarm the flesh with its earthly preoccupations. In essence, Paul appealed to the believers to follow the way of the Holy Spirit in opposition to the desires of the flesh. Such change of mind moves believers to become more like Jesus because their focus is on the resurrected and glorified Christ. They aim to be like Him.

Believers have died, says Paul. When Christ died, the believers also died. Identification with Christ's death is just as real as any earthly reality. The concurrent reality is that your life is hidden with Christ in God. In other words, a person is safe in Christ since they are identified with Him in faith. Their real lives are hidden in Him.

When Christ who is our life appears, then you also will appear with Him in glory (v. 4).

A believer's life shall not be hidden with Christ forever. In fact, at the *parousia*, when Christ appears in full glorification and perfection, so also will the believers. The word *appears* (Greek, *phaneroo*) signifies *to reveal, to uncover,* and *to make known what was hidden.* So, believers who once were hidden with Christ will be made known to all in all the perfect glory of Christ. Christ is our death and our

---

[34] Jack W. Hayford, general editor; consulting editors, Sam Middlebrook . . . [et.al.], *Spirit-filled Life Study Bible* [computer file], electronic ed., Logos Library System, (Nashville: Thomas Nelson) 1997, © 1991, p. 1803.

future life. He paves the way and gives grace and power for us to participate with Him in glorification.

Therefore put to death your members which are on the earth: fornication, uncleanness, passion, evil desire, and covetousness, which is idolatry (v. 5).

The first step in the process of being conformed to the image of Christ is to recognize the truth of believers' identification with Christ in His death and resurrection. The second step is to seek the things that are above. In other words, our minds are to be set to the agenda of the Holy Spirit. The third step is to activate the will to bring to end the actions that deny the truths of our identification with Christ. This process is very similar to what Paul presents in Romans 6:11–14.

Paul lists the types of sins that so commonly are associated with an earthly focus. These six items are not an exhaustive list of all sins. In fact, Paul continues to build this list in verses 8 and 9. These sinful behaviors obviously belie a mind that is concentrated on the flesh. So, Paul commands the believers to put to death any parts of the body that may have these tendencies.

CROSS REFERENCE
Galatians 5:19—21

"Now the works of the flesh are evident, which are: adultery, fornication, uncleanness, lewdness, idolatry, sorcery, hatred, contentions, jealousies, outbursts of wrath, selfish ambitions, dissensions, heresies, envy, murders, drunkenness, revelries, and the like; of which I tell you beforehand, just as I also told you in time past, that those who practice such things will not inherit the kingdom of God."

God gives us an organized, categorized list of vices in Galatians 5:19–21. While we might add more to the list, this section of Scripture includes sexual sins (adultery, fornication, uncleanness, lewdness), religious sins (idolatry and sorcery), relational sins (contentions, jealousies, outburst of wrath, selfish ambitions, dissensions, heresies, envy, murders), and indulgences of the body (drunkenness and revelries). Paul concludes by saying, "and the like," to include other sins not listed. We may add greed or covetousness to the list (Col. 3:5) and have a complete list. Often people have specific areas of weakness in one or more of these areas. The way we can support each other in our weaknesses is to focus on repentance, encouragement, and prayer.

CROSS REFERENCE
Romans 6:11–14

"Likewise you also, reckon yourselves to be dead indeed to sin, but alive to God in Christ Jesus our Lord. Therefore do not let sin reign in your mortal body, that you should obey it in its lusts. And do not present your members as instruments of unrighteousness to sin, but present yourselves to God as being alive from the dead, and your members as instruments of righteousness to God. For sin shall not have dominion over you, for you are not under law but under grace."

According to Romans 6:11–14, our reality is the same as Jesus' resurrected reality. God works in each of us to cause our living to mirror the resurrected Christ. In these verses, the Holy Spirit gives us one of the few commands in the Book of Romans: We are to reckon (Greek, *logizomai*) ourselves dead to sin.

In Romans, Paul explained how God reckons our faith as righteousness. Our reckoning relates to everyday life because we have been made righteous by faith. We now bring that reality into existence moment by moment. We bring into the physical realm what is true in the spiritual realm. Thus, the first step is to reckon, consider, and fix in our minds the fact that God's work of release from slavery to sin is complete. The flip side to this is to reckon that we are "alive to God in Christ Jesus our Lord." We do not move from slavery to sin to simply do whatever we wish. No, we belong to Christ. We belong to the one who makes us alive to God. Thus, the lordship of sin is replaced with the lordship of Christ. Once the reckoning is complete, we then can move on to the will and the body.

Since the reign of Christ is secure in our lives by faith, we now move into the area of our will. We have the ability by the Holy Spirit to refuse sin's desire to rule us. We have a long history of sin's deadly reign with all of the havoc it wreaks. Our bodies are still mortal due to the pervasive effects of the fall of humanity. But that does not mean we are doomed to live in continual misery. Sin still wishes to rule in us, however, even though its chains are broken. Its reign as a despotic ruler has been broken, but it still wishes to rule as an outlaw. We feel this in the pull of sin in our lives. Nonetheless, the power, as the Spirit of God, rests in us, not in sin. So, we have moved from the reckoning of the mind to the decision of the will to not let sin reign. The individual parts of the body are addressed in the next verse.

The essence of the phrase *do not present* is better captured with the command *stop presenting*. Stop presenting the members of your body as instruments of unrighteousness. Paul intends that the believers stop something that is heavily ingrained in their very being. But sin's reign is over, so what we do with our physical members is now up to us! No longer will sin carry deadly force so that we inevitably do evil with our bodies. In fact, just as Christ is alive from the dead, so, we too must carry ourselves in that same power. We have Christ's resurrection power through the Holy Spirit to make a difference in the physical realm through the reign of righteousness in our bodies. So, we take our feet, our hands, our fingers, and every part of our body and present them to God as His instruments for righteousness' sake. This is immensely practical. Every morning we present our bodies as offerings for righteous duty by the power of the Holy Spirit.

We may easily see the progression of thought in this way:

1. To *reckon* is a movement in the mind of the believer (v. 11).
2. *Don't let sin reign* is an action of the will of the believer (v. 12).
3. *Stop presenting* and *present* are done with the body of the believer (v. 13).

Thus, the mind, will, and body are the focus of Paul's concern to bring righteousness into the believers' lives.[35]

Because of these things the wrath of God is coming upon the sons of disobedience, in which you yourselves once walked when you lived in them (vv. 6, 7).

God's judgment of humankind is based upon sin. Since Romans 3:23 states that we all sin, we all deserve wrath from God. Sinners bring wrath upon themselves because of their sin, God's wrath is just. It is the consequence of not acknowledging God and His ways. So, the wrath of God is declared as coming (in the present tense). People who choose to live according to the way of darkness reap the fruits of darkness. Presently, people find wrath in a life surrounded with such fruit. In the future, there is an expectation of final wrath from God when He judges the earth.

Paul describes the Colossians as sons of disobedience before they came to

---

[35] David P. Seemuth, Spirit-filled Life New Testament Commentary, *Romans* (Nashville: Thomas Nelson Publishers, 2004).

Christ. While God clearly communicates that the Jews deserve wrath due to disobedience (Rom. 10:21; 11:30–32), reference here is to Gentiles. Verse 5 indicates behavior that describes the Gentiles more specifically. The connection of immorality and idolatry, while present in Israel's past, was less prevalent among the Jews in Paul's day. Most of the Colossians were Gentiles. To be sons of disobedience implies a familial relationship with evil. As a father acts, so do the children.

Of course, the Colossians believer used to *walk* in such a fashion as the unregenerate Gentiles. But they have been made alive in Christ. So, they live in a new manner in Christ. Paul points out that in their previous life they did not just do evil deeds, they lived in them. This means that the sinful life goes deeper than deeds. The sinful life conforms to the ways of the dominion of darkness. People choose to live in that dominion along with all its ways.

But now you yourselves are to put off all these: anger, wrath, malice, blasphemy, filthy language out of your mouth (v. 8).

Believers are to *put off* (Greek, *apothesthe*) the old manner of living. They must abandon or rid themselves of the behaviors that characterize life in the dominion of darkness. They are no longer sons of disobedience. God made them alive to walk in ways of life and light, not the ways of death and darkness. Each of the characteristics listed here refers to a sin in human relationships.

Anger (Greek, *orge*) is the emotion and reaction of outrage responding to the actions of others. Believers are to be *slow to anger* (James 1:19–20) for such displays of anger destroy the well-being of the community of faith. *Wrath* (Greek, *thumon*) is often translated "rage" or "bad temper." Anger and

GOD'S RIGHTEOUS JUDGMENT

Paul in Romans 1:18—3:20 describes the evil state and demeanor of the Gentiles as well as the Jews. Ethnicity does not shield the Jew from God's judgment if the Jew sins. Nor does the lack of having the explicit Law of Moses shield the Gentile from righteous judgment. The Gentile will be judged justly through the law of the heart written on the conscience. The Jew will be judged according to the Mosaic Law. Each will be found guilty based on sinful behavior as measured by the law they have. None will be declared righteous before God by behavioral standards that God demands because people do not meet such standards. Thus, all are justly destined for the wrath of God.

CROSS REFERENCE
Ephesians 2:1–2

"And you He made alive, who were dead in trespasses and sins, in which you once walked according to the course of this world, according to the prince of the power of the air, the spirit who now works in the sons of disobedience."

Paul emphasizes people's sorry state before God invaded their lives through grace. While the word order in the text above puts the focus on being made alive, the original word order puts a spotlight on the trespasses and sins that bound these believers before coming to Christ. The pervading influence of evil overshadows any sense of absolute freedom of choice that may be claimed by someone who does not know Christ. The power of evil wishes to continue enslavement to sin through diabolical means. Yet it is these people, even with such evil influences and tendencies, that God made alive.

Several words require focus in this text. First, the duo of *trespasses* and *sins* covers the spectrum of misdeeds. The word *trespasses* (Greek, *paraptoma*) indicates general transgressions of explicit commands of God. It is also used when a person violates what is known to be right in the conscience. *Sins* (Greek, *harmartia*) denotes missing the mark as if simply falling short of what God expects. Paul intends to show that the breadth of sinfulness is part and parcel of the experience of the believers before coming to know Christ. Paul also uses the word *walked* here to describe the manner of life of the unbelievers. In other words, sins and trespasses are not one time, or even rare actions; rather, sins and trespasses are a manner of continued behavior daily lived out. Paul often uses the idea of walking as part of the Christian's experience. Both the sinner's walk and the Christian's walk highlight the continuous nature of root behavior patterns that bear fruit in obvious ways.

The phrase *according to the course of this world* means "according to the ways of the world." The prince of the power of the air is Satan. Here the word *air* does not refer to the atmosphere, but to the general climate of the culture. These people lived like dead people because they were dead in sin. They had no recourse. A person that is unregenerated in Christ is under the domination of the adversary. This does not mean that every unbeliever is demon-possessed or that they overtly worship Satan. Rather, their whole thought system, pattern of life, and conduct is motivated, animated, and manipulated by the adversary. People that live on their own in sin think that they are living a marvelously liberated life. Yet this verse states that this self-willed way is a deception as people are being managed by a master marionette, the adversary of the soul who leaves enough slack on the strings for people to assume that they are in control. But if they ever try to get free, they find that the strings are stronger than they thought.

Paul uses the word *spirit* here to refer to Satan. It is rare to use spirit in this way. But Paul shows the distinction between the Christ who is seated at the right hand of God and under whom are all powers and authorities over against the puny dominion of Satan. The Holy Spirit contrasts mightily with the Evil One who is likewise spirit. Certainly, Satan has some power over evil to inflict further evil. But Christ's dominion is sure and infinitely more powerful as shown by the Holy Spirit's power in and through Christ and the church.

wrath share the element of negative emotional reactions. *Malice* (Greek, *kakian*) carries with it the ideas of "ill will" and "wickedness." Wickedness is not a general doing of wrong, but is particularly related to acting with destructive intent toward others. *Blasphemy* describes the act of cursing, slandering, reviling or showing contempt or lack of reverence for God. In the Old Testament, blaspheming God was a serious crime punishable by death (Lev. 24:15–16). It was a violation of the third Commandment, which required that the name and reputation of the Lord be upheld (Ex. 20:7).[36] Finally, Paul rounds out the list with *filthy language*. Shameful or deceitful speech damages human relationships. We should not limit our understanding of this phrase to indecent sexual language. The term is broader than that. Any language which damages human relationships is shameful and to be put off.

---

[36] Ronald F. Youngblood, general editor; F. F. Bruce and R. K. Harrison, consulting editors, *Nelson's New Illustrated Bible Dictionary*: An authoritative one-volume reference work on the Bible with full color illustrations [computer file], electronic edition of the revised edition of *Nelson's Illustrated Bible Dictionary*, Logos Library System, (Nashville: Thomas Nelson) 1997, © 1995, p. 220.

QUESTIONS FOR PERSONAL REFLECTION AND GROUP DISCUSSION

Read Colossians 3:1–8 and then answer the following questions.

1. What is the link between the resurrection of Christ and the everyday life of the believer as Paul describes in verses 1–4?

2. What practical steps toward proper behavior are necessary according to verses 2 and 5? How would you explain these concepts to people not familiar with the Book of Colossians?

3. What is the difference between the lists in verses 5 and 8?

4. Why does the wrath of God come upon the disobedient (v. 6)?

Supremacy of Christ in the Church

Colossians 3:9–17

Paul rounds out the contrast of the old life with the new by moving into the realm of the new man, the church. Yes, personal characteristics that put off the old and put on the new are important. Now Paul changes the sphere of proper behavior to the church as a whole. His Spirit should display edifying behavior within the church as it is the place where God dwells. The church, with kingdom behavior and dynamics, moves forward to bring forth the expansion of the kingdom of God.

Do not lie to one another, since you have put off the old man with his deeds, and have put on the new man who is renewed in knowledge according to the image of Him who created him (vv. 9, 10).

Paul includes one final command to eschew destructive behaviors: Do not lie to one another. Deceptive living conflicts with the new way of life found in Christ. Paul contrasts what believers had in the old man with that in the new man. The old man is gone, having been put to death at the Cross. Thus, the misdeeds of the old man are to be no longer tolerated. The new man is the church. This is described as one new man (Eph.

2:16) as God brings Jew and Gentile together in Christ, obliterating distinctions based on the flesh.

Paul here uses three important phrases: *put off*, *be renewed*, and *put on*. Followers of Christ exhibit behaviors motivated from their "learning." They put off old conduct, are renewed in their minds, and they put on the new man. This must be understood in the overall context of the letter. In Colossians, Paul urges the believers to bring into their lives the truths of the spiritual realm. Christ is already the exalted ruler over everything and believers are in Christ. So, we display the rule of Christ in our lives.

First, believers jettison the old man, abolishing all the conduct that was part of that former reality. This old man is equivalent to the body of death that Paul refers to in Romans 7:24. However, believers may think that the old man is still in control. This is a lie. The new man is in charge. This new man is in Christ. Paul describes the conduct they pursued previously (vv. 5, 8) as a natural outgrowth of the old man. The behaviors simply emanate from the old nature.

Paul uses the past tense to describe the putting off of the old man and the putting on of the new man. This shows the Colossians that reality is already here, at least from a heavenly point of view. God, in Christ, already accomplished this work. Now it is time to be renewed in the knowledge of the truth of this new reality. All of this knowledge is according to the image of Him who created the new man. In Genesis 1:26, 27 God made man in His image. God built part of Himself into humankind. People have carried this image continually, though it has been marred by sin's power. When God created the new man, the church, the divine was again included. But this time it is the image of the resurrected Christ with power, glory, and dominion. In this way, the church has the power to progress and become the glorious church of God's plan.

Where there is neither Greek nor Jew, circumcised nor uncircumcised, barbarian, Scythian, slave nor free, but Christ is all and in all (v. 11).

Paul reminds the Colossian believers that the new man, the church, cannot be classified with old distinctions. All these have been destroyed through the work of Christ. The new man that God fashioned has no earthly distinctions that separate and isolate people from one another and from God.

WORD STUDY
BARBARIAN

Barbarian—*a person who is different from the dominant class or group.* Originally, this term had no negative connotation. The Greeks used it to describe anyone who did not speak the Greek language. Later, when Rome conquered Greece and absorbed its culture, the word *barbarian* signified those whose lives were not ordered by Greco–Roman culture.

When the apostle Paul referred to Greeks and barbarians in Romans 1:14, he was speaking of all mankind. The barbarians (Acts 28:4, KJV) who aided the apostle Paul on the island of Melita do not appear to have been uncivilized. In this instance, the word meant something very similar to the word *foreigner*. It is good to remember the apostle Paul's declaration that in Christ all human distinctions disappear (Gal. 3:26–29).

Scythian—*a barbaric race that lived in Scythia, an ancient region of southeastern Europe and southwestern Asia, now generally identified as Russia.* In biblical times, the Scythians were a tribe of nomadic raiders notorious for their cruelty and barbarism.[37]

---

[37] Ronald F. Youngblood, general editor; F. F. Bruce and R. K. Harrison, consulting editors, *Nelson's New Illustrated Bible Dictionary: An authoritative one-volume reference work on the Bible with full color illustrations* [computer file], electronic edition of the revised edition of *Nelson's Illustrated Bible Dictionary*, Logos Library System, (Nashville: Thomas Nelson) 1997, © 1995, p. 161.

WORD STUDY
MEEKNESS

Meekness—an attitude of humility toward God and gentleness toward people that springs from the recognition that God is sovereign—that is, in control. Although weakness and meekness may rhyme, they are not the same. Weakness is due to negative circumstances, such as lack of strength or lack of courage. But meekness is due to a person's conscious choice. It is strength and courage under control, coupled with kindness.

The apostle Paul pointed out that the spiritual leaders of the church have great power, even leverage, when confronting a sinner. But he cautioned them to restrain themselves in meekness (Gal. 6:1; 5:22–23). The people of God should be meek, even toward evil people, knowing that God is in control.

Meekness is a virtue practiced and commended by our Lord Jesus (Matt. 5:5; 11:29). It is part of every believer's equipment (2 Cor. 10:1; Gal. 5:23; 6:1; Eph. 4:1–2).[38]

Ethnic distinctions are gone. Religious distinctions are gone. Class and socioeconomic divisions are gone. There is simply one new man.

In Galatians 3:28, Paul also states there "is neither Jew nor Greek, there is neither slave nor free, there is neither male nor female; for you are all one in Christ Jesus." The Holy Spirit through Paul declares the great message of equality in Christ. No human distinctions exist in Christ. The church is the place where oneness in Christ is celebrated and lived out in everyday life.

Therefore, as the elect of God, holy and beloved, put on tender mercies,

kindness, humility, meekness, longsuffering (v. 12).

It is one thing to understand that the church is one new man and that old distinctions are gone. But long-held prejudices and segregation create a poor atmosphere for spiritual growth. So, Paul gives specific commands to show the church what the new man looks like.

These believers are the elect of God. They are a called out people to live for God Himself. Paul points to the amazing truth of the choice God made to establish the church. We must be careful to note two aspects of this choosing. It is a choice to create a group through whom He can work

---

[38] Jack W. Hayford, *Hayford's Bible Handbook* [computer file], electronic ed., Logos Library System, (Nashville: Thomas Nelson) 1997, © 1995, p. 698.

out His eternal plan. God's joy is to enable everyone the opportunity to enter by faith into the community of believers. This choice occurred even before the world began. In other words, God had a redemptive plan of grace even before creation.

The elect are holy and blameless. God created this group to live for Him, set apart to demonstrate the power of God to overcome evil in their lives. God does this because of His unconditional love toward those who believe. He knows that true peace and health can come only when the set-apart people of God live the kingdom life here on earth. When they do that, they experience and demonstrate the love of the Father. Some commentators say God chose the elect individually to be saved; others were to be damned. Instead, God graciously chose to have a group of people through whom the message and ministry of salvation may come. The individual is not in view. Paul calls the church the elect, the object of God's love.

The characteristics God wishes for the church to embrace are:

- Tender mercies (Greek, *splagxna oiktirmou*)—The deep inner movements of compassion.
- Kindness (Greek, *xrestoteta*)—The goodness resulting from the embrace of God's goodness and generosity.
- Humility (Greek, *tapeinophrosunen*)—A deep sense of modesty; a humble spirit.

- Meekness (Greek, *prauteta*)—The gentleness characterized by Christ's meekness and gentleness (2 Cor. 10:1).
- Longsuffering (Greek, *makrothumian*)—The patience exhibited when harmed by others.

Bearing with one another, and forgiving one another, if anyone has a complaint against another; even as Christ forgave you, so you also must do (v. 13).

The phrase *bearing with one another in love* is closely related to the word *longsuffering*. The attitude of a believer toward other believers is one of love, unconditional love. The church is to be a new society with new relationships. True forbearance brings with it a forgiving attitude. Here the Greek word is *charizomenoi*, which comes from the word *charis*, "grace." We are to show grace to one another, even when we have complaints.

Just as *Christ forgave you, so you also must do*. Perhaps this phrase is better understood this way: Just as Christ has fully poured out Himself for you, even though you didn't deserve it, so also you should pour grace upon your fellow believers.

But above all these things put on love, which is the bond of perfection (v. 14).

WORD STUDY
PEACE

Peace—The Old Testament meaning of peace is completeness, soundness, and the well-being of the total person. This peace is God-given and obtained by following the Law (Ps. 119:165). Peace sometimes has a physical meaning in the Old Testament, suggesting security (Ps. 4:8), contentment (Is. 26:3), prosperity (Ps. 122:6–7), and the absence of war (1 Sam. 7:14). The traditional Jewish greeting, *shalom*, is a wish for peace.

In the New Testament, peace often refers to the inner tranquility and poise of the Christian whose trust is in God through Christ. This understanding was originally expressed in the Old Testament writings about the coming Messiah (Is. 9:6–7). The peace that Jesus Christ spoke of was a combination of hope, trust, and quiet of mind and soul brought about by reconciliation with God. The host of angels proclaimed such peace at Christ's birth (Luke 2:14). Christ Himself expressed this in the Sermon on the Mount (Matt. 5:9) and throughout His ministry. He also taught about this peace at the Lord's Supper, shortly before His death (John 14:27). Such peace and spiritual blessedness is a direct result of faith in Christ (Rom. 5:1).[39]

Unconditional love binds believers together and becomes the crowning glory of the church. Since God's posture toward humanity is love, believers express themselves in the same way. As 1 Corinthians 13 says, the most gifted believers are impoverished if love does not direct the church.

And let the peace of God rule in your hearts, to which also you were called in one body; and be thankful (v. 15).

Peace must rule since God has destroyed the divisions that mark earthly prejudices. Most people regard peace as the absence of conflict. This is not so with Paul. For him, peace marks the presence of God. It describes the state of full integration in the kingdom of God in a person's soul, a home, or a society.

Thankfulness also marks believers' interpersonal relationships. When thankfulness leads, complaints, jealousies, and factions fade away. Certainly, believers will hold various opinions on various issues. But when

[39] Jack W. Hayford, *Hayford's Bible Handbook* [computer file], electronic ed., Logos Library System, (Nashville: Thomas Nelson) 1997, © 1995, p. 720.

thankfulness is a part of the character of the church, peace rules the day.

> Let the word of Christ dwell in you richly in all wisdom, teaching and admonishing one another in psalms and hymns and spiritual songs, singing with grace in your hearts to the Lord (v. 16).

The phrase *let the word of Christ dwell in you richly in all wisdom* parallels Paul's command to be filled with the Spirit in Ephesians 5:18. The word of Christ and the movement of the Holy Spirit are in concert, never in conflict. Here, as in Ephesians 5:18–20, the command to *let the word of Christ dwell in you richly* is modified by the words *teaching, admonishing,* and *singing.*

Paul shows the manner in which the Holy Spirit's fullness is made manifest to the church. First, it is found in the new way of relating to one another. Here the believers are to be known for the style of speech resident in their interactions with each other. Their involvement is first focused around worship. The Psalter functioned as the "hymn book" of the Old Testament. It is no wonder that Paul picks up the importance of such scriptural songs. Paul does not limit these *psalms* to the Old Testament psalms. In fact, this is a broad category of songs often accompanied by various musical instruments. Paul also does not give us a strict definition of what a hymn is. That it is sung is a given, as is the overall context: public worship. The believers are together in praise to God. The third element mentioned regarding singing is spiritual *songs.* These may be thought of as songs motivated by the Holy Spirit Himself. The word that modifies *song* is *pneumatikois,* which is probably better translated as "in the [Holy] Spirit."

ACCENT ON APPLICATION
What Is Worship?

Our praise and worship must be in spirit and truth (John 4:23). Songs can be used to help in the memorization of Scripture and the fixing of doctrinal truth in the believer's heart and mind. However, Jesus taught us about the spirit of worship as well. Our worship is not simply the statement of propositional truth, but the passionate expression of love, trust, obedience, and joy between people and their Creator.[40]

---

[40] Jack W. Hayford, *Hayford's Bible Handbook* [computer file], electronic ed., Logos Library System, (Nashville: Thomas Nelson) 1997, © 1995.

WHAT IS PRAISE?

Praise is an act of worship or acknowledgment by which the virtues or deeds of another are recognized and extolled. Praise is revealed as the means by which God's rule and presence may be invited into the midst of any group or private situation or circumstance: The Lord is "enthroned in the praises of Israel" (Ps. 22:3). The praise of man toward man, although often beneficial (1 Cor. 11:2; 1 Pet. 2:14), can be a snare to man (Prov. 27:21; Matt. 6:1-5). But the praise of God toward man is the highest commendation a person can receive. Such an act of praise reflects a true servant's heart (Matt. 25:21; 1 Cor. 4:5; Eph. 1:3-14).

The praise of man toward God is the means by which we express our joy to the Lord. We are to praise God both for who He is and for what He does (Ps. 150:2). Praising God for who He is we call adoration; praising Him for what He does is known as thanksgiving. Praise of God may be in song or prayer, individually or collectively, spontaneous or prearranged, originating from the emotions or from the will.

The godly person will echo David's words, "My praise shall be continually of You... And [I] will praise You yet more and more" (Ps. 71:6, 14).[41]

We were created to live and breathe in an atmosphere of praise-filled worship to the Creator. The avenue of sustained inflow of divine power was to be kept by the sustained outflow of joyous and humble praise. The severance of the bond of blessing that sin brought silenced humanity's praise-filled fellowship with God and introduced self-centeredness, self-pitying, and complaint (see Gen. 3:9–12). But we have salvation and life in Christ. Upon receiving Jesus Christ as Savior, we are called to prayer and the Word of God for fellowship and wisdom in living. Our daily approach to God in that communion is to be paved with praise: "Enter into His gates with thanksgiving, and into His courts with praise" (Ps. 100:4). Such a walk of praise-filled openness to Him cultivates deep devotion, faithful obedience, and constant joy. Praise can bring steadfastness and godliness to a believer's walk. This way of living is not fanatical, glib, or ritualistic. Instead, it draws on the divine life, giving power to the believer (see Appendix).

Having been filled with the Spirit (v. 18) we are to worship in the Spirit.

Psalms are scriptural songs, hymns are songs that have a lyric with a doctrinal

---

[41] Jack W. Hayford, *Hayford's Bible Handbook* [computer file], electronic ed., Logos Library System, (Nashville: Thomas Nelson) 1997, © 1995.

content, and spiritual songs are born by the Holy Spirit in the spiritual realm and are able to penetrate into it. Such worship and fellowship guarantees a new manner of interpersonal relationships, for those relationships are rooted in the worship of God.

There is also a private element to worship connected to the heart of individuals. Thus, making melody in one's heart enables the Christian to carry worship into everyday life. It is not limited to the public setting. Private, heart adoration is portable.

All of this is done "with grace in your hearts to God." This indicates that the root of true worship in the Holy Spirit is deep gratitude towards God. Worship is God-focused. We give Him our attention first, then we also give gracious attention to fellow believers.

And whatever you do in word or deed, do all in the name of the Lord Jesus, giving thanks to God the Father through Him (v. 17).

Worship is not simply an event on a Sunday morning. Worship controls the life of the believer. Words and deeds, thoughts and actions, ideally bring glory and honor to Christ. Thankfulness distinguishes believers who live in God's grace—giving thanks to God, being gracious toward others, and incorporating praise into their lives.

Questions for Personal Reflection and Group Discussion

Read Colossians 3:9–17 and then answer the following questions.

1. What is the new man and why is it so important to Paul (vv. 10–11)?

2. Who are the elect of God? What is a proper understanding of election? Does God elect some to be saved and others to be lost? Explain.

3. What aspect of the characteristics listed in verses 12–14 is most important to you at this time?

4. What does it mean to let the word of Christ dwell in you richly (v. 16)?

5. What are the differences between psalms, hymns, and spiritual songs (v.16)?

6. How does one live a life of praise and thanksgiving as mentioned in verse 17? (*See* Appendix 1.)

Supremacy of Christ in the Family

Colossians 3:18–21

Wives, submit to your own husbands, as is fitting in the Lord. Husbands, love your wives and do not be
bitter toward them. Children, obey
your parents in all things, for this is
well pleasing to the Lord. Fathers, do
not provoke your children, lest they
become discouraged (vv. 18–21).

Paul here condenses what he said
in Ephesians 5:22—6:4 into four
verses. Perhaps Paul knew that the
Ephesian letter would be read in the
Colossian congregation as a so-called
traveling epistle. It is appropriate to
refer to the Ephesian section for a
more extensive understanding of this
section. Looking at this larger passage,
with its sociological context, helps us
to unpack this short section. Here is
Ephesians 5:22—6:4:

Wives, submit to your own husbands, as to the Lord. For the husband is head of the wife, as also
Christ is head of the church; and He
is the Savior of the body. Therefore,
just as the church is subject to
Christ, so let the wives be to their
own husbands in everything. Husbands, love your wives, just as Christ
also loved the church and gave Himself for her, that He might sanctify
and cleanse her with the washing of
water by the word, that He might
present her to Himself a glorious
church, not having spot or wrinkle
or any such thing, but that she
should be holy and without blemish.
So husbands ought to love their own
wives as their own bodies; he who
loves his wife loves himself. For no
one ever hated his own flesh, but
nourishes and cherishes it, just as the
Lord does the church. For we are
members of His body, of His flesh
and of His bones. "For this reason a
man shall leave his father and
mother and be joined to his wife,
and the two shall become one flesh."
This is a great mystery, but I speak
concerning Christ and the church.
Nevertheless let each one of you in
particular so love his own wife as
himself, and let the wife see that she
respects her husband. Children, obey
your parents in the Lord, for this is
right. "Honor your father and
mother," which is the first commandment with promise: "that it
may be well with you and you may
live long on the earth." And you, fathers, do not provoke your children
to wrath, but bring them up in the
training and admonition of the Lord.

Life lived under the power of the
Holy Spirit maintains a certain order.
This order is not marked out with le-
galistic boundaries or rigid demands.
On the contrary, God desires individ-
uals in the fellowship of believers to

bear testimony to His life. In so doing, His troops are prepared for the battles that are to be waged in a winsome way. Thus, guidelines, instructions, and requirements regarding our pathway toward domestic order and ethical professional lifestyle are not ends in themselves, but preparatory to being effective in confronting the powers of evil.

These verses about wives submitting to husbands have provoked many to decry the apostle Paul's un-liberated and chauvinistic view of women. Nothing could be further from the truth. Ephesians 5:22 does not contain the word *submit* in the original text. It is implied from verse 21 and appropriately carried through in this verse. But Paul specifically provides practical instruction for both wife and husband on mutual submission. Why was this necessary? It was necessary because in Paul's day, the subjugation of women was a fact of everyday life. Domination by the husband was simply assumed. So, when Paul says to the church, "submit yourselves to one another," this inaugurated a radical cultural shift in which wife and husband are on the same level in Christ. She can function in the body of Christ according to her gift and faith. She can pray and prophesy in the public fellowship (1 Cor. 11:2–16) as long as she does it in a culturally sensitive way, not calling attention to herself. In Christ, there is no hierarchy of man over woman. Cultural domination by men ceased.

But Paul also knew that a certain order must be maintained under God's authority. So, wives are to voluntarily submit themselves to their husbands as to the Lord. This was a spiritual issue, not a matter of men selfishly getting what they want at the expense of women. In fact, when Paul addresses husbands, submission on their part is extremely demanding. In Christ, there is no hierarchy. In the home, Paul says, order is appropriate.

It is hard to communicate the revolutionary aspect of the Spirit-filled life in relation to husbands and wives. In the first century, domination on the part of the husband was assumed. In the Spirit, it is rejected. In Christ, the wife has new standing, but she voluntarily submits, not because the culture demands it, but because it is the will of God. This does not mean that a wife is forced to do anything against the will of God. She is under the Lord and voluntarily submits herself to her husband only after the Lordship of Christ is assured.

Paul revolutionizes the relationship of husbands toward wives in this section. Love (Greek, *agape*), in all of its unconditional facets, is demanded of the husband. If you were a Greek living in Ephesus, your first response to this would be, "I have to do *what*?" The expectation of submission on the part of the wife was easy in that male dominated culture. That a husband would voluntary submit to his wife through sacrificial love was ridiculous. To think that a husband must totally give himself as Christ gave Himself to the church was beyond the imagination of an Ephesian husband.

The goal of Christ's giving of Himself was to provide purity and wholeness for the church. Jesus did everything possible so that the church would have all the benefits of purity and redemption. So, Holy Spirit-motivated husbands are to seek the same wholeness for their wives. This is radical.

The husband needs to submit to the Lord Jesus Christ so that he becomes the mirror of the person, character, and the love of God through Jesus. Just as the love of Jesus attracts us to Him, the love of Jesus in the man will attract the wife.

Paul's emphasis on husband and wife leads to a second couplet, children and parents. The command to obey was a given in first-century Ephesus and Colosse. But Paul adds a twist for Spirit-filled children. Their motivation for obedience is not cultural. The new society of the people of God includes new motivations for behavior. The biblical reason for obedience springs from the command to honor parents. Obviously, obedience does not equal honor. A child can obey through hard heartedness. But Paul urges children to be in the Spirit and listening to the Spirit's word from Deuteronomy 5:16. In almost the same way as a husband would care for his own body (and therefore his wife) so a child would obey out of honor as a

way of caring for him or herself. The promise of living well and long is linked to honoring parents.

This promise is twofold, that people would have success in life and enjoy a long life. There is a law that is woven into the fabric of the universe. People cannot dishonor parents and realize fruitfulness or fullness in life. God desires children to realize a life that is filled with all the benevolence, goodness, and blessing that God created humankind to enjoy. A child's experience of those blessings will be dependent upon the parent developing a child that obeys his or her parents.

Paul's second admonition may seem odd to the twenty-first century reader. Paul only addresses fathers. While we certainly can expand the understanding of this verse to parental authority in general, Paul specifically admonishes fathers. Paul urges them not to exasperate their children, provoking them to wrath. A Spirit-filled father knows how to provide godly encouragement and training in the home. This radicalized the role of the first-century father. In those days, fathers did little to raise children. They had more important business affairs to tend to. So, children were largely ignored or simply nuisances to be bossed around.

If a parent is to be honored, then a parent who understands this principle ought to be leading and training a child in a way that engenders that honor. You cannot demand it, though their training can be demanding. The Greek word translated *training* here has to do with discipline and correction. Not provoking children to wrath does not mean that they will like everything that they are asked to do as they are trained. To provoke means that something is done intentionally, insensitively, or ignorantly. This is a provocation rather than an instruction. What this verse communicates is that there should not be anything done that provokes them by being inconsiderate, unbalanced, or cruel. We are not to provoke them to the type of anger that would not exist if a parent were dealing with a child sanely, sensitively, and scripturally.

When we see the radical nature of these commands in the full context of the Colossian social setting, we realize that Spirit-filled living leads to order in the household without domination or destruction. God wishes for the family who lives under God's authority to exhibit a radical reorientation that dismisses power struggles.

Supremacy of Christ in Relation to the World

Colossians 3:22—4:6

This final section before the conclusion of the letter to the Colossians focuses on how the church is to behave in matters of connection with the world. It is one thing to develop good inner characteristics. It is another to exhibit such characteristics in the church. It is yet another thing to show Christ's love and lifestyle to a world postured against Christ and His people. But Paul wants the Colossian believers to live a Christ-honoring life in the world as well.

> Bondservants, obey in all things your masters according to the flesh, not with eyeservice, as men-pleasers, but in sincerity of heart, fearing God. And whatever you do, do it heartily, as to the Lord and not to men, knowing that from the Lord you will receive the reward of the inheritance; for you serve the Lord Christ. But he who does wrong will be repaid for what he has done, and there is no partiality. Masters, give your bondservants what is just and fair, knowing that you also have a Master in heaven (3:22—4:1).

Here again, we see the parallels with Ephesians 6:5–9. The essence of each person in the couplet of bondservant and master is that each lives under a Lord who does not show partiality. He watches both and is master of both. The word *partiality* (Greek, *prosopolepsia*) means "favoritism," "partiality," "distinction," "bias," or "conditional preference." The word denotes a biased judgment, which gives respect to rank, position, or circumstances instead of considering the intrinsic conditions. God shows no partiality in justice, judgment, or favorable treatment when

Accent on Application
Relationships in Christ

Employee-employer relationships in some ways parallel the slave-master relationship of the first century. Of course, many differences exist as well. But the principles of what makes a good employee and a good employer certainly emanate from this section. Each serves Christ as the Lord who sees these relationships. Employees must fully comply with requests as much as it is in their power (and as long as the requests don't require employees to violate biblical standards). Goodwill in every encounter rules the day. Employers realize that in Christ there is no distinction between employee and employer. God is the great leveler of life. The high are brought low and the low lifted up.

dealing with people, and He expects us to follow His example.[42]

Paul does not condone slavery in these verses. He addresses a cultural reality within the church. He re-characterizes the master-slave relationship since both are in Christ, just as Philemon and Onesimus were (Philem. 15, 16). Paul was not out to change entire cultural social structures. He did obliterate slave-master distinctions in the church, however, because in Christ, there is neither slave nor free. There is simply oneness in Him.

But slaves were becoming followers of Jesus. Many of them were bound to non-Christian masters. So, they must act in a way that is totally in line with Spirit-filled living. Yes, they are to obey. Not to obey could easily lead to their death. But their obedience springs from

a new well. Their relationship with Christ, and their ultimate responsibility to Him translates into a different kind of obedience on earth. Yes, they obey, but with sincerity of heart. Their motivation changes—they are serving Christ Himself. The service they do to earthly masters reflects their service to their heavenly Master. God is a rewarder of those who do right, even to those servants who obey in the context of an evil institution of slavery. God is not bound by the culture.

As is the pattern, Paul again revolutionizes the cultural norm. Masters must behave entirely differently as Spirit-filled people. When urged to "do the same things to them" many believing masters must have balked at the thought. They were the ones in control. But mutual submission re-orients the master-slave relationship. The entire

---

[42] Jack W. Hayford, general editor; consulting editors, Sam Middlebrook. . . [et.al.], *Spirit-filled Life Study Bible* [computer file], electronic ed., Logos Library System, (Nashville: Thomas Nelson) 1997, © 1991, p. 1818.

Accent on Application
Continuing in Prayer

Believers, recognizing their dependence upon their Creator and Savior, cultivate all forms of prayer: praise, worship, thanksgiving, confession, adoration, holy meditation, petition, supplication, intercession, and spiritual warfare. Prayer should not be thought of as a mystical experience in which people lose their identity in the infinite reality. Effective prayer must be a scripturally informed response to the living God who can hear and answer on the basis of Christ's redemption. Prayer involves several important aspects:

1. *Faith.* The most meaningful prayer comes from a heart that places its trust in God who has acted and spoken in the Jesus of history and the teachings of the Bible. God speaks to us through the Bible, and we in turn speak to Him in trustful, believing prayer. Assured by the Scriptures that God is personal, living, active, all-knowing, all-wise, and all-powerful, we know that God can hear and help us. A confident prayer life is built on the cornerstone of Christ's work and the words of the Spirit-inspired writings of the Bible.

2. *Worship.* In worship we recognize what is of highest worth. This is not ourselves, others, or our work. It is God. Only the highest divine being deserves our highest respect. Guided by Scripture, we set our values in accord with God's will and perfect standards. Before God, angels hide their faces and cry, "Holy, holy, holy is the Lord of hosts" (Is. 6:3).

3. *Confession.* Awareness of God's holiness leads to consciousness of our own sinfulness. Like the prophet Isaiah, we exclaim, "Woe is me, for I am undone! Because I am a man of unclean lips, and I dwell in the midst of a people of unclean lips; for my eyes have seen the King, the Lord of hosts" (Is. 6:5). We must confess our sins to God to get right with Him, and He promises to forgive us of all our unrighteousness (1 John 1:9).

4. *Adoration.* God is love, and He has demonstrated His love in the gift of His Son. The greatest desire of God is that we love Him with our whole being (Matt. 22:37). Our love should be expressed, as His has been expressed, in both deeds and words. People find it difficult to say, "I love you." But when love for God fills our lives, we will express our love in prayer to the One who is ultimately responsible for all that we are.

5. *Praise.* The natural outgrowth of faith, worship, confession, and adoration is praise. We speak well of one whom we highly esteem and love. The one whom we respect and love above all others naturally receives our highest commendation. We praise Him for His "mighty acts ... according to His excellent greatness!" (Ps. 150:2) and for His "righteous judgments" (119:164). For God Himself, for His works, and for His words, His people give sincere praise.

6. *Thanksgiving.* God has forgiven our sins, granted us acceptance as His people, and given us His righteous standing and a new heart and life. What reasons to thank Him! While ingratitude marks the ungodly (Rom. 1:21), the believer lives thankfully, seeing God in countless ways. So, in everything we give thanks (Col. 3:17; 1 Thess. 5:18).[43]

social structure may not change, but the manner of the household must change. God has no partiality. He sees no distinction between slave and free. In the Lord, there are no such class differences. Masters who are Spirit-filled must act accordingly. Yes, they may be regarded as traitors in a society obsessed with power structures. But Spirit-directed life demands revolutionary behavior in the midst of such evil.

Continue earnestly in prayer, being vigilant in it with thanksgiving; meanwhile praying also for us, that God would open to us a door for the word, to speak the mystery of Christ, for which I am also in chains, that I

may make it manifest, as I ought to speak (vv. 2–4).

Paul admonishes these faithful Colossians to be continually *in prayer with thanksgiving*. Praise, prayer, and thanksgiving ought to be the marks of the Spirit-filled church. Paul provides a focus to their prayers. He wishes to be effective in his ministry to people while he is imprisoned, perhaps even while waiting for his own execution. But Paul's circumstances do not bind the effectiveness of his ministry. He wants to speak boldly of *the mystery of Christ* which refers, as we recall, to what once was hidden but is now revealed to all the world: Christ as King reconciling the world to Himself. He

---

[43] Jack W. Hayford, *Hayford's Bible Handbook* [computer file], electronic ed., Logos Library System, (Nashville: Thomas Nelson) 1997, © 1995, pp. 725–25.

wants the gospel to be made *manifest*. That is, he wants it to be shown to all. He will do this through his proclamation, even if he is in chains.

Walk in wisdom toward those who are outside, redeeming the time. Let your speech always be with grace, seasoned with salt, that you may know how you ought to answer each one (vv. 5, 6).

Paul here urges these believers to walk in the wisdom that is found in Christ. He has established throughout the epistle that believers do not need to follow rigid legalistic practices or seek esoteric knowledge through various rituals. Wisdom is found by being connected to Christ by the Holy Spirit.

As he also stated in Ephesians 5:16, Paul admonishes them to be redeeming the time. The believers have a choice. They can live right along with the times without any care or discernment, or they can live in wise fashion. Paul urges the believers to watch how they are living this life. They are to watch the path as one might take extra care in walking an unknown path at night. This may be common sense, but not in this present age. The present age is marked with evil and its deception. The Evil One is a master at deceiving people into thinking that all is well, when it isn't. Believers are to redeem the time. The word *redeeming* here (Greek, *exagorazomenoi*) means to "buy back." There is an ever-present tendency to see time slip away without giving attention to the purpose for which God has called us. Thus, we are to keep sensitive to what is going on around us and keep on target with God's plan for the ages.

Believers are to live wisely and redeem the time; so, their speech is to be with grace, seasoned with salt. Gracious speech that is witty and engaging is combined with salt as seasoning for conversation for the sake of the gospel. In this way, the believers give effective answers to each one.

QUESTIONS FOR PERSONAL REFLECTION AND GROUP DISCUSSION

Read Colossians 3:18—4:6 and then answer the following questions.

1. How should we understand the radical nature of verses 18–21?

2. How does Ephesians 5:21—6:4 help our understanding of verses 18–21?

3. Why should masters and slaves behave differently than the world around them would expect according to 3:22—4:1?

4. Why does Paul want prayer from the Colossian believers?

5. What does it mean to redeem the time in verse 5?

Colossians 4:7–18

CONCLUDING REMARKS

Paul provides final direction for the Colossians that gives insight into his heart. He is deeply concerned for the welfare of the Colossian believers. He wishes to do whatever he can to build them up.

Tychicus, a beloved brother, faithful minister, and fellow servant in the Lord, will tell you all the news about me. I am sending him to you for this very purpose, that he may know your circumstances and comfort your hearts, with Onesimus, a faithful and beloved brother, who is one of you. They will make known to you all things which are happening here (vv. 7-9).

Tychicus was "a Christian of the province of Asia" (Acts 20:4), a faithful friend, fellow worker, and messenger of the apostle Paul (Eph. 6:21–22; Col. 4:7–8). Along with other disciples, Tychicus traveled ahead of Paul from Macedonia to Troas, where he waited for the apostle's arrival (Acts 20:4). Paul also sent Tychicus to Ephesus to deliver and perhaps to read his epistle to the Christians in that city (Eph. 6:21). He did the same with the Epistle to the Colossians (Col. 4:7). Paul sent him as a messenger to Titus in Crete (Titus 3:12) and afterward to Ephesus (2 Tim. 4:12).[44]

Paul viewed Tychicus as a beloved brother, faithful friend, and fellow servant in the Lord. Obviously, Paul treasured this partner in the Lord's service. Paul probably would have preferred to keep this brother with himself. But he unselfishly gives Tychicus to these Colossian believers to encourage them and to bring information to them about his circumstances.

Likewise, Paul sends Onesimus to the Colossians. He was a slave of Philemon and an inhabitant of Colosse (Col. 4:9; Philem. 10). When Onesimus fled from his master to Rome, he met the apostle Paul. Paul witnessed to him, and Onesimus became a Christian. In his letter to Philemon, Paul spoke of Onesimus as "my own heart" (Philem. 12), indicating that Onesimus had become like a son to him. Paul convinced Onesimus to return to his master, Philemon. He also sent a letter with Onesimus, encouraging Philemon to treat Onesimus as a brother rather than a slave. Paul implied that freeing Onesimus was Philemon's Christian duty, but he stopped short of commanding him to do so. Onesimus

accompanied Tychicus, who delivered the Epistle to the Colossians as well as the Epistle to Philemon.[45]

Aristarchus my fellow prisoner greets you, with Mark the cousin of Barnabas (about whom you received instructions: if he comes to you, welcome him), and Jesus who is called Justus. These are my only fellow workers for the kingdom of God who are of the circumcision; they have proved to be a comfort to me (vv. 10, 11).

We find here four more of Paul's fellow workers. Aristarchus was a Macedonian of Thessalonica who traveled with the apostle Paul on his third missionary journey through Asia Minor (Acts 19:29; 20:4; 27:2). He was with Paul during the riot at Ephesus (Acts 19:29); later, he preceded Paul to Troas (Acts 20:4–6). A faithful companion and friend, Aristarchus accompanied Paul to Rome (Acts 27:2), where he attended the apostle and shared his imprisonment.[46] Here Paul describes him as a *fellow prisoner*. We are not told why he

---

[44] Ronald F. Youngblood, general editor; F. F. Bruce and R. K. Harrison, consulting editors, *Nelson's New Illustrated Bible Dictionary: An authoritative one-volume reference work on the Bible with full color illustrations* [computer file], electronic edition of the revised edition of *Nelson's Illustrated Bible Dictionary*, Logos Library System, (Nashville: Thomas Nelson) 1997, © 1995, p. 1281.

[45] Ronald F. Youngblood, general editor; F. F. Bruce and R. K. Harrison, consulting editors, *Nelson's New Illustrated Bible Dictionary: An authoritative one-volume reference work on the Bible with full color illustrations* [computer file], electronic edition of the revised edition of *Nelson's Illustrated Bible Dictionary*, Logos Library System, (Nashville: Thomas Nelson) 1997, © 1995, p. 926.

is imprisoned, but Paul considers him a valuable asset in his ministry.

Mark and Barnabas are also with Paul. Here Paul urges the Colossians to welcome Mark, who assisted Paul and Barnabas on their first missionary journey as far as Perga (Acts 13:5). He probably arranged for travel, food, and lodging and may have done some teaching as well.

At Perga John Mark gave up the journey for an undisclosed reason (Acts 13:13); this departure later caused a rift between Paul and Barnabas when they chose their companions for the second missionary journey (Acts 15:37–41). Paul was unwilling to take Mark again and chose Silas. They returned to Asia Minor and Greece. Barnabas persisted in his choice of Mark, who was his cousin (Col. 4:10) and returned with him to his homeland of Cyprus (Acts 15:39; also Acts 4:36).

This break occurred about A.D. 49–50, and John Mark is not mentioned in the Scriptures until a decade later—in favorable terms. Paul asked the Colossians to welcome Mark (Col. 4:10) not as his assistant but as a fellow laborer (Philem. 24). During his imprisonment in Rome, Paul told Timothy to bring Mark with him to Rome, "for he is useful to me for ministry" (2 Tim. 4:11). One final reference to Mark is from Peter in Rome; Peter affectionately referred to him as "my son" (1 Pet. 5:13). Thus, in the later references to Mark in the New Testament, he appears to be reconciled to Paul and laboring with the two great apostles in Rome.[47] Perhaps what is most encouraging about Paul's mention of Mark is his willingness to embrace him after a seeming failure.

Barnabas was an apostle in the early church (Acts 4:36–37; 11:19–26) and Paul's companion on his first missionary journey (Acts 13:1—15:41). A Levite from the island of Cyprus, Barnabas's given name was Joseph, or Joses (Acts 4:36). When he became a Christian, he sold his land and gave the money to the Jerusalem apostles (Acts 4:36–37).

Early in the history of the church, Barnabas went to Antioch to check on the growth of this early group of Christians. Then he journeyed to Tarsus and brought Saul (as Paul was still called) back to minister with him to the Christians in Antioch (Acts 11:25). At this point Barnabas apparently was the leader of the church at Antioch, because his name is repeatedly mentioned before Paul's in the Book of Acts. But after Saul's name was changed to Paul, Barnabas's name is always mentioned after Paul's (Acts 13:43).

Because of his good reputation, Barnabas was able to calm the fear of Saul among the Christians in Jerusalem

---

[46] Ibid, p. 113.

[47] Youngblood, op. cit., p. 802.

(Acts 9:27). He and Saul also brought money from Antioch to the Jerusalem church when it was suffering a great famine (Acts 11:27–30). Shortly thereafter, the Holy Spirit led the Antioch church to commission Barnabas and Paul, along with John Mark, Barnabas' cousin (Col. 4:10), to make a missionary journey (Acts 13:1–3) to Cyprus and the provinces of Asia Minor.[48] Barnabas's name means "son of encouragement." It is no wonder that Paul valued this friend and coworker.

Justus is also mentioned here. We know little about him other than that he, along with Aristarchus, Mark, and Barnabas, were all Jewish followers of Jesus who ministered to the Gentiles.

Epaphras, who is one of you, a bondservant of Christ, greets you, always laboring fervently for you in prayers, that you may stand perfect and complete in all the will of God. For I bear him witness that he has a great zeal for you, and those who are in Laodicea, and those in Hierapolis. Luke the beloved physician and Demas greet you. Greet the brethren who are in Laodicea, and Nymphas and the church that is in his house (vv. 12–15).

Obviously, Paul values Epaphras's ministry as a fellow bondservant of Christ. He is a model of prayer for others and of zeal for the Lord. His ministry extended beyond Colosse and included the believers in Laodicea and Hierapolis, cities in the vicinity of Colosse. Epaphras remained in Rome with Paul as a fellow prisoner (Philem. 23).

Luke and Demas are also mentioned here. Luke is described as the beloved physician. Luke traveled extensively with Paul on his journeys. He is the author of the New Testament books of Luke and Acts.

Luke apparently was a humble man, with no desire to sound his own horn. More than one-fourth of the New Testament comes from his pen, but not once does he mention himself by name. He had a greater command of the Greek language and was probably more broadminded and urbane than any New Testament writer. He was a careful historian, both by his own admission (Luke 1:1–4) and by the judgment of later history.[49]

Demas, however, began well, but didn't finish well. In 2 Timothy 4:10 Paul says, "Demas has forsaken me, having loved this present world, and has departed for Thessalonica." Here in Colossians, Paul simply extends greetings sent by Demas.

Just as Paul brings greetings from these individuals, so he extends them as well. Paul wishes formal greetings

---

[48] Youngblood, op. cit., p. 161.

[49] Youngblood, op. cit., p. 777.

QUESTIONS FOR PERSONAL REFLECTION
AND GROUP DISCUSSION

Read Colossians 4:7–18 and then answer the following questions.

1. What are some characteristics we should aspire to as we look at how Paul describes his fellow-workers?

2. What do we learn about the worship services of the Colossians from verses 16–18?

3. How is the admonition given to Archippus applicable to believers today?

to be extended not only to the Colossian believers, but also to those in Laodicea at the church located in Nymphas's house. We know nothing of Nymphas other than that he hosted the church of God. Of course, it is an important reminder here that the church was the gathered community of believers and not a building.

Now when this epistle is read among you, see that it is read also in the church of the Laodiceans, and that you likewise read the epistle from Laodicea. And say to Archippus, "Take heed to the ministry which you have received in the Lord, that you may fulfill it." This salutation by my own hand—Paul. Remember my chains. Grace be with you. Amen (vv. 16–18).

Here we get a glimpse into the operation of the churches in Paul's day. First, the reading of Paul's letters highlighted the gatherings. In essence, this was the public reading of Scripture before the church. The epistle from Laodicea very well may have been the same as the letter to the Ephesians. The church listened to the apostle and, in most cases, carried out his wishes.

We don't know much about Archippus. That he holds an important position in the church in Colosse is assured. Paul's command to him is simple: fulfill the ministry given to you. This is perhaps an obvious command, but it was something that Archippus needed to hear. In Philemon 2 Paul calls Archippus his fellow soldier.

Finally, Paul notes that he writes these final commendations with his own hand. An assistant penned most of the letter at Paul's request. But he cares so much for the Colossians that he wants the letter to bear his own mark in some way beyond the ideas and truths communicated here. He wants them to remember him in prayer (just as he requested prayer before). As he began, he also ends. He wants grace to be extended to these beloved believers in Christ.

Appendix

The Value of Praise in the Christian Life

Throughout the Scriptures, we read of people who praise the Lord. Their examples provide the modern believer with numerous lessons in the value of praise:

1. The name *Judah* means "praise" (Gen. 29:35). In Genesis 49:8–12 Jacob speaks important words over Judah, giving him the highest blessing. His brothers will praise him. He will triumph over all his enemies. Verse 10 says Judah will have royal authority ("the scepter") and legal authority ("a lawgiver") and will bring forth the Messiah ("until Shiloh comes"). Out of Judah, through David, came Christ, who in every action and detail is praise to the Father (Luke 3:23–33). The tribe of Judah led Israel through the wilderness (Num. 2:3, 9) and led in the conquest of Canaan (Judges 1:1–19). Judah is the first tribe to praise David, making him king (2 Sam. 2:1–11).

2. Praise is the cure for the dry times that come to every believer (Num. 21:16–17). Here the praise of God caused waters to flow from a well. Note four truths: (1) God's instruction—"Gather the people together." There is unity and power in corporate gathering. (2) God's promise—"I will give them water [i.e. life]." (3) The people's responsibility—They sang, "Spring up, O well! All of you sing to it." (4) Our lesson—In times of pressure, anxiety, or depression, do not stay alone. Gather with God's people,

especially a praising people. Regardless of your personal feelings, join in audible praise, and sing to your well—the living God. Let your song be one of thanksgiving for past blessings and a song of faith in God's promises for the present and the future!

3. There is power in unity of praise (2 Chr. 5:13). This text demonstrates the power in unity of praise, thanksgiving, and music: (1) The trumpeters and singers were in oneness. (2) They made one sound in praise and thanksgiving to the Lord, saying "For He is good, for His mercy endures [lasts] forever." (3) The house (temple) was filled with a cloud, which is the glory of God's presence.

Remember, even in praise, thanksgiving, and worship, "God is not the author of confusion" (1 Cor. 14:33). Anything said or done that draws attention to the worshiper and away from God should be reconsidered.

4. Powerful praise births victory (2 Chr. 20:15–22). Here is a great lesson on the power of praise. Mortal enemies, Moab and Ammon, confronted Judah. The people sought God in prayer and with faith in His Word (20:1–14). Then came the word of the prophet: "Do not be afraid ... for the battle is not yours, but God's" (v. 15).

The victory came in a strange but powerful manner. The Levites stood and praised "the Lord God of Israel with voices loud and high" (v. 19).

Then some were actually appointed to sing to the Lord and praise Him in the beauty of holiness. These went before the army, saying: "Praise the LORD, for His mercy endures [lasts] forever" (v. 21). The result of this powerful praise was total victory!

5. Praise stops the advancement of wickedness (Ps. 7:14–17). This short passage contains two truths about praise.

First, praise is the answer when wickedness and iniquity come against the believer. Temptation to sin and live wickedly will soon disappear in the face of sincere, powerful, and audible praise. This will bring the glorious presence of Jesus, driving out the desire to identify with the sinful act and/or thought.

Second, in verse 17 the writer declares, "I will praise the LORD." Praise is an act of the will. It is not merely an exuberance overflowing with words, but a self-induced declaration of thanksgiving—a sacrifice. The praiser *chooses* to praise.

Here are two important points to understand about praise: (1) Do not wait until all conditions and circumstances are favorable, but (2) offer a thanksgiving of praise because God is worthy and it is right (*see also* Is. 12:1–3 and Jer. 33:11).

6. Praise spotlights God (Ps. 18:3). Here is the most basic reason for our praise to God: He is "worthy to be praised." The most primitive meaning of "praise" (Hebrew, *halal*) is "to cause to shine." Thus, with our praise,

we are throwing the spotlight on God, who is worthy of praise and deserves to be glorified. The more we put the spotlight on Him, the more He causes us to shine. Modern medicine attests to the value of bringing a depressed person into a brightly lighted room, acknowledging that light greatly helps to heal their depression. How much more will praise introduce the light of God and bring us into the joy of the Lord.

7. Praise is the pathway to God's presence (Ps. 22:3–4). Unquestionably, one of the most remarkable and exciting things about honest and sincere praise is that it brings the presence of God. God is everywhere present, but there is a distinct manifestation of His rule in the environment of praise. Here is the remedy for times when you feel alone, deserted, or depressed. Praise! However simply, compose your song and testimony of God's goodness in your life. The result: God enters! His presence will take up residence in your life. The word *inhabit* means "to sit down, to remain, to settle, or marry." In other words, God does not merely visit us when we praise Him, but His presence abides with us and we partner with Him in a growing relationship. Let this truth create faith and trust, and lead to deliverance from satanic harassments, torment, or bondage. Notice how this text ties three words together: "praises," "trusted," and "delivered"!

8. We must sing praises with understanding (Ps. 47:7). The word *understanding* is linked to wisdom and prosperity. Proverbs 21:16 provides contrast to such understanding: "A man who wanders from the way of understanding will rest in the assembly of the dead." But when we sing praises with understanding, we are giving testimony to God's love for us and our love for Him. Life results instead of death. Others, listening to us praise God, hear testimony of our salvation and our joyful relationship with Him, which often leads to their own salvation.

9. Praise is the road to success (Ps. 50:22–23). This psalm relates God's power, majesty, and glory, and is summed up in these closing verses, which apply to us as well as to the people of Israel. If we leave God out of our lives and live in rebellion, destruction follows. In contrast, the simple road to success is set forth: (1) To praise is to glorify God. The focus of praise is directed toward God, but in His wisdom, we are the ultimate beneficiaries. (2) We receive power to order our conduct. Thus, our lifestyle comes into obedience to God. (3) We receive a revelation (understanding)—that is, insight into God's salvation. Our praise becomes a vehicle for God to come to us and to minister through us.

10. Praise releases blessings and satisfaction (Ps. 63:1–5). This classic passage teaches how expressed praise releases the blessings of praise. Notice,

this is not a silent prayer: "My mouth shall praise You with joyful lips." The fruit of such praise is: (1) "O God, You are my God" (affirmed relationship); (2) "Early will I seek You" (clear priorities); (3) "My soul thirsts... My flesh longs for You" (deep intensity); (4) "I have looked for You in the sanctuary, to see Your power and glory" (desire for corporate involvement); (5) "Because Your lovingkindness is better than life, my lips shall praise You" (appropriate gratitude); (6) "My soul [the real me] shall be satisfied as with marrow and fatness" (personal needs met).

11. Creative praise stays lively (Ps. 71:14). Here the psalmist makes a commitment: "I ... will praise You [God] yet more and more." The idea expressed is beautiful, saying, "I will find fresh and new ways to express my praise toward God." This does not mean to abandon the old ways but to become as creative in our praises to God as God is creative in meeting our needs. Thus, we will not fall prey to careless praise, which becomes dull and boring and ends in merely mouthing phrases. God wants us to be creative in our praise.

12. Teach your children to praise (Ps. 145:4). This verse emphasizes the importance of passing on the praise of God from one generation to another. Praise is to be taught to our children. The Bible enjoins us to raise a generation of praisers. We must not suppose that children will grow up and desire God. We must be careful. Whatever

we possess of God's blessing and revelation can be lost in one generation. We must consistently praise Him and we must teach by example, as well as by words. Then our children and our children's children will do the same.

13. The Psalms conclude with a mighty appeal to praise the Lord (Ps. 150:1–6). Some psalms are desperate cries, while some are filled with thanksgiving. Some have theologically or historically based instructions to praise the Lord for His person, holiness, power, or goodness. But the climax is a command to praise the Lord. We are to praise God (1) in His sanctuary—that is, His earthly temple and throughout His created universe and (2) for His mighty acts and according to His excellent greatness. Then a list of instruments and ways to praise follows. This list is not exhaustive but demonstrates how creative our praise is to be. Finally, in case even one person feels less than inclined to praise Him, the instruction is clear: If you have God's gift of life-breath, you should praise Him. Hallelujah!

14. Put on the glorious garment of praise (Is. 61:3). The Hebrew root for "garment" is 'atah. This word shows praise as more than a piece of clothing casually thrown over our shoulders. It literally teaches us to wrap or cover ourselves with praise. The garment of praise is to leave no openings through which hostile elements can penetrate. This garment of praise repels and replaces the heavy spirit. This special

message of instruction and hope is for those oppressed by fear or doubt. Put on this garment. When distressed, be dressed with praise!

15. Perfected praise produces power (Matt. 21:16). In response to the criticism leveled against verbal praise, which was powerful, vocal, and strong, Jesus quoted Psalm 8:2 and so reminded us of a great secret. Perfected praise will produce strength! It is powerful! At the very moment the religious leaders rejected Jesus, the full meaning of who Jesus was captivated the people. Capturing this revelation about Him causes loud and powerful praise to come forth. How heartening this must have been to Jesus as He marched toward the Cross!

16. Praise opens prison doors (Acts 16:25–26). Study this example of the power of praise, even in difficult circumstances. Beaten and imprisoned, Paul and Silas responded by singing a hymn of praise from their hearts to God. The relationship between their song of praise and their supernatural deliverance through the earthquake cannot be overlooked. Praise directed toward God can shake open prison doors! Then, a man was converted, his household saved, and satanic captivity overthrown in Philippi. Today praise will cause every chain of bondage to drop away. When you are serving God and things do not go the way you planned, learn from this text. Praise triumphs gloriously!

17. Encourage one another in praise (Eph. 5:18–19). This text instructs interaction in our praise. Paul tells the Ephesians to speak to one another using psalms and hymns and spiritual songs. Entering a gathering of believers, even with a small offering of praise, our worship begins to be magnified as we join with others. Their voices encourage us, and we inspire them. Separation from the local assembly deprives a person of this relationship and its strength. Let us assemble often and praise much—encouraging one another in praise.

18. Praise releases the spirit of prophecy (Heb. 2:11–12). This text quotes the messianic prophecy in Psalm 22:22, showing how the Spirit of Christ fills the New Testament church. It reveals how Christ identifies Himself with His people when they sing praises. As they do this, two important things happen: (1) He joins in the song Himself, and (2) this praise releases the spirit of prophecy. The latter is in the words "I will declare Your name to My brethren." As we joyfully sing praise to our God, Christ comes to flood our minds with the glory of the Father's character. There is no doubt about it—the praises of the people in the church service release the spirit of prophetic revelation—the magnifying of God through Jesus Christ. Thus, praise introduces edification, exhortation, and comfort to bless the whole body.

19. Offer the sacrifice of praise (Heb. 13:10–15). Why is praising God a sacrifice? The word *sacrifice* (Greek, *thusia*) comes from the root *thuo*, a verb

meaning "to kill or slaughter for a purpose." Praise often requires that we kill our pride, fear, or sloth—anything that threatens to diminish or interfere with our worship of the Lord. We also discover here the basis of all our praise: the sacrifice of our Lord Jesus Christ. It is by Him, in Him, with Him, to Him, and for Him that we offer our sacrifice of praise to God. Praise will never be successfully hindered when we keep its focus on Him—the founder and completer of our salvation. His Cross, His love, gift of life, and forgiveness keep praise as a living sacrifice!

20. Walk worshipfully with God (1 Pet. 2:9). This text not only appoints praise, but represents a basic revelation of the Bible: God wants a people who will walk with Him in prayer, march with Him in praise, and thank and worship Him. Note the progression in Peter's description of the people of the New Covenant: (1) We are a chosen generation—a people begun with Jesus' choice of the Twelve, who became 120, to whom were added thousands at Pentecost. We are a part of this continually expanding generation, chosen when we receive Christ. (2) We are a royal priesthood. Under the old covenant, the priesthood and royalty were separated. We are now—in the Person of our Lord—kings and priests to His God (Rev. 1:6), a worshiping host and a kingly band, prepared for walking with Him in the light or warring beside Him against the hosts of darkness. (3) We are a holy nation, composed of Jews and Gentiles—of one blood, from every nation under heaven. (4) We are His special people. God's intention from the time of Abraham has been to call forth a people with a special mission—to proclaim His praise and to propagate His blessing throughout the earth.[50]

---

[50] Jack W. Hayford, *Hayford's Bible Handbook* [computer file], electronic ed., Logos Library System, (Nashville: Thomas Nelson) 1997, © 1995, p. 720–24.

A SYSTEMATIC REVIEW OF THEMES IN
EPHESIANS AND COLOSSIANS

The purpose of a commentary on a biblical book is primarily to understand what the inspired text is saying in its own context. Once this is embraced, the reader can, under the guidance of the Holy Spirit, move to the realization of what God would have people do with specific principles and applications of the text in the current era. This process of interpretation protects people from simply identifying and excising verses or phrases from the Bible and creating non-biblical ideas that were never intended. People often find "proof-texts" to support unusual ideas and this leads to all manner of errors.

It can be very instructive, however, to organize specific verses focusing on particular topics to see how God wishes us to embrace these truths from a thematic perspective. In this section we wish to examine some of these themes that are present in the epistles of Paul to the Ephesians and Colossians in order to gain overall portraits that may not be seen from a simple reading of the text. In a sense, we systematize these truths for the benefit of celebrating and appropriating God's truth for us. We will look at what God is saying more broadly about Himself, about the person and work of Jesus Christ, the Holy Spirit and about humanity. We will also look at the response of believers to God's truth in salvation and in living as His people as revealed in Ephesians and Colossians. This is not a re-telling of the epistles but an organized examination of these truths along thematic lines.

God the Father

Paul presents the work of God the Father prominently in these epistles. In Ephesians and Colossians we see that the Father:

- Wills Paul to be an apostle (Eph. 1:1)
- Is the Father of the Lord Jesus Christ (Eph. 1:3; Col. 1:3)
- Grants blessings (Eph. 1:3)
- Gives wisdom and understanding about Himself (Col. 1:9–10, 27: 2:2)
- Delivers us from the powers of darkness (Col. 1:13)
- Chose believers before the world began (Eph. 1:4)
- Promises that we might become like Jesus (Eph. 1:5)
- Is full of glory and will receive glory (Eph. 1:6, 17)
- Is rich in mercy and full of love for humanity (Eph. 2:4)
- Makes believers alive in Christ and prepares us to walk in good works (Eph. 2:1–10)
- Brings the glory of the church to the world (Eph. 3:10–12)
- Is in every believer by the Spirit (Eph. 4:6)
- Expects believers to be engaged in kingdom warfare fully endowed with His power (Eph. 6:10–20)

While there is certainly much about Jesus Christ in the letters, one cannot but be impressed at how involved the Father is in the working out of His plan for humanity. It is clear that God carefully constructed His plan not only to bring the world back to Himself, but to also use the church to reach the world. Thus, the church is advancing as an instrument of the Father in order to show His love and mercy to those who are far off, separated from God. God delights in revealing Himself to people. His goal is to bring people who were in utter despair and darkness into the glorious kingdom of light. As the Spirit says in Col. 2:15: "Having disarmed principalities and powers, He made a public spectacle of them, triumphing over them." Of course, this is all wrought by the working of Christ by the power of the Holy Spirit. But we see that Paul begins with the Father and them moves on in His thinking to the work of Christ.

Jesus Christ

It is only "in Christ" that any of God's benefits become realized in the life of any human being. That is fundamental to Paul, the apostle, who is called by the will of God the Father (Eph. 1:1). So, when we look at the multifaceted work of Christ, we recognize that God planned redemption with the focus on the person and ministry of His Son Jesus Christ the Lord (Eph. 1:3). In Ephesians and Colossians we see these truths about Jesus Christ:

- Every spiritual blessing comes in Christ (Eph. 1:3).
- Redemption comes through the blood of Christ, along with the forgiveness of sins (Eph. 1:7; Col. 1:13, 14).
- Christ is creator (Col. 1:16).
- Unity and peace in God's plan is found in Christ (Eph. 1:10; 2:14–17).
- Power is seen in the resurrection of Christ (Eph. 1:20).
- Only "in Christ" is there hope for the sinner (Eph 2:1–10; Col. 2:13, 14).
- Kindness and grace is focused on the person of Christ (Eph. 2:7).
- Access to the Father is through Christ (Eph. 2:18).
- Jews and Gentiles together have been made into a new entity (Eph. 2:6, 15; 4:24; Col. 3:10, 11).
- Christ is the giver of gifts to the church (Eph. 4:7–16) and is the head of the church, His body (Eph. 5:23; Col. 1:18).
- He is God incarnate, ruler over all creation (Col. 2:9–10).

If this were the Epistle to the Romans, Paul would burst out into doxology, giving praise for the glorious work of his Savior. We see the power and nature of Jesus Christ to impact the world through His working out of the divine plan made long ago. Through such a list above we are brought to the realization that humanity had no hope other than to have the God of the universe enter this world through the Incarnation and perform the perfect act of sacrifice to bring sinners to Himself.

The Holy Spirit

As we shift to the work of the Holy Spirit we see how the work of Christ becomes profoundly evident in the world. Only through the working of the Holy Spirit does the continuing ministry of Jesus penetrate darkness through His church. The Holy Spirit:

- Seals the believer (Eph. 1:13,14; 4:30)
- Reveals the Father (Eph. 1:17; 3:5)
- Provides the link to the Father (Eph. 2:18)
- Builds up the church as His dwelling place as one body (Eph. 2:22; 4:3, 4)
- Provides strengthening for the believer (Eph. 3:16, 17)
- Brings renewal (Eph. 4:23)
- Fills believers for effective living as the people of God (Eph. 5:18)
- Provides power through spiritual language (Eph. 6:18)

The extensive description of the manner by which the Holy Spirit transforms the societal structures is seen also in Ephesians 5:18—6:9. Relationships that were based on power and class are profoundly altered because of the work of the Holy Spirit in and through the church. By the Spirit the body of Christ advances and brings light to the darkness.

The Human Condition and the Believer's Response

People who were without Christ are described as "dead in trespasses and sins, in which you once walked according to the course of this world, according to the prince of the power of the air, the spirit who now works in the sons of disobedience . . . by nature children of wrath" (Eph. 2:1–3). This is not good news. In Colossians 1:21 Paul says that those who are without Christ are "alienated and enemies" of God. Thus, God presents a picture through the Holy Spirit of people who gladly preferred the way of darkness. Only powerful grace in the person of Jesus could break through to bring any hope at all to lost humanity. Such people are further described as "without Christ, being aliens from the commonwealth of Israel and strangers from the covenants of promise, having no hope and without God in the world" (Eph. 2:12). But, indeed, God has broken through the barrier of darkness to bring light to those who were "near and far off" (Eph. 2:17).

But now believers in Christ are brought into a new relationship with God through Christ. They:

- Through faith have been saved by grace (Eph. 2:8; Col. 2:5)
- Sit together in heavenly places in Christ Jesus (Eph. 2:6)
- Are intended to do good works for God in response to salvation (Eph. 2:10)
- Constitute the church, mobilized for ministry in this age (Eph. 2:18–22)
- Testify to the power of God to the "principalities and powers in the heavenly places" (Eph. 3:10)
- Are to walk in humility and unity, worthy of the Lord's calling (Eph. 4:1–6; Col. 3:12–17)
- Have been granted gifts from the Son of God to become a more effective body of Christ (Eph. 4:11–16)
- Have been called to live in holiness in contrast to the world of darkness (Col. 3:5–11; Eph. 5:1–16), to live with new views of social norms (Eph. 5:17—6:9; Col. 3:18—4:1), and in the power of the Holy Spirit to assault the kingdom of darkness (Eph 6:10–18)

Thus, the picture we receive from Paul's Spirit-inspired letters ought to provoke sincere and deliberate examination as to whether or not the church in this present age is really embracing all that we should be. The convicting Word prods us to thinking of how effectively the current church engages powers of darkness. We are granted grace and favor from God the Father. We are given untold blessings from the Son of God. We are mightily empowered by the Holy Spirit in this age to bring assault upon the powers of darkness. These epistles challenge every believer in Christ to a new look at God's benefits and our own responsibilities with His power.

NOTES

Notes

NOTES

NOTES

NOTES

NOTES

NOTES

NOTES

NOTES

NOTES

NOTES

CPSIA information can be obtained
at www.ICGtesting.com
Printed in the USA
LVHW082119181121
703656LV00006B/14

9 780785 249436